Three Minutes a Day

VOLUME 59

THREE MINUTES A DAY
VOLUME 59

Tony Rossi
Editor-in-Chief

The Christophers
264 West 40th Street, Suite 603
New York, NY 10018

www.christophers.org

Our founder, Father James Keller, M.M., chose the following prayer attributed to St. Francis of Assisi as the Prayer of The Christophers because it represents the potential for good that God instilled in each of us.

Lord, make me an instrument of Your peace.
Where there is hatred, let me sow love;
where there is injury, pardon;
where there is doubt, faith;
where there is despair, hope;
where there is darkness, light;
and where there is sadness, joy.

O Divine Master, grant that I may not so much seek
to be consoled as to console;
to be understood as to understand;
to be loved as to love.
For it is in giving that we receive;
it is in pardoning that we are pardoned;
and it is in dying that we are born to eternal life.
Amen.

PRAYER OF ST. FRANCIS
(ADOPTED AS THE PRAYER OF THE CHRISTOPHERS)

The Christophers warmly thank
all our friends, sponsors, and supporters
who have made this 59th volume of
Three Minutes a Day possible.

Contributing Writers

Tony Rossi

Sarah E. Kostopoulos

Joan Bromfield

Melissa Kuch

Garan Santicola

Dear Christopher Friend,

Welcome to Volume 59 of our annual *Three Minutes a Day* book series! Whether you are a longtime reader or a first-timer, rest assured that the stories and reflections contained in these pages will add wisdom, hope, and faith to your life, as well as help you live out the Christopher motto, "It's better to light one candle than to curse the darkness."

One of the strengths of our *Three Minutes a Day* books is that they have broad appeal. For instance, we recently heard from a priest named Father Mike, who works in various ministries. He praised our book, saying, "Stories of many ordinary people leading faith and hope-filled lives can and do generate a lot of light and powerful impacts. I am continuing to distribute copies here…at the Alcohol and other Drug Recovery Center, to graduates from high school and college, and in various parishes as well as a health care facility…May God continue to bless all the work of The Christophers."

From high school and college students, to those recovering from addiction, to parishioners at churches, to those enduring illness, *Three Minutes a Day* can serve as a spiritual aid to them all, says Father Mike. And we heartily agree! We pray that Volume 59—and all our Christopher literature and media work—inspires you to more actively love God and love your neighbor, thereby creating a better world.

Mary Ellen Robinson, President

Father Edward M. Dougherty, M.M., Board of Directors

Save the World, Do the Dishes

Author, speaker, and former high school teacher John Perricone shared a story on social media about inviting a monk to speak to his class several years ago. Its lesson for the new year can apply to people of any faith or no faith.

"As he entered the room, he didn't say a word," Perricone recalled. "He just walked to the board and wrote this: 'EVERYONE WANTS TO SAVE THE WORLD, BUT NO ONE WANTS TO HELP MOM DO THE DISHES.'

"We all laughed. But then he went on to say this to my students: 'Statistically, it's highly unlikely that any of you will ever have the opportunity to run into a burning orphanage and rescue an infant. But, in the smallest gesture of kindness—a warm smile, holding the door for the person behind you, shoveling the driveway of the elderly person next door—you have committed an act of immeasurable profundity, because to each of us, our life is our universe.'

"This is my hope for you for the New Year—that by your smallest acts of kindness, you will save an other's world."

Show kindness and mercy to one another. (Zechariah 7:9)

Remind me that little acts of kindness mean a lot, Father.

God Doesn't Make Bums

Ellen Cheng works with LAMP Catholic Ministries in New York, offering material and spiritual support to those who are poor. One day, while out in LAMP's truck serving sandwiches, a man named Angel approached her group and told them he couldn't stop drinking despite trying various programs.

Ellen questioned whether Angel had ever asked God for help. He responded, "God won't help me. I'm a bum." Ellen then revealed that she, too, once had a drinking problem, and believes that God helped her. Angel noted that Ellen was "not a bum." She replied, "My family thought I was when they threw me out. Bosses, friends, and others called me that. But I discovered that God doesn't make bums."

Angel stepped aside to eat his sandwich and ponder Ellen's words. Before leaving, he told her, "A lot of people come by with food, but that's it. You come here, you see us, look us in the eye, and talk to us. You listen. [We] appreciate it so much." Ellen prayed that Angel would experience God's unconditional love and move forward towards recovery.

My steadfast love shall not depart from you. (Isaiah 54:10)

Guide alcoholics towards help and healing, Messiah.

Mr. Bill's Village

Despite the fact that he is legally blind, Bill Moczulewski of Cabot, Arkansas, never missed a day of work. A store janitor during the overnight shift at Walmart, he always began his five-mile walk to his job in the early evening. And yes, you read that right! Bill walked to and from work every day, regardless of the weather. At least he did.

As reported by Steve Hartman of *CBS News,* Christy Conrad saw Bill walking one day three years ago and offered him a ride. She got to know him and started giving him a lift whenever she was able. But, of course, she wasn't always available, so she created a Facebook page called "Mr. Bill's Village," looking for volunteers to help him out.

Christy hoped the page would attract a few people willing to do a good deed. Instead, it generated 1,500 followers and a large group of volunteers competing to drive Bill to Walmart.

Today, Bill gets a ride to work almost every day. He concluded, "There's a lot of good people in this world, all over the place."

Each of us must please our neighbor for the good purpose of building up the neighbor. (Romans 15:2)

Jesus, help me to go out of my way to be a good neighbor.

No More Bad Days for Jeremy Renner

Actor Jeremy Renner, who played Hawkeye in Marvel's *Avengers* movies, endured a major accident in 2023. After seeing that his nephew was about to be crushed by a runaway snowplow, Renner tried jumping onto the vehicle to gain control. His jump fell short, and he got run over himself, resulting in 38 broken bones in his legs, spine, face, and ribs.

The fact that Renner survived at all is something of a miracle. And though his recovery process will never fully be over, he is walking and talking normally again. The experience gave him a new perspective on life.

On *The Tonight Show with Jimmy Fallon*, Renner noted, "There's so many great gifts that being tested to your limits [brings]...I won't have a bad day for the rest of my life...Also, the idea of learning how not to panic and how to focus."

"In order to walk, you have to put one foot down, then the other foot in front of it, then you're walking...I think it's a great reminder of what we all should be looking at in life. If we get too stressed or if things get too difficult...just put one foot down, then put another foot down, and then move towards it."

Suffering produces endurance. (Romans 5:3)

In times of struggle, Lord, help me to keep moving forward.

The Collective Goodness of People

Actor Jeremy Renner's recovery from getting run over by a snowplow not only gave him a new perspective on life, it introduced him to a more positive view of humanity.

Renner was on life support for several days in the hospital. His loved ones didn't know if he would survive. When he regained consciousness, the amount of love he received felt overwhelming to him, and he wasn't comfortable with it at first.

"It was sort of like a living wake kind of thing," Renner told Jimmy Fallon. "Everyone's coming to say their goodbyes...To receive that much love is also, I think, a very difficult thing for anybody to do. I was terrible at it.

"But because there was so much goodness and good will that came my way, I tell you, Jim, it's not goodness that I really believed existed. I just didn't think that existed. And I certainly believe it now. I think it's ultimately what got me to survive and come back and be strong. I will be stronger than I've ever been as I continue in my recovery. The collective of goodness in people, it's astounding."

Endurance produces character, and character produces hope. (Romans 5:4)

May humanity's goodness shine and flourish, Savior.

Jesus and Java

You might not think of a coffee shop as an appropriate place to pray, but that's one of the goals at St. James Coffee in Rochester, Minnesota. It was founded in 2012 by Father Matt Fasnacht, who wanted to offer the general public a "non-intimidating" venue to "encounter Christ," reported Joe Slama in *Our Sunday Visitor*.

Today, the shop attracts both believers and non-believers looking for great coffee and deep conversations. St. James even houses an adoration chapel and offers themed drinks like "Capuchin-O." Melissa Scaccio, who runs St. James, said, "Some of my best customers are actually atheists."

Brandon Hendrickson, an agnostic who was raised Protestant, noted he loves St. James because "it allows people to open up to one another. So, it easily becomes a more friendly place, even for people who are not part of that tradition...The assumption is not that everybody is strangers, and maybe they have radical disagreements...but rather that people like each other and know each other. And that is infectious."

They devoted themselves to...fellowship, to the breaking of bread and...prayers. (Acts 2:42)

Teach me to grow in fellowship with all, Father.

Connecting Despite Dementia

When her late father was battling dementia, actress Nikki DeLoach went to visit him, but he was unable to recognize her. Nikki then remembered something they had always done when she was a child. Because they had the same size hands, they would put them palm to palm as a way of connecting.

Nikki now had her father put his palm up against hers, and she told him, "We have the same size hands!" He examined and traced her fingers slowly. Then, he looked up and started crying. "You know who I am now, don't you?" Nikki asked him. He nodded his head.

Several weeks later, when Nikki was leaving, her father walked her to her truck, and they hugged goodbye. As soon as she sat in the driver's seat, Nikki burst into tears, overwhelmed by the emotion of her father's condition. Suddenly, she heard a knock on the window. It was her father, putting his palm up against the window. Nikki returned the gesture.

On the show *Comfort Food with Kelly Rizzo*, Nikki said she shared that story to tell people, "Don't give up on [your loved one with dementia]. They are in there."

He gives power to the faint. (Isaiah 40:29)

Bless all dementia patients and their caregivers, Father.

A Naples Tradition of 'Hanging Coffee'

A century ago in Naples, Italy, when a customer at a café had a bit of good fortune, that person would buy a "caffè sospeso" for someone in need. In the past decade, this Neapolitan tradition has spread to coffee houses around the world and has become known as the practice of "hanging coffee."

Despite the name, hanging coffee does not involve a bunch of mugs dangling from the ceiling. Rather, customers can request that hanging coffees be added to their bill. These purchases then act as a credit for anyone coming into the shop who needs a hot coffee, but lacks the means to pay for it. The barista can serve this person a fresh brew, and even food, courtesy of the client who bought a spare in advance.

This generous act has spread far beyond Naples, thanks to a social media post that went viral, reported *Aleteia*. The post read, "Small kindnesses like this can impact so many lives, in ways we could never imagine. Maybe we should all try it."

Let them drink and forget their poverty. (Proverbs 31:6-7)

God, help me to pay it forward and spread kindness today!

Two Brothers, Two Choices

Many years ago, the publication *Bits and Pieces* shared a story about two brothers convicted of stealing sheep. As punishment, the letters ST, for Sheep Thief, were branded on their foreheads.

One brother couldn't stand the shame. He moved away, but wherever he went, he was asked about the letters and what they meant. Eventually, he became embittered and died a lonely forgotten man. But the other brother stayed put. "I can't run away from my past," he reasoned, "but I can try and win back the respect that I once had."

This brother began to build a reputation for kindness and fair dealing. He went out of his way to be friendly and helpful. Years later, he was a revered member of the community.

One day, a stranger came to town and asked a villager about the letters on the old man's forehead. The villager said, "It happened a long time ago. I've forgotten the details. But the letters are an abbreviation for saint."

This son of mine...was lost and is found! (Luke 15:24)

May I honestly confront my mistakes, Redeemer, and work towards becoming the good person You created me to be.

Wall Streeter Found New Direction

The late John Kennedy Bingham embodied the values of love and service that he learned from his Catholic parents and at his alma mater, St. John's University in Queens, New York. For instance, during the 1980s, he secured a high-level job at a Wall Street firm. However, when John discovered an insider trading scandal, he exposed it and decided to leave the finance industry.

As reported by *St. John's Magazine*, John "headed to Thailand to work as a $248-a-month Catholic Church volunteer with his uncle, [a] Jesuit missionary, to assist refugees from Cambodia's 'Killing Fields.'" In addition, he met his wife, Agnes, there, with whom he went on to have four sons.

John returned to New York after eight years to work with Catholic Charities on behalf of immigrants and refugees. His friend, Salvatore Barcia, R.Ph., said John's work "in the Cambodian refugee camps reminds me of Jesus' gospel encounter with the rich young man. Unlike the young man, who could not eschew his wealth to follow Jesus, John literally gave away his suits and headed off to a life of service."

Store up almsgiving in your treasury. (Sirach 29:12)

God, may we remember true wealth comes from helping others.

Foxworthy Focuses on the 85 Percent

Comedian Jeff Foxworthy, best known for his "You Might Be a Redneck" jokes, has been making people across America laugh for more than three decades. And that's just how he likes it because he wants to appeal to a broad audience.

During an appearance on the podcast *Mayim Bialik's Breakdown,* Foxworthy explained, "I think, for the style of comedy I do, that we're looking for that connection. I think if you gathered everybody in this country together, sat them down, and said, 'What is it that you want out of life?'—and I'm talking about pegging left and right politically—I bet you people would agree on 85 percent of the same things. So, that's what I look for.

"Even though, Mayim, you grew up Jewish, I grew up Christian; you grew up in California, I grew up in Georgia; I'm gonna look for those things that we have in common...As a country now, we don't focus on that 85 percent...We focus on the 15 percent where we differ, and we yell at each other about that. But there's basic human wants and needs that are universal. You want to be able to take care of your kids. You want to be able to eat today...That's the part of it that I [focus on]."

Maintain constant love for one another. (1 Peter 4:8)

Help us focus on what we share in common, Creator.

Food for Hope, Part 1

Food banks are a blessing to hungry people around this country and around the world. But did you ever wonder how they got started? Well, a Christopher Award-winning children's book has the answer. Written by Jeff Gottesfeld and illustrated by Michelle Laurentia Agatha, *Food for Hope* tells the story of John van Hengel, the Catholic man who created food banks.

During the early part of van Hengel's life, there were no indications he would ever go hungry. He grew up in Wisconsin during the Great Depression, but his family never lacked food. He attended college and grad school, moved to California, married a model, had two children, and thrived as a salesman.

Then, it all fell apart. Van Hengel lost his job, got divorced, lost custody of his children, and endured a spinal injury while breaking up a fight. Despite surgery, he was in pain and needed rehabilitation, so he moved to Arizona, where the warm weather might help his recovery. That's where he found a new path in life.

He was...a man of suffering and acquainted with infirmity. (Isaiah 53:3)

When I lose my way, Jesus, guide me towards the light.

Food for Hope, Part 2

After getting divorced, losing his job, and sustaining a serious injury, John van Hengel was left destitute. That's how he wound up in Phoenix, Arizona, in 1967, at a St. Vincent de Paul-run soup kitchen at St. Mary's Catholic Church.

In the Christopher Award-winning children's book *Food for Hope*, author Jeff Gottesfeld writes, "John liked people. He talked with everyone in the dining room—disabled veterans, the homeless, and kids whose parents had to choose between rent and food. Their stories opened his heart. He found work at the kitchen, shelter in a cheap room above a garage, and faith in prayer with Father Ronald at St. Mary's Church."

The menu at the soup kitchen was minimal (soup, rice, beans, powdered milk), so van Hengel took the initiative to ask a local citrus orchard if he could collect the grapefruits that had fallen off their trees and would otherwise be thrown away. They agreed, and fresh fruit made its way onto the menu. But it was an encounter with a woman on one of his food runs that changed the course not only of van Hengel's life, but of our country.

Contribute to the needs of the saints; extend hospitality to strangers. (Romans 12:13)

May my misfortunes lead me to help others, God.

Food for Hope, Part 3

One day in 1967, while collecting fruit for St. Mary's soup kitchen, John van Hengel met a woman who told him she had plenty of food for her 10 kids, and she didn't pay for any of it.

He was skeptical, but she led him to the dumpster behind a supermarket, which was full of discarded food that was completely edible. The woman said, "I just wish I could put this stuff in a bank."

Excited by this idea, van Hengel went back to St. Mary's and told Father Ronald, a Franciscan priest, that they should start a bank to store food. Father Ronald agreed and told van Hengel, "Do it."

Van Hengel protested that he already worked at the soup kitchen and didn't have time. But Father Ronald insisted, "You heard the call, John. Decide if you want to listen."

Van Hengel did listen. Father Ronald allowed him to use an abandoned bakery on Phoenix's Skid Row for the project. That first year, they collected 125,000 pounds of food.

He looked up to heaven, and blessed and broke the loaves...And all ate and were filled. (Matthew 14:19-20)

I can't multiply loaves and fishes like You, Jesus, but help me do my part in feeding hungry bodies and souls.

Food for Hope, Part 4

After John van Hengel opened the St. Mary's Food Bank, it quickly became successful. During an interview about his Christopher Award-winning children's book *Food for Hope*, author Jeff Gottesfeld said, "I had the opportunity to speak at St. Mary's...I met a number of people who knew van Hengel, and they're proud as can be."

"This past year, St. Mary's Food Bank [collected] 125 million [pounds of food]...They have a couple of hundred full-time employees... and they're helping people get job training."

Above his desk, van Hengel wrote a Biblical quote, but gave it his own twist: "The poor we shall always have with us, but why the hungry?"

Motivated by his faith, van Hengel kept growing the food bank idea and turned it into the nonprofit America's Second Harvest, which helped create food banks around the country. He also chose to live in relative poverty because he looked back on his life and realized that money had not made him happy.

Is not this the fast that I choose...to share your bread with the hungry? (Isaiah 58:6-7)

Remind me that money alone doesn't bring happiness, Lord.

Food for Hope, Part 5

Jeff Gottesfeld was thrilled to share the story of Catholic hero John van Hengel in his Christopher Award-winning children's book *Food for Hope*. And as a person of faith himself, albeit a different faith, Gottesfeld admires the spiritual motivations that governed van Hengel's life.

Gottesfeld said, "Not only am I Jewish, I'm pretty observant. I go to synagogue on Saturdays, I read Hebrew, I study Torah...But I'm interested in religion, and my respect for the Roman Catholic Church is enormous."

Gottesfeld hopes that children and families who read *Food for Hope* are motivated to make a difference. He said, "Don't take food for granted. It is not automatic for big segments of our society...Volunteer, whether it's for food or something else."

"What's great about food: it's completely nonpartisan. All it has to do with is feeding people. And there are plenty of things like that out there that are nonpartisan. Get in there, do the work. Know that you're working alongside other Americans doing the same thing...What matters is your energy and your goodness."

If you offer your food to the hungry...your light shall rise in the darkness. (Isaiah 58:10)

Help me direct my energy towards good works, Abba.

Life for the Bereaved

When a person loses a spouse, friends and relatives often form a "casserole brigade," rallying around the bereaved. This usually lasts about two months. Then, the widow or widower is on her own or his own.

Consider Mrs. Geneva Broadhurst. After her husband died many years ago, she felt her whole world crash around her.

Mrs. Broadhurst, who lived in Atlanta, heard about a program for widows and widowers called Life Enrichment. When she first attended, others in the program helped her through the grieving process. Later on, she became a volunteer coordinator.

"Getting involved changed my life," she said. "By reaching out to others during my grief, I found a new meaning to my own life."

Mrs. Broadhurst learned that death is a part of life—a painful part—and that we need support when a loved one has passed from this world, just as others need us in their grief.

Bear one another's burdens, and so fulfill the law of Christ. (Galatians 6:2)

Jesus, make my shoulders strong enough and broad enough to ease another's burdens.

Jesus Was Observant and Sensitive

Jesus was both observant and sensitive. Nothing was too insignificant for Him to notice. Consider the time He was on His way to help someone who had sought Him out.

Though Jesus was surrounded by a crowd, a woman hoping to be cured of the bleeding that had troubled her for 12 years touched the hem of His garment. Jesus noticed this light touch, turned to the woman, and told her, "Daughter, your faith has made you well."

On another occasion, Jesus was teaching in the temple and watched as people put money into the treasury. Some put in large sums, but a poor widow came along and put in two copper coins. Jesus noticed her generosity and observed that she had given more than everyone else because she donated out of her poverty, not abundance.

In these two stories, Jesus is teaching us to be observant, to notice even the smallest events of each day. He is also telling us to develop our sensitivity, our ability to respond. The observant, sensitive individual is the person who makes things happen. Count yourself among their number.

Let us work for the good of all. (Galatians 6:10)

Lord, help me to be an observant, sensitive person.

Teacher's Words Save Young Man's Life

When Anthony Swann was nine years old, the Department of Social Services abruptly took him out of his classroom to be placed in foster care. His fourth-grade teacher, Jerretta Wilson, told him everything was going to be alright. Little did Swann know at the time how this teacher would impact his life.

Wilson never forgot about her student, but in those pre-Internet days, it took her five years to find him. His life was in a downward spiral at the time, so Wilson told him to "make something of himself, to take the bitterness and hatred and make something of it." When Swann said he wanted to become a teacher, Wilson supported him every step of the way.

As reported by the *Chatham Star-Tribune*, Swann was named Virginia's Teacher of the Year in 2021. In a speech to teachers at G.L.H. Johnson Elementary School, he noted that it was Wilson's words that saved him: "It's the power of your influence that is going to change the trajectory of a child's life. That's what happened with me."

Your word is a lamp for my feet, a light on my path. (Psalm 119:105)

Loving Lord, bless all teachers as they guide the trajectory of a child's life.

Tuskegee Airmen Legacy Remembered

The Tuskegee Airmen, also known as the Red Tails for their illustrious red jackets and red-tailed aircrafts, were the first African American military aviators in the United States. In 2023, centenarian fighter pilot Lt. Col. James Harvey—one of the only Tuskegee Airmen still alive—remained committed to sharing stories of the group's triumphs for future generations.

Before World War II, it was not an option for a Black man to become a fighter pilot. So, when the opportunity arose to be one of the Red Tails, Harvey jumped at it. The pilots faced racial prejudice, but despite the tough training, Harvey told *ABC 10 News San Diego*, "We knew what we were capable of."

The Red Tails brought down more than 100 enemy aircraft in WWII, and their success contributed to the military being desegregated. They even won the first Top Gun competition in their category in 1949. This victory was finally recognized 73 years later in 2022. Present at the ceremony was 100-year-old Harvey, still making sure the Red Tails are not forgotten.

Thanks be to God! He gives us the victory through our Lord Jesus Christ.
(1 Corinthians 15:57)

Lord, bless the Red Tails for their service to our country.

Healers Come in Many Guises

Bob A. was a man with intellectual challenges who made the world a better place. He worked as an orderly in a Birmingham, Alabama hospital, performing routine tasks with great care to make patients comfortable and cheer them up. Bob treated them with consideration and respect, remembering their preferences and problems.

More importantly, he cared deeply about their welfare. His interest and concern had a way of warming the impersonal atmosphere of the hospital whenever he came into a room. If a patient had no family or friends who visited regularly, Bob often brought a small gift, such as a few flowers or a newspaper.

When one of his patients was moved to another part of the hospital for some reason, he found time to stop by for short visits during his lunch hour or when he went off duty.

"It's my calling to help the sick," he once said. "It wasn't God's will that I could be a doctor, but I help the doctors."

Handicapped? Not Bob! He used his talents well and found fulfillment in his work by brightening the lives of others.

Blessed are the merciful, for they shall obtain mercy. (Matthew 5:7)

Help me make one person's life better, Redeemer.

Keeping a Prayer Journal

Several years ago, when she was studying abroad in London, Sarah Zentner began keeping a diary because she wanted to remember her experiences accurately. It became more than a record of events, however, because her writing also expressed gratitude to God for the blessings she was receiving.

In an article for *Busted Halo,* Zentner recalled that the experience became so "inviting and restorative" that she kept it up, even after she returned home. She calls her efforts "prayer journaling," and encourages others to do the same.

Zentner said, "A prayer journal can take any shape, really, but for me, it's always been most helpful to think about it as a written dialogue with God…An entry in your prayer journal can address anything and everything on your heart. You can celebrate, or you can grieve. You can ask questions or state bold truths inspired by Bible verses."

"You can speak, and you can listen. A prayer journal is simply another avenue for expressing your relationship with God, and there's no right or wrong way to do that."

O Lord, let Your ear be attentive to the prayer of Your servant. (Nehemiah 1:11)

Messiah, may we always keep the lines of prayer open.

The Older Woman in the Pew

When she was a young wife and mother, Maria Morera Johnson remembers chuckling whenever she saw the older women at daily Mass praying their rosaries. Now, a couple of decades later, Johnson laughs because she herself has become "the older woman in the pew."

In reflecting on the past at *CatholicMom.com*, she treasures the years she spent raising her kids, but also wonders if she could have carved out a little more time for practical and spiritual self-care, maybe by going on a weekend retreat occasionally instead of simply learning about the Catholic faith from books.

Johnson wrote, "It is not selfish to take a small break in the day and breathe. To set aside for a moment the many hats and remember who we are. It is all the more important to remember whose we are...I need to tend to my own continuing spiritual well-being. To seek those groups of women with whom...I can pray, and learn, and let down my hair, and even explore new devotions and new experiences related to growing in relationship with Christ."

See what love the Father has given us, that we should be called children of God. (1 John 3:1)

Remind me to slow down and seek You, Jesus.

Salvation Comes to Girls Town

In Chalco, located on the outskirts of Mexico City, the Sisters of Mary seek out girls in need, between the ages of 11 and 16, throughout the Mexican countryside. These young women are then offered an education and home at the boarding school, Girls Town, for five years.

Father Christopher O'Connor, pastor of Blessed Virgin Mary Help of Christians Parish in Woodside, New York, recently paid a visit to Girls Town. He was impressed by the spiritual enthusiasm of the "3,000 young girls" he ministered to, particularly when it came to the sacrament of reconciliation.

"The whole set-up they have at Girls Town is amazing," Father O'Connor explained to *The Tablet's* Paula Katinas. "Each dorm is like a family, with a Sister serving as a mother to the girls in that dorm."

"A lot of [the girls] came from broken homes," Father O'Connor concluded. "There were a lot of tears. The main thing was to listen to them and allow them to tell their story...to make sure each girl knew she was loved."

I will instruct you and teach you the way you should go. (Psalm 32:8)

Abba, send us loving and humble examples of service.

Strawberry Brings Hope to Prisoners

"Heathen, womanizer, alcoholic, addict." That's how former baseball player Darryl Strawberry described himself to inmates at Maryland Correctional Institution in Hagerstown. At least, that's how he acted before he got into recovery and accepted God in his life. Now, he gives talks to others who have gone down the same wrong roads that he traveled, encouraging them to make better choices.

Regarding his visits to prisons, Strawberry told *MLB.com's* Anthony DiComo, "I get a chance to speak with a lot of broken people, hurting people, because once upon a time, that was me." Warden Gregory Werner added, "[Strawberry is] a living example of change. I hope that the incarcerated population takes that to heart."

Strawberry plans to speak more to juveniles in the future because an increasing number of them believe "going to prison is cool." He concluded, "It brings them hope for someone like me to come in there…and deliver a message to them about their life…and how they can make the best out of their situation."

Remember those who are in prison, as though you were in prison with them. (Hebrews 13:3)

Guide the incarcerated toward rehabilitation, Jesus.

House of the Good Samaritan, Part 1

The House of the Good Samaritan in Fatima, Portugal, was buzzing with joy and purpose the day journalist Leopoldina Reis Simões came to visit to write a story for *Global Sisters Report*. She quickly learned that this is the norm at the facility.

Its 87 female residents—ranging in age from 18 to 94—all have some form of mental challenges, but that doesn't stop them from leading fulfilling lives. They especially love greeting visitors with warm hugs and smiles.

Sister Ana da Paz Nunes runs the facility for the Franciscan Sisters of Divine Providence, and noted it was created 40 years ago for "the service of the poorest." The physical capabilities of "the girls," as all residents are called, varies, so each takes part in tasks that match what they can do. That includes helping with services, embroidering, reading, painting, singing, and more.

"Here, no one is more important than anyone else," Sister Nunes said. "We live like a family, and everyone has their mission and role." More tomorrow...

By wisdom a house is built, and by understanding it is established. (Proverbs 24:3)

May we love and learn from people with mental challenges, Savior.

House of the Good Samaritan, Part 2

Residents and staff at the House of the Good Samaritan are a culturally and religiously diverse group. As Sister Ana da Paz Nunes told *Global Sisters Report,* "Here, we learn to look at everyone as a person, as a being created by God."

The nine Portuguese and Timorese Sisters who run the facility are able to do so by staying grounded in their faith. "We do everything we can on our part, and what we can't, we hand over to God so that God can do His part," Sister Nunes said.

The residents, all women with some form of mental disability, find purpose and guidance through the daily celebration of the Eucharist. Sister Nunes added, "Some residents also have catechesis. The spiritual aspect is important in their lives. They are sensitive to the problems of the world, pray, are informed, and like to watch the news. I have a lot of confidence in their prayer. It's pure."

In the end, the House of the Good Samaritan is a visible testament to the ways that love and acceptance can bring forth the Kingdom of God on earth.

It is to such as these that the Kingdom of God belongs. (Mark 10:14)

Teach me to see Your image in all people, Creator.

From Shy Freshman to Confident Senior

When Antonia Dey entered Archbishop Molloy High School as a freshman, she initially felt shy and unsure of herself. By the time she became a senior at the Queens, New York institution, she had gained confidence and mapped out a clear vision of her future.

An immigrant from Guyana, Dey had never been in a school with as many teachers and opportunities as Molloy. She took advantage of them all, joining up to 16 different clubs, reported Bianca Basone in *Stanner Life* magazine.

In addition, Dey displayed a talent for computer science, and was encouraged by teachers and staff to pursue that road. She plans to study engineering at Northwestern University, where she has received a scholarship. Dey explained, "I want to help engineer sustainable housing and agricultural practices, so that I can give back to Guyana."

Noting she felt "cared for right away" after starting at Molloy, Dey is a testament to how talented teachers can guide students. She is grateful to those who "always have my back."

Teach the righteous and they will gain in learning. (Proverbs 9:9)

Guide students towards wise, encouraging mentors, Lord.

The World Needs Great Responders

The late journalist Bette Dewing pointed out the need for what she called "great responders," people who have learned the art of listening sympathetically, and responding with caring words.

The victims of violent crime or tragic accidents, people who have lost loved ones, and people who are depressed about some family or personal problem are among those who need the moral support of a caring listener.

Too often, our well-meaning response to someone's sorrow is, "Don't worry. Forget about it." But taking a positive approach doesn't mean denying the existence of sorrow. Acknowledging the feeling is a first step in moving through it.

By listening with love, we can help heal the emotional wounds of others. We can all learn to be great responders to those in need of God's comfort—and ours.

Comfort, comfort My people, says your God. (Isaiah 40:1)

Jesus, may we comfort others with the understanding and compassion with which You comfort us.

Puppies Behind Bars

Some police dogs sniff out drugs or catch criminals, but the canines in the NYPD's Employee Assistance Unit have a different job: to make people happy. These dogs, from Puppies Behind Bars, were recognized for their service at MetLife Stadium in East Rutherford, New Jersey in 2023, and they are lifting the spirits of cops and civilians, one wagging tail at a time.

Puppies Behind Bars is a nonprofit organization that has raised more than 3,000 dogs. As puppies, they are trained by incarcerated individuals. The program's approach is twofold: helping to rehabilitate prisoners, while also giving back to communities by training these service animals. The dogs then go out into the world as therapy dogs for wounded veterans, for police officers, and for others who are in need.

Susan Lobel of Puppies Behind Bars told *WABC-TV* that these dogs have a positive effect on the community, and that it is also great watching incarcerated individuals give back to society "and do something wonderful that keeps on giving."

Let Your steadfast love become my comfort according to Your promise to Your servant. (Psalm 119:76)

Merciful God, bless the therapy dogs who provide healing and comfort to so many in need.

The Power of Music Therapy

The time that Julene Johnson spent working at a senior center during her college years was life-changing. In an interview with *AARP Bulletin,* she recalled that she was studying performance and music therapy. But one day, she witnessed a woman with dementia begin playing the piano at the center.

Johnson said, "Everyone in the room came to life and started moving, tapping their feet, and dancing. I was struck by how impactful something as simple as playing a tune had on the whole room. That inspired me to better understand what it is about music that affects us."

Today, Johnson works as a cognitive neuroscientist at the University of California, San Francisco's Institute for Health and Aging. She points out that music can help people get a good night's sleep and give seniors meaningful moments throughout the day. "Dancing with music will improve physical function," she added. "And our research shows singing in a choir eases loneliness and improves self-esteem. If you're a caregiver, music is something you should think about as part of your care plan."

Be filled with the Spirit...singing and making melody to the Lord in your hearts.
(Ephesians 5:18-19)

Allow music to fill me with joy and life, Lord.

**The Lord is my rock,
my fortress,
and my deliverer.**

(Psalm 18:2)

Free and Equal in God's Sight

The year 2023 saw the city of Savannah, Georgia, rename a town square for a courageous, faith-filled Black woman: Susie King Taylor. In fact, this was the first time a Savannah square had been specifically named after a woman and a person of color.

Born to enslaved parents in 1848, Taylor learned to read and write through an underground system due to Georgia's severe restrictions on educating slaves. When taken into custody by Northern soldiers during the Civil War, she became an Army nurse, who also organized schools to teach emancipated slaves how to read and write. Taylor later wrote a memoir, titled *Reminiscences of My Life,* detailing her experiences as an African American woman during the war.

Taylor's grandmother gave her a religious education and spiritual foundation as a child. Those lessons stayed with her throughout her life. Taylor wrote, "God is just; when He created man He made him in His image, and never intended one should misuse the other. All men are born free and equal in His sight."

Moses was educated in all the wisdom of the Egyptians and was powerful in speech and action. (Acts 7:22)

Lord, may we learn from the mistakes of the past to create a more unified future.

Bus Driver Chose to Spread Goodness

Govan Brown used to begin his days at 2:45 a.m. in Bay Shore, Long Island, to make it to work by 6:30 a.m. as a New York City bus driver. Over a period of 20 years, he logged 220,000 miles, enough to go to the moon.

If you rode his bus, you'd hear him say, "I'd like to take this opportunity to wish each and every one of you a nice day. Keep warm in spirit, and may God bless you in each and every way." Such was Brown's trademark. He is remembered for spreading cheer on Route M101.

The general manager of the Manhattan bus division said in an interview with *The New York Times* that Brown had "so mastered being happy with himself, happy with life, and happy with people that nobody can touch him."

Brown retired in 1988, but his approach to life continues to provide lessons for us all. Every day, we can choose how we respond to a situation, what we want to contribute, how we can make a difference. If we respond out of our goodness, we can guide ourselves and others down a route towards happiness.

A glad heart makes a cheerful countenance. (Proverbs 15:13)

Holy Spirit, lead me in spreading goodness to all I meet.

How Other People Pray

Many years ago, *Catholic News Service* asked people, "When do you pray? How do you pray? Where?" The answers were featured in a newspaper column. Here are a few of them:

- "When I obey warmhearted impulses, I am praying, and also when I graciously let someone help me. When I smile and cause another to smile, I am praying."

- "Out on a teeming highway with its risks and dangers, prayers for the safety of all in transit become second nature."

- "I pray whenever I need to express my feelings, whether they may be gratitude or the need for comforting. It never matters where I am when I pray; what does matter is that I do."

- "My life is a prayer, moment by moment. I use images, a statue in the window above the kitchen sink, a prayer taped to the mirror."

- "I'm a quadriplegic. I can't do anything for myself. But I can pray for others."

Prayer is both a natural impulse and a learned habit. It can be spontaneous or deliberately planned. Draw strength and consolation from the knowledge that God is always listening.

Pray without ceasing. (1 Thessalonians 5:17)

Lord, hear my prayer.

Tech Boy Initiative

High school freshman and comic book author DeJuan Strickland recently gave his former school, McCurdy Elementary in St. Louis, Missouri, a generous parting gift: a check covering the "school lunch debts of every student."

Strickland's generosity was featured on *KMOV4 News,* and his thoughtful donation proved to be an inspiration to many. One Missouri resident, Yolanda Duncan, was so moved by this youngster's actions, she decided to present him with a personal check matching what he gave to his elementary school.

"Sometimes a kid's only meal they eat during the day is at school," Strickland pointed out. "[As a kid], I didn't even know what could... be my next meal...and it definitely was a struggle."

That's how Strickland came up with the "Tech Boy" initiative, named after his 2021 comic book. It includes a *GoFundMe* page, created with the sole purpose of paying "lunch balances every year for different schools in the area." Strickland concluded, "I am only one person, but when everyone starts coming together...it will spark some change."

If you offer food to the hungry...your light shall rise in darkness. (Isaiah 58:10)

Messiah, may we strive to be a shining example to others.

NFL Star Helps Save Woman on Airplane

Baltimore Ravens tight end Mark Andrews has Type 1 Diabetes. As a result, he wound up helping a woman experiencing an emergency on a Southwest Airlines flight from Maryland to Phoenix, Arizona.

When a woman on the airplane started losing consciousness, a nurse and doctor were summoned by the flight attendants. As they were trying to figure out what was wrong, Andrews, who was sitting behind the woman, said, "Could her blood sugar be low? I have a diabetic test kit."

Andrews showed the medical staff how to use the kit, and after giving the woman some orange juice, she felt better.

Andrews said in a statement to *WJZ TV*, "In addition to the fast-acting flight attendants, the real heroes are the nurse and doctor who also happened to be on the plane. Thankfully, they were able to provide the woman the quick assistance she needed."

The mind firmly resolved after due reflection will not be afraid in a crisis. (Sirach 22:16)

Jesus, help me to think and act wisely in a crisis.

Christian Bale's Foster Care Mission

Actor Christian Bale is known for roles such as Batman in *The Dark Knight* trilogy, but now he's playing a real-life hero by creating foster homes to keep siblings together.

Sixteen years ago, Bale heard that Los Angeles County had one of the largest numbers of foster children in the country, and that many brothers and sisters were separated in the system.

Bale, the father of a three-year-old daughter at the time, couldn't imagine his child in that situation. He vowed to do something, thinking it would be a simple process. But, as he told the *Associated Press,* he learned it was quite complex: "These are people's lives. And we need to be able to have them land on their feet when they age out. There's so much involved in this."

Bale persevered and, 16 years later in 2023, he broke ground on what will become a dozen homes for foster children and a community center in Los Angeles. Bale hopes this will inspire similar projects to help more children in the future and keep siblings in foster care together.

Let Your steadfast love become my comfort according to Your promise to Your servant. (Psalm 119:76)

Loving Lord, bless all children who are in the foster care system, and please keep families together.

Firefighter Reunited with Boy He Rescued

When their Dorchester, Massachusetts house caught on fire 45 years ago, three-year-old Umar Fox and his sister were rescued by a firefighter. In 2023, Fox reunited with that firefighter who saved his life.

Fox, now 48 and a father of three with two stepchildren, managed to locate retired Boston firefighter Joseph Gilmore and arrange an in-person meeting. Gilmore remembered rescuing Fox from that fire, but had no idea that his act of bravery had saved so many others.

During the meeting, Fox revealed that he saved someone from drowning as a teen, and later managed to talk two people out of suicide while working as a recovery coach. As reported by *The Boston Globe*, Fox told Gilmore, "We wouldn't be here [without you]. What you did, in turn, saved other people's lives and brought more into the world."

One life truly can make a difference.

Yes, Father, for such was Your gracious will. (Matthew 11:26)

God, thank You for all first responders, and please watch over them and keep them safe.

The Saint of Schio, Part 1

During World War II, the town of Schio in northern Italy endured several bombings. This happened even after the overthrow of Mussolini due to the Nazi occupation. But in the bombings of Schio, not a single death was recorded.

The townspeople credited this to Mother Josephine Bakhita of the Canossian Daughters of Charity, who was living amongst them and had already been identified by many as a saintly figure. She was canonized in 2000 by Pope John Paul II, and today her image hangs over the front door of the Church of the Holy Family, adjacent to the Canossian convent in Schio.

Born in Sudan, Africa, Bakhita was kidnapped into slavery as a child and endured years of abuse. She was eventually sold to an Italian consular agent stationed in Africa. While this man and his family treated her in a kindlier manner, they still maintained an unjust sense of ownership over her. Nevertheless, when the family was returning to Italy, Josephine requested to go with them, so they brought her along as their servant. Italy is where her life changed for the better.

Many are the afflictions of the righteous, but the Lord rescues them from them all. (Psalm 34:19)

Save victims of modern day slavery, Holy Spirit.

The Saint of Schio, Part 2

In Italy, Josephine Bakhita had the opportunity to learn about Jesus through the Canossian Daughters of Charity. They also lobbied for her to be granted freedom, which she won in a court case, enabling her to devote herself to learning the faith.

In 1890, Bakhita received baptism, confirmation, and first communion from the patriarch of Venice, who had been instrumental in helping her attain freedom. In 1902, she made her profession as a Canossian Daughter of Charity and was asked to serve in the town of Schio.

Over the next 45 years, Bakhita became known for her devout prayer life and the tremendous mercy she showed to others. She contributed to her community through simple tasks of cooking and sewing, her artistry as an embroiderer, and her selfless service to the many visitors they received.

As she grew older, the future saint began to suffer physical pain, but she was known for the joy she displayed even amid her suffering. She died in 1947, but the people of Schio maintain a permanent exhibit dedicated to her memory.

**For freedom Christ has set us free.
(Galatians 5:1)**

May I use my freedom to be of service to others, Jesus.

Fun from The Toy Lending Library

Children checking out books from their local library has been a common experience for many years. But recently, the idea of lending out toys in the same manner has become increasingly popular. The Toy Lending Library of South Dakota, which was founded in 2015 by Anelis Coscioni, offers just one example.

The Library allows families who can't afford toys to offer their children something fun and educational. The nonprofit collects donated playthings for kids, ranging in age from newborn to five years old. The toys are then sanitized, packaged with a book, and sent to different locations, such as regular libraries, where parents can check out the box and take it home for their kids to enjoy for a few weeks.

Coscioni told *Costco Connection* magazine that they have "900 toy boxes in circulation," and interest is increasing. And in 2023, the Toy Lending Library established a headquarters at First United Methodist Church in Sioux Falls, which rents them space for one dollar a year because the church wanted to partner with a ministry that is making a positive difference.

The streets of the city shall be full of boys and girls playing in its streets. (Zechariah 8:5)

May children enjoy the pleasures of playtime, Father.

Wood That Would Last

Some people might think that the age of 85 is too late to start a new chapter in your life, but Maurice Clifton of Boise, Idaho, has proven them wrong. Clifton spent 14 years working as a bank executive, and the next 45 years as a real estate broker.

Once he retired, he found time to devote to his hobby of woodworking. He told *Costco Connection* magazine, "I work with ancient olive wood that comes from Jerusalem, and new, sustainable wood, cultured and grown recently."

Soon, woodworking wasn't just a hobby for Clifton, but a new business called Wood That Would Last. He explained, "I make jewelry/keepsake boxes, furniture, and everything in between. The goal I have is to make a tree have a life past its growing years."

Clifton also teaches woodworking to young people so they can acquire a useful skill they might not have considered developing. His message for people of all ages: "If you have a hobby or anything that has sustained you in body and spirit, go for it!"

A skilled woodcutter may saw down a tree... [and] make a useful vessel. (Wisdom 13:11)

Jesus, may we seek to develop talents at every stage of life.

X Marks the Kiss

The custom of using Xs in letters to represent kisses had an unromantic origin. It grew out of a legal practice.

When legal agreements were signed in medieval times, the signers put a cross—the sign of St. Andrew—under their name as an indication of their honesty and good faith.

The cross was often a little tilted and resembled an X. As a further guarantee that they would honor the agreement, signers were required to kiss the document.

In time, after the practice was no longer observed, the X came to be associated with the kiss.

This shift in association seems a natural one. Honesty and good faith in all our dealings are signs of our love for others.

Let us live honorably. (Romans 13:13)

Holy Spirit, guide our conduct so that it will reflect our faith.

Paralyzed Bride Surprises Groom

Chelsie Hill always dreamed of walking down the aisle on her wedding day. But that dream seemed impossible after a 2010 car accident, caused by a drunk driver, left her paralyzed from the waist down.

Still, as Hill's wedding to her fiancé, Jay Bloomfield, approached in 2021, she yearned to make her dream a reality. The 29-year-old, who founded the Los Angeles wheelchair dance team the Rollettes, told *Business Insider*, "I want to stress there's nothing wrong with sitting down in your chair. But for me growing up, I always imagined myself walking down the aisle."

On the day of the wedding, Hill used leg braces and a walker to surprise Bloomfield, who had his back turned before she entered the ceremony. When Bloomfield saw his bride-to-be walk down the aisle, his "jaw dropped" in surprise and elation! Together, the couple said their vows eye-to-eye.

"I just felt like that whole time, our souls were locked in on each other," Hill said. "I didn't see anybody else around me. I just saw him."

Put on the full armor of God, so...you may be able to stand your ground. (Ephesians 6:12-13)

Help me, Lord, to persevere and make my dreams a reality.

Couple Reaches Oak Anniversary

We know that a couple's 50th anniversary is called golden—and both the 60th and 75th anniversaries are dubbed diamond. But what about the 80th? It is a rare accomplishment, but for those who reach it, the designation is oak.

Leroy and Julia Kayser of East Hampton, New York, celebrated their 80th in 2024. They met as teens and fell in love right away, never even dating anyone else. The Kaysers survived the Great Depression, World War II, and the ordinary challenges of life. They had two children and are now great-grandparents.

What are some of their secrets of both living and staying together for so long? Leroy told *CBS 2 News's* Jennifer McLogan, "We plagiarize from an old Johnny Mercer song: 'Accentuate the positive; eliminate the negative.' That's our goal... [And] we are not couch potatoes. We do get outside and get our old bones moving, with rakes and shovels." They also volunteer in their community.

Their motto is, "Compromise. Loyalty. Communication."

Clothe yourselves with love, which binds everything together in perfect harmony. (Colossians 3:14)

Lord, help couples practice compromise, loyalty, and communication.

A Path Toward Racial Healing, Part 1

John Blake and his brother, Pat, grew up in an African American neighborhood in inner city Baltimore during the late 1960s/early 1970s. Their father, who was Black, worked as a merchant seaman and was away from home most of the year. As a result, the boys often found themselves in foster homes because their mother was not around. All they were told was that she was White, her name was Shirley, and her family hated Black people.

For John, the hatred went both ways. Though no one in his community specifically told him he should hate White people, "it was just something I absorbed like the humidity," he explained. "It's the conversations I overheard. It's what I saw."

John's perspective evolved significantly in later years because he experienced radical changes in himself and other family members from both sides of the Black/White divide. He shared his powerful story in his Christopher Award-winning memoir, *More Than I Imagined: What a Black Man Discovered About the White Mother He Never Knew.* More tomorrow...

Whoever says, "I am in the light," while hating a brother or sister, is still in the darkness. (1 John 2:9)

Inspire us to move past hate toward love, Creator of All.

A Path Toward Racial Healing, Part 2

During John Blake's childhood, one person stood out as a shining light: his paternal Aunt Sylvia. During a *Christopher Closeup* interview, he said, "She was an unmarried woman who never had children. She worked as a secretary. To the eyes of the world, she was perhaps nobody…but she was like my lighthouse in the sea of chaos… that surrogate mom who helped me believe in myself, who taught me the value of books and faith."

Faith became an important part of John's life, but he wasn't a willing churchgoer in his youth. With Aunt Sylvia, however, he didn't have a choice: "She took us to a Black church, but it's more like we were drafted," he reminisced.

"Outside of Sunday, a lot of [the people in church] were considered nobodies: blue-collar workers who were dealing with discrimination, who grew up in Jim Crow. But when they came to church, they had this dignity and love of God that, even as a kid, I could sense. So…my Aunt Sylvia and some of those people I met in the Black church made God more tangible."

Set the believers an example in speech and conduct, in love, in faith, in purity.
(1 Timothy 4:12)

May my love for You, Jesus, make Your love more tangible to others.

A Path Toward Racial Healing, Part 3

At age 17, John Blake's life changed when his father asked him if he wanted to meet his mother. Three days later, John and his brother, Pat, were driven to Maryland where they entered "a menacing red brick building. It's the saddest place I've ever been," he recalled in an interview about his Christopher Award-winning memoir, *More Than I Imagined: What a Black Man Discovered About the White Mother He Never Knew.*

"I could feel the misery, but I couldn't quite put it together. I'm hearing people moan in pain in the background, while others are just laughing hysterically...[I learned] we were in the waiting room of a...notorious mental institution called Crownsville, and they were known for abusing patients. They would chain them to beds, subject them to medical experiments."

A hospital orderly brought a thin White woman into the room. Her eyes lit up, and she exclaimed, "Oh, boy! John and Pat, it's so good to see you!" It was their mother, Shirley. She hugged her sons, but John felt awkward, having never even used the word "Mom" before. Despite the discomfort of the situation, that meeting resulted in several epiphanies for John.

Can a woman forget her nursing child?
(Isaiah 49:15)

Reunite separated families, Abba.

A Path Toward Racial Healing, Part 4

After learning that the White mother he never met had been locked in a mental institution for years, John Blake was shocked and experienced several revelations.

During an interview with The Christophers, the *CNN* correspondent explained, "No one told us that our mom had this severe form of mental illness called schizophrenia. We didn't make that discovery until that day in the waiting room. People didn't talk about mental illness.

"What was [also] significant about that meeting...is that before I met my mom, I didn't think that any White person could understand or empathize with what it meant to be Black, to grow up in a poor, violent neighborhood like I did, to be looked down upon because of nothing that you have control over.

"But when I met my mom, I thought, 'Wow, I've never seen a Black person suffer like that.' She began to shatter these assumptions about White people that I had in that meeting, without even saying a word. That was the first time that I developed empathy for a White person."

There is no longer Jew or Greek...for all of you are one in Christ Jesus. (Galatians 3:28)

Remind us we are all part of one human family, Creator.

A Path Toward Racial Healing, Part 5

Before John Blake left that visit, his mother made one request of him. She asked him to send her a St. Jude prayer book. At the time, John didn't know who St. Jude was, but he soon learned he was the patron saint of hopeless causes for Catholics like his mom. She considered herself a hopeless cause and relied on St. Jude to help and guide her.

As he shared in his Christopher Award-winning memoir, *More Than I Imagined: What a Black Man Discovered About the White Mother He Never Knew,* John developed a good relationship with his mother, and he believes St. Jude helped improve her condition and life in the ensuing years.

Beyond that, John also saw St. Jude's effectiveness in other areas. For instance, some might consider those who hold racist beliefs, such as his mother's family, to be hopeless causes. But John soon discovered that the power of human relationships can genuinely change people's hearts and minds—and that Christian faith can serve as the motivating force for acting with mercy and humility.

The hope of the righteous ends in gladness. (Proverbs 10:28)

Be my guiding light when hope seems lost, Jesus.

A Path Toward Racial Healing, Part 6

Despite the racial strife in the U.S., *CNN's* John Blake believes that healing can be found, based on his own experiences as a Black man getting to know the White half of his family.

During an interview about his memoir *More Than I Imagined,* he explained, "I've spent a lot of time covering the worst racial upheavals in this country...[but] I have never seen such pessimism about racism in this country [as now]. There's so many people who believe that racism is a permanent part of being American, that we won't ever get past our racial divisions. One guy told me that racism is embedded in our DNA."

"I have not seen that to be the case," John continued. "I've seen people in my mother's family who denied they were racist...even though they used the N-word...I've seen them change... There's a Scripture...in the New Testament where Paul talks about, we're all new creations in Christ."

"I do wonder, though, if a lot of Christians still believe that. But I have seen it. People can change. Racism is not embedded in our DNA. That's one of the things I try to show in my book."

If anyone is in Christ, there is a new creation. (2 Corinthians 5:17)

Open our hearts to the possibility of positive change, Lord.

Caregiving Made Actor a Better Man

Actor Brennan Elliott has starred in many *Hallmark* movies, including the Christopher Award-winning *The Gift of Peace*. In real life, his most important role has been caregiver for his wife, Cami, who has endured several diagnoses of cancer.

In 2022, Cami learned she had stage four gastric cancer, leading to more surgery and treatments for her—and even more anxiety for their family, which includes two children. Elliott would share periodic health updates with his fans on social media, and his fans continued to pray for Cami's healing.

In March 2023, good news finally arrived. He revealed that Cami's latest pathology report showed no cancer. Elliott added, "It's been such an impossible journey, but today is a day to rejoice in God's mercy and grace. From the bottom of my heart, thank you to every one of you who has prayed for us and encouraged us along the way."

"To care for, love and support my better half through this dreadful disease, as difficult as it has been and continues to be, it has made me grow to being a better man, husband and father."

Husbands, love your wives, just as Christ loved the church and gave Himself up for her. (Ephesians 5:25)

Bring strength to families dealing with cancer, Lord.

Surprise Gift for Security Guard

James Mogaji, an overnight security guard at Providence College's Raymond Hall, is originally from Nigeria. Members of his family remain there, but he had not been able to travel to see them in more than 10 years.

When students heard about this problem, they set out to fix it by setting up an online fundraiser without Mogaji's knowledge. One week later, they had collected $3,000 and presented it to him. A video of the gift's presentation showed a surprised Mogaji falling down in shock, joy, and gratitude.

Daniel Singh, a resident assistant at Raymond Hall, told Mogaji that students there support one another: "As long as I've been here, they've done that for me, and we've done that for each other, so now we're doing it for you."

Student organizer Brandon Reichert told an interviewer that Mogaji "is just the kindest soul anyone has ever met in this building. He means so much to us."

Because a campus community responded to a call for donations, there's a family that no longer has to wait to see their loved one.

It is more blessed to give than to receive. (Acts 20:35)

Teach us, Jesus, to respond to the needs of others.

Retirement Doesn't End Divine Compassion

The Sisters of the Divine Compassion devoted their lives to sharing God's kindness and love through their work as teachers, principals, spiritual counselors, therapists, and more. And they didn't stop in retirement!

A number of the nuns live in community at Wartburg (a senior facility in Westchester County, New York), notes the Sisters' 2023 Annual Report. Many continue to share their charism of compassion with residents, staff, and visitors.

The Sisters may help with special events, shopping, gardening, visiting memory-care patients, and leading prayer groups. "Our Sisters bowl, sing and dance, walk, practice Tai Chi, and so much more," the report states.

Retiring from a full-time work schedule can often mean more time to share spiritual and other gifts with others. The Sisters continue to find meaning in their lives in their senior years, and hope to inspire others to do the same.

Whoever pursues righteousness and kindness will find life and honor. (Proverbs 21:21)

Lord, may we value the contributions of our elders.

Shirt-sleeve Solutions

Back in the 1970s, Bill Lindsey went to Fort Lauderdale as a VISTA volunteer. VISTA, now a part of AmeriCorps, is the domestic equivalent of the Peace Corps. Lindsey's job was to work with poor people in their neighborhoods.

A decade later, Lindsey became executive director of the Fort Lauderdale Housing Authority. Urban planners from around the country came to see him because he had done something few had been able to accomplish. He rehabilitated slum areas.

How did he do it? Well, when he first went to Fort Lauderdale, Lindsey lived with the people, and he continued doing so. He knew them and the problems they faced. And he learned what to do about them by rolling up his shirt sleeves.

There's nothing like first-hand knowledge in solving problems.

God gave knowledge and skill. (Daniel 1:17)

Redeemer, we need Your wisdom, as well as first-hand knowledge, to solve pressing social problems.

Port in a Storm

A devastating storm in Far Rockaway, New York, completely destroyed Salome Williams-El's barber shop. Initially, she started a GoFundMe site to raise money to open a new shop, but she quickly realized she needed to do more.

That's when a unique idea popped into her head: Williams-El decided she would cut people's hair on a New York City subway platform. She spoke with the New York City Police Department about where to put her temporary work space in the subway system, and they worked out a plan.

Williams-El's longtime patrons came by to help in whatever ways they could. They handed out fliers, cleaned up hair clippings, and sat for haircuts so passersby could see her work. "Of course, I was compelled to come out and help her," Donny Bellmon told *NY1 News*. "She's the best barber I know."

Instead of charging clients, Williams-El asked them to donate to her GoFundMe. In time, she hopes to have a new shop that's convenient for everyone. She also demonstrates that when we get tossed by life's storms, it is possible to find safe harbor.

Rescue me...from the deep waters.
(Psalm 69:14)

Guide me through life's storms to safe harbor, Abba.

Because We Exist

Sister Julia Walsh realizes that "Gospel living is messy," and certainly not easy, so she created the blog *Messy Jesus Business* to explore "the struggle of faith." The idea of putting our faith into action is a common theme in many of her posts.

In one reflection, Sister Julia noted, "We are commissioned to serve, to give, to be people of joy, light, salt: we are meant to share the Good News. When we look around at the suffering and injustice in our communities, neighborhoods, and ecosystems, it is obvious we have work to do."

Sister Julia then issues a call to action, a call to recognize the inherent dignity of everyone created by God: "It doesn't matter who you are, or what you did, or how you live—all of us are completely worthy of love and care because we exist...We do this by what we teach, speak, and how we are with people and all of creation; by the sharing of food, space and care. Every person is worthy of honor and respect because they are an image of God."

In the Lord you are light. Live as children of light. (Ephesians 5:8)

May I see Your image in everyone equally, Creator.

A Runaway's Return, Part 1

Manndi DeBoef was fed up. She can't recall what exactly she was fed up about because she was only six years old at the time, but she decided to run away from home. She took her mother's red overnight bag, packed a few items, then told her mother she was leaving. "My mother didn't seem overly concerned," DeBoef wrote at *BustedHalo.com*. "She said she would miss me and hoped I would visit."

DeBoef walked to the end of her street, then sat down on the red suitcase, hoping her mom would come after her. She didn't. Frustrated, the six-year-old finally returned home, where she was greeted by her mother, who knelt down and said to her:

"Manndi, I watched you from the bedroom window. You were never out of my sight. Do you really think I would let my precious little girl run away? I gave you some space. But I am very happy that you came back home."

Those words taught Manndi that no matter where she went, her mother would always welcome her back. That incident also taught her a truth about God. More tomorrow...

As a mother comforts her child, so I will comfort you. (Isaiah 66:13)

May children gain wisdom from their parents, Paraclete.

A Runaway's Return, Part 2

After Manndi DeBoef ran away from home at age six, her mother welcomed her back with "open, loving arms." Over the course of her life, DeBoef—now a mother of two herself—has found the same holds true with God.

Writing at *BustedHalo.com,* she recalled that she experienced dark spiritual times following two miscarriages, an unwanted divorce, and the death of a loved one. But God gave her space and welcomed her back when she was ready.

DeBoef wrote, "No matter how much we screw up, how long we stay away, and how deeply our faith has fallen, [God] truly desires each of His children to come home; whether for the first time or the 10th. Each time I have faltered or faced what I felt was bitter defeat, I found grace, peace, and healing when down on my knees in heartfelt prayers."

"In much the same way my mother served as an example of Christ's never-ending love for me as a young child, I am hopeful that my two sons know...that no matter how far they wander, roam, and explore, their mother's love will not only go with them, but be...waiting for them to find their way back home."

God has welcomed them. (Romans 14:3)

May I welcome the lost with open, loving arms, Paraclete.

Cannonball Moments, Part 1

"Winning wars and wooing women." That may not seem like the kind of life that would lead a man to sainthood, but that's how St. Ignatius of Loyola started out during the late 1400s and early 1500s. Everything changed when he was a soldier at the battle of Pamplona.

During a *Christopher Closeup* interview about his book *Cannonball Moments: Telling Your Story, Deepening Your Faith,* author Eric Clayton explained, "[Ignatius is] defending the castle against the superior French forces, who offer terms of surrender to which Ignatius says no...So, he gets the rest of his troops to go along with him. And it's a terrible outcome.

"[Ignatius] gets a cannonball to the legs, but everyone else is killed or grievously wounded...He realizes, 'My pride has brought about devastation unnecessarily.' He spends 11 months in bed recovering in his castle in Loyola, and it's there that he's given two books: one on the life of Christ and one on the saints."

Those two books set Ignatius on a new path towards God.

When pride comes, then comes disgrace; but wisdom is with the humble. (Proverbs 11:2)

Help me resist being prideful, Lord. May I instead embrace a humble attitude.

Cannonball Moments, Part 2

While recovering from the injuries he sustained after being hit in the legs by a cannonball, Ignatius of Loyola was given two books to read: one on the life of Christ and one on the saints. They allowed Ignatius to consider a different path for his life.

Eric Clayton, author of the book *Cannonball Moments,* explained, "God is inviting him to imagine these different paths. One is his old way of life, and one is this potential new way of thinking, of being a pilgrim for God.

"The cannonball moment is just one moment, and it gets held up as, 'He was knocked down a soldier, and he stood up a saint.' That's not it at all. He was knocked down, and then he had a very long time to pray, to think, and to grapple with different ways his life could unfold, his vocation story.

"Then, [Ignatius] has to go out and try it and begin the journey. It's not like he gets the answers all at once...He has quite a journey ahead of him, but it's one that he does carefully through discernment in the company of the Spirit."

Clothe yourselves with the new self, created according to the likeness of God. (Ephesians 4:24)

If I am on the wrong path, Lord, lead me to a better way, to Your way for me.

Cannonball Moments, Part 3

Another key moment in St. Ignatius's journey occurred while he was living in a cave, both meditating and working on his new path in life. Though he wrote his acclaimed Spiritual Exercises there, he also struggled mightily.

During a *Christopher Closeup* interview about his book *Cannonball Moments,* Eric Clayton explained, "[Ignatius is] having these profound experiences of God, and he's also going out and serving God's people in the nearby town of Manresa. At the same time, the evil spirit is tempting him…[Ignatius] struggles with depression, he struggles with suicide, he struggles with thinking God wants him to suffer."

Eventually, God wins out in Ignatius's heart, mind, and soul. Eric noted, "The greatest thing he does in that cave is remember that he's the beloved of God and treat himself that way. [He realizes]…'I should be out in the world because God still has dreams for me,' as opposed to allowing the evil spirit to hold him fast with shame and guilt…I think it's important for all of us to release ourselves from our own cavernous experiences."

The Lord God helps me…I know that I shall not be put to shame. (Isaiah 50:7)

Remind me of Your dreams for me, Creator.

Cannonball Moments, Part 4

During his time as an undergraduate at Fairfield University, a Jesuit school, Eric Clayton felt a deep connection to St. Ignatius's life and the way he practiced his faith. And as someone with a talent for writing stories—as well as enjoying them in books, TV, and film—Eric has been greatly shaped by the spirituality of storytelling.

Eric observed, "As we think about our own lives and our own vocations as stories, and you pair that with Ignatian Spirituality...you're called to remember God is in all things. God is in all stories. God is in all the details, as mundane and ordinary and nitty-gritty as they may be. Then, everything is worth sifting through and exploring to find God."

"Thinking about stories on the screen, even these so-called godless stories, we might [say], 'God is necessarily there because God is everywhere.' And so, stories...are ways for us to put ourselves in these other worlds and think about, 'How is God speaking in this fantastical language that might be relevant to me in my very real, mundane world.'"

The whole crowd stood on the beach. And [Jesus] told them many things in parables. (Matthew 13:2-3)

Reveal Your presence to me through stories, Creator.

Lenten Journey in Guatemala

During Lent 2024, writer Mary DeTurris Poust traveled to Guatemala for a retreat. Though the U.S. State Department had cautioned visitors to beware of crime, Mary "found only love" among a people who had endured "forced conversion, a stripping of their Mayan culture, enslavement, civil war and far more than we can imagine," she wrote in the newspaper *The Evangelist*.

In addition, Mary witnessed moving displays of faith as homes, businesses, and churches flew purple Lenten banners to commemorate Jesus's walk to Calvary. Residents also prepared "large scale Stations of the Cross...for street processions."

The experience brought a newfound sense of enlightenment to Mary's Lenten journey. She wrote, "In a place where people live in corrugated tin shacks and where street vendors sell their wares with babies strapped to their chests and blankets stacked on their heads, faith and joy and generosity are rampant...I never met a rude or cranky Guatemalan, even in the airport after hours of delay, even among the beggars on the street. Instead, I was met with a pureness of heart that exemplified the Gospel."

Blessed are the pure in heart, for they will see God. (Matthew 5:8)

Jesus, grant me a pure and grateful heart.

Making a Family in the NICU

The Neonatal Intensive Care Unit (NICU) at Methodist Women's Hospital in Elkhorn, Nebraska, had already played a major role in the lives of Taylor and Drew Deras. It's the place the two nurses met while working the overnight shift, leading to their marriage in 2020.

Then, in 2021, a baby girl named Ella, born premature at 23 weeks, came under their care. Ella faced numerous health issues, including chronic lung disease. The doctor wasn't sure she would even survive. But under Taylor and Drew's loving care, Ella began to improve.

When Ella's birth mother retreated from the scene, Ella was made a ward of the state, reported *People* magazine. By then, Taylor and Drew had grown to love the child, so they took steps to become her foster parents—and adopted her in 2023.

Taylor said, "I feel like it's a total God thing, that He's kind of like, 'This is your path with nursing, this is your place, and here's your husband. And then, here's your daughter that you've been praying for.'"

He destined us for adoption as His children through Jesus Christ. (Ephesians 1:5)

Lord, may we trust in Your divine timing.

Bocelli's Priceless Gift

Singer Andrea Bocelli has become a superstar around the world due to the talent, heart, and soul he puts into his songs. He is also a person known for embracing his Catholic faith. But as Bocelli revealed to George P. Matysek Jr. in an interview for the *Catholic Review*, this wasn't always the case.

Although Bocelli grew up as a churchgoer in his small Tuscan village in Italy, he went through an agnostic period as a teenager because of the "arrogance of youth." Age brought more wisdom, and the singer eventually chose to believe in God again.

Bocelli now calls his faith a "priceless gift," explaining, "Whoever has this same gift improves their own life and the world around them. I believe that having faith means believing in the power of good, and at every crossroad choosing the road that leads to it."

Music, he adds, can help us in that regard: "When we touch our spiritual chords, we create a bridge across which to access, at any time and in all simplicity, what is hidden behind the veil of everyday life. Personally, when I interpret a holy song or one that is spiritually elevated, I experience it as a form of prayer."

I believe; help my unbelief! (Mark 9:24)

Jesus, strengthen the priceless gift of my faith.

A Teen's Beliefs and Doubts

After attending a Christian grade school and going to Mass every week, Alessandra Harris's son declared that he no longer believed in God, following his first year in high school. Harris felt shocked and unsure of how to handle this, so she prayed. And despite her son's objections, she made sure he continued to attend his Confirmation preparation classes.

One weekend, the Confirmation class headed off to a weekend retreat "which included Mass, keynote speakers, adoration, praise and worship, confession, and small group discussions," Harris wrote in *U.S. Catholic.* She was happily surprised when her son returned home having had "a personal encounter with God" thanks to the teens' honest discussions about faith and the challenges in their lives, as well as a transcendent experience with Eucharistic adoration.

Harris knows her son's faith may undergo ebbs and flows over the course of his life, but she does "feel confident the [students] who have received the sacrament of Confirmation will carry that grace with them for the rest of their lives."

Draw near to God, and He will draw near to you. (James 4:8)

Open young people to the gift of Your grace, Jesus.

Amish Neighbors Lend a Hand

A fierce windstorm and falling trees in March 2024 seriously damaged The Martyrs Chapel in Auriesville, New York. The wooden structure had been built in 1894.

Contractors estimated that the cost to renovate the chapel, which often hosts small pilgrimages, would be $300,000. The insurance payment covering the damage was far less, so the board of Our Lady of Martyrs Shrine wasn't sure what to do.

As reported by *The Evangelist,* that's when the nearby Amish community offered to do the repairs themselves. They already helped maintain the wider property by mowing grass and weeds in exchange for hay that they could take and use.

Bill Baaki, board member of the nonprofit that operates the Shrine, expressed gratitude and admiration for the help: "The Amish have the craftsmanship at the same level that [the chapel] was built...Even though it is not an ornate structure...it was built with a lot of love and care. We have [the Amish] as the neighbors right up the road, and they can apply the same love and care and do the repairs at a cost that is manageable."

They restored the house of God to its proper condition. (2 Chronicles 24:13)

May we be open to interfaith friendships, Creator of All.

In My Father's Kitchen, Part 1

We've all heard the adage, "Charity begins at home." John and Leigh-Ann Tumino of Syracuse, New York, truly took these words to heart when they created "In My Father's Kitchen" 23 years ago. It all started when John was driving and saw a seemingly homeless man holding a sign pleading for help.

John told *The Catholic Sun's* Eileen Jervis, "I heard the Holy Spirit tell me, 'You know, he thinks he's invisible, and I see him. I want you to feed him.' So, I...bought a sandwich, water, and cookies, and took them back to the man."

For 20 minutes, John sat with the gentleman, whose name was Tim, as he ate. Tim revealed the "traumatic childhood experiences" that led him to addiction and homelessness.

John continued, "I went home and said to Leigh-Ann, 'I know what we are supposed to do... Find these individuals, tell them they are not invisible, and feed them...' We thought we were just going to be feeding folks. And then we find it's not just feeding them, but...getting them connected to the services they need. A sandwich opened the door." More tomorrow...

I was hungry and you gave me food. (Matthew 25:35)

Father, open our hands and hearts to those in need.

In My Father's Kitchen, Part 2

John and Leigh-Ann Tumino's charity In My Father's Kitchen has expanded greatly over the last two decades. As reported in *The Catholic Sun,* it now has "three arms to its faith-based nonprofit organization."

The first arm is Street Outreach, a program geared towards "individuals who...have a disability that prevents them from adequately caring for themselves." Nonprofits, such as the one the Tuminos established, give people a "hand up, not a handout," by directing them towards the right places to get further assistance and changing their lives for the better.

The second arm, Life House, exemplifies this by providing "a safe, comfortable home for women who are victims of human trafficking." Leigh-Ann explained, "By collaborating with professionals, community agencies, trauma-informed staff and Human Trafficking Courts, we are able to help women navigate the system, so their journey to healing can begin."

"People don't choose to live outside," Leigh-Ann added. "There is always some type of trauma...that led them to using drugs." More on one such individual's story tomorrow...

Defend the rights of the poor. (Proverbs 31:9)

Abba, may we strive to protect and defend the rights of all.

On Hire Ground, Part 1

The final arm of In My Father's Kitchen's outreach efforts is aptly named On Hire Ground. It is a mobile program, which offers nine different homeless individuals a day a more "healthy alternative to panhandling," in the form of free community work.

Kevin Batsford serves as the manager of On Hire Ground. When he first met John and Leigh-Ann Tumino 12 years ago, he was in an extremely low place. Bad choices had led Batsford to crack cocaine and alcohol addictions.

He was "sleeping under a bridge" and "holding a cardboard sign" when John Tumino approached him. It was just like the situation back in 2003, when Tumino went up to the homeless man on the street.

"I asked myself, 'Who is this guy?'" Batsford told *The Catholic Sun*. "John gave me lunch, and a few days later, he brought me another lunch, and prayed with me. We got to know each other, and over time, became friends."

After losing his brother, who was also homeless, in a house fire, Batsford felt providentially inspired to seek more serious means of help. More on this tomorrow...

The...Lord directs the steps. (Proverbs 16:9)

Messiah, may we listen for Your call in all stages of life.

On Hire Ground, Part 2

Three months after the death of his brother, Kevin Batsford was walking past the Salvation Army Adult Rehab Center in Syracuse, New York, and felt the tug of God's guiding hand.

"I had probably walked past there 1,000 times on my journeys while getting drugs or whatever," Batsford recalled in *The Catholic Sun.* "But that day...I heard a voice in my head that told me to go in."

As it happened, the Salvation Army had a bed available for Kevin. A few weeks later, a visit to the chapel, during which he "gave it all to God," proved to be a turning point.

After months of intense rehab, the Salvation Army took a chance on hiring Kevin. John Tumino remained his "mentor through it all," and eventually hired Kevin himself to manage On Hire Ground.

"It's been almost 10 years since I've been clean and off the streets," Kevin concluded. "I have my daughters back in my life, and we live as a family...When you're ready to get help, know you're not alone...God helped me get clean so that I could help other guys...He just continues to bless me."

You have been born anew. (1 Peter 1:23)

Creator, may we believe in the power of second chances.

So Much to Give

Maureen Stanko was lying in bed one night, worrying about what would happen to her 20-year-old son, Nick, once he graduated from school. Because Nick has autism, she wondered if there would be a place in the world for him. Then, Maureen recalled her father's favorite saying: "When you have a problem, pray like hell, then get off your knees and do something."

That was the inspiration Maureen needed to open So Much to Give Inclusive Café, which employs people with disabilities as waiters, cooks, and greeters. As reported by CBS News' *The Uplift,* the café in Cedars, Pennsylvania, has also become a safe space for people with disabilities to dine without stress.

Hostess and sign language teacher Lauren Oppelts is hearing impaired. Her job at the café has transformed her tremendously. She said, "I have grown so much self-confidence."

Nick has also started working at So Much to Give. Before opening one day, he set the entire room up himself, without being asked. Maureen observed, "The level of pride in him was just incredible."

Let us love, not in word or speech, but in truth and action. (1 John 3:18)

Help me turn my prayers into action, Holy Spirit.

Service in the Time of Cholera

In 1832, the citizens of Baltimore, Maryland, fell prey to the cholera epidemic, an intestinal illness which killed more than 800 people and sickened thousands more. By today's standards, cholera is easy to treat. But when the Oblate Sisters of Providence volunteered to care for the sick, that wasn't known.

As reported by *Catholic News Service*, the Oblate Sisters are "the world's first sustained religious community for Black women, founded in Baltimore by Mother Mary Lange, a candidate for sainthood." Until then, the order's focus had been on educating children. Dennis Castillo, a professor of church history at St. Mary's Seminary, explained, "Here you have these women...getting into this unknown terror. They put their faith in God and were ready to be martyrs of charity."

The Sisters received little recognition at the time due to racism, but they are finally being honored by the government and the Archdiocese. Sister Rita Michelle Proctor, the order's current superior general, observed, "Our sisters were motivated by their love for God...and the need to serve God's people."

Bear one another's burdens, and in this way you will fulfill the law of Christ. (Galatians 6:2)

Father, guide me in serving Your people.

The Five Keys of Stewardship

What does it mean to be a steward of your parish? Most people believe it is a combination of donating your time, money, and/or talents. While this is true to an extent, the nature of stewardship encompasses more than that. To that end, Susan M. Erschen of *OSV News* presents us with "five keys" or guidelines "for living as good stewards":

- **Spend time with God.** As with any significant relationship, forging a lasting bond with our Lord requires consistent time and effort.

- **Realize God has chosen us.** God has a plan for each one of us to be stewards in our own unique capacity, through the use of our "different gifts."

- **Contribute something for God.** Be it financial support or skill, each of us has something to offer our church.

- **Trust in God's abundance.** It's easier to give selflessly when we trust that God will provide for our needs.

- **Love and serve.** "When we love and serve others...we build up a community that will love and serve us."

> **Think of us in this way, as servants of Christ and stewards of God's mysteries.**
> **(1 Corinthians 4:1)**

Father, may we build upon a legacy of faithful stewardship.

Look For Me There, Part 1

The late *Meet the Press* moderator Tim Russert was admired both for his interviewing skills and the person he was off camera. His son, Luke, believes this stems from the way he was raised.

Tim's dad—Big Russ, as he was called—was a churchgoing World War II veteran with a "servant's heart" and an optimistic attitude. His jobs included driving a truck and working for the Sanitation Department in Buffalo, New York, for 40 years. During a *Christopher Closeup* interview, Luke recalled that one of his grandfather's favorite phrases was, "It's nice to be important, but it's more important to be nice."

This mindset had a huge impact on Tim. Luke noted, "He tried to make sure that no matter how famous he became...that he kept up a connection with where he came from, which was the small Irish Catholic community of South Buffalo."

Tim also decried TV personalities who used "highfalutin language" to make themselves sound smart. He once told Luke, "That's not authentic. Talk how you talk, act how you act, and be respectful."

God...gives grace to the humble. (James 4:6)

Remind me to be humble and kind, Savior.

Look For Me There, Part 2

Two days before Tim Russert's death in 2008, he was on vacation at the Vatican with his wife, writer Maureen Orth, and his son, Luke. They attended a prayer service with Pope Benedict XVI before Tim returned to the U.S. for work, while Maureen and Luke remained in Rome. That's where they received the tragic news about Tim's fatal cardiac arrest.

Because Tim was a public person, Luke had the eyes of the country on him as he experienced his own grief. That fact had its positives and negatives. For instance, as Luke and Maureen drove to Tim's wake in Washington, D.C., they saw a long line of thousands of people. At first, Luke thought there might be an event at the National Cathedral that day, but he soon learned they were all there to pay their respects to Tim.

"It had the full ensemble of the American quilt," Luke said, "meaning President Bush stopped by, as well as the short order cook who is an immigrant from Sierra Leone from the diner near *NBC*. So, it was really a beautiful thing to witness and see all these people come through."

We...are one body in Christ, and individually we are members one of another. (Romans 12:5)

May we support each other in times of loss, Father.

Look For Me There, Part 3

Luke Russert was heartened by the huge turnout for his father, Tim's, wake. During a *Christopher Closeup* interview about his memoir *Look For Me There,* Luke recalled, "I ended up staying for nine hours and shaking everyone's hand because I felt a sense that I was helping. I was bringing comfort to people. But then, I was also getting strength from people as they walked through."

Looking back on this period, Luke realizes he was being strong for others, but he never processed his own feelings of grief. He took a job with *NBC News* shortly thereafter, partially because it helped him stay connected to his father. And though he demonstrated both a hard work ethic and natural talent in being an on-air correspondent, there was an element of Luke's career that remained grounded in pleasing his father.

It wasn't until Luke had an encounter with an unexpected source, acting like an Old Testament prophet, that he reconsidered what he was doing.

You have pain now; but I will see you again. (John 16:22)

Give me strength during times of grief, Jesus.

Look For Me There, Part 4

After several years of working as a correspondent for *NBC News*, Luke Russert got called in to meet with Speaker of the House, John Boehner, one day. Luke thought he was going to get chewed out for some negative coverage, but instead Boehner questioned whether Luke was really happy with his job.

"I've seen people that are here 20, 30, 40 years in the cycle that is American politics," Boehner said. "You might benefit from...[getting] out of Washington to see how the rest of the country lives, the rest of the world lives. Just do something that affirms that you actually want to be here for the long term."

Boehner's observations became an eye opener for Luke, who said, "I believe that God has messengers out there. And I think in that case, [Speaker Boehner] was somebody who had a very similar upbringing to my father: working-class Catholic family from the Rust Belt...It was worthwhile advice, and it ended up being a catalyst for me to do some self-evaluation and decide that I needed to take a step away to figure out, who am I independent of all this and what am I about?"

Test everything; hold fast to what is good.
(1 Thessalonians 5:21)

Send Your messengers to guide me, Creator.

Look For Me There, Part 5

Luke Russert knew he was privileged to be able to travel around the world on his voyage of self-discovery and processing grief. Though his mom, Maureen, joined him for a few trips, he mostly ventured to foreign lands alone.

"I believe in something called the power of aloneness," Luke explained during a *Christopher Closeup* interview about his memoir *Look For Me There*. "I am into community...We are better together. But I do think there is a time for aloneness, where you block out the rest of the world. This is why we see so many retreats in our own Catholic faith, especially silent retreats. Or Jesus, 40 days and 40 nights.

"There is something to be said about taking a moment for yourself...and being perceptive, thinking about what the Jesuit Examen [says]: What did I do well today? What did I do bad today? What did I learn today? Where do I see myself fitting in today? I realized that traveling was going to open up some of that by the environment being new—and me being curious and away from the comforts of home."

The human mind plans the way, but the Lord directs the steps. (Proverbs 16:9)

Teach me to be more perceptive, Abba.

Look For Me There, Part 6

During his travels around the U.S. and the world, Luke Russert came to a new appreciation of his Catholic faith, experiencing elements of it like never before, especially pertaining to the communion of saints, the Catholic belief that we are still spiritually connected to our departed loved ones.

For instance, a friend suggested to Luke that he could still talk to his father, even though he wasn't physically present anymore. That sounded odd to Luke at first. "It wasn't until I got off the hamster wheel of work," he recalled, "and it wasn't until I got to a place of deep, meditative peace through prayer that I realized you can communicate with your lost loved ones.

"You can have these deeply spiritual, impactful meditative sessions where you can imagine conversations. You can go through the sort of things you went through in the day and imagine what they would say to that or how they would approach it…There's a real component of that in the communion of saints, and there's a reason why it's so prevalent in our faith and why so many people are affected by it every single day."

We are surrounded by so great a cloud of witnesses. (Hebrews 12:1)

Lord, may I remember that love can transcend even death.

Look For Me There, Part 7

One piece of wisdom Luke Russert learned during his travels around the world has to do with the nature of humanity. While it might seem Pollyanna-ish to say we are more alike than we are different, his experiences confirmed that belief.

During an interview about his memoir *Look For Me There,* Luke said, "I traveled to over 67 places, and I didn't have any bad experiences. I wasn't attacked by anybody, I wasn't discriminated against. Most every interaction I had was decent enough. And I went to places where America, at least in their government stance, is not an ally. It's not liked."

"If people feel respected and…that you're trying to be understanding of them, you're trying to be kind to them, they'll open up a little bit. They will try to put their best selves forward. You're always going to run into mean people. You're always going to run into some people that unfortunately are bad people. But I would say the vast majority, all they're looking for is a semblance of respect. And if you give off respect and kindness, it'll come back to you. I've lived it, and I've seen it."

In everything do to others as you would have them do to you. (Matthew 7:12)

May I treat all people with respect, Savior.

Look For Me There, Part 8

Though Luke Russert's memoir, *Look For Me There*, was mostly inspired by the loss of his father, *NBC News's* Tim Russert, his mom Maureen Orth's influence also plays a major role.

At the time she graduated from college, the main career options for women were nurse and teacher. But Maureen felt called to something different, so she joined the Peace Corps and worked to build rural schools in Medellin, Columbia.

"It was a deeply impactful moment in her life that I kind of say is her origin story," Luke explained during an interview with The Christophers, "because it was there where she literally was living out the gospel. She was doing God's work, if you will.

"She always saw that as the most important work she ever did. She went on to become a very accomplished writer at *Newsweek,* and now *Vanity Fair.* But she saw that helping people and trying to bring a sense of virtue to as many people as possible was why she was on Earth. I described in the book that she had the passion of a fiery Jesuit priest."

We are what He has made us, created in Christ Jesus for good works. (Ephesians 2:10)

Lead me to do Your work serving others, Father.

Look For Me There, Part 9

Luke Russert admits that he found his mother's passion and purpose difficult to deal with when he was growing up because she was always pushing him towards doing more and gaining a wider perspective.

He realizes now that she was trying to convey the message, "You're living this life of comfort [and] privilege. You're in this bubble. You might see how Americans live, but Americans aren't the only people in the world. There's a huge spectrum of poverty, of suffering, of a lack of opportunity that you need to be mindful of and carry with you."

In light of his travel experiences, Luke does now carry that understanding with him and has gained a deeper respect for his mom as well. He has also discovered the peace he was looking for by finally coming to terms with the loss of his father.

Luke knows that Tim's message to him would be akin to, "Don't be angry. Do good. Live life to the best of your abilities. Be happy. Don't be sad. And go forward living. Take the lessons we've given you, and do the best you can with them."

Be transformed by the renewing of your minds, so that you may discern what is the will of God. (Romans 12:2)

Abba, guide me in using my gifts in the best way I can.

Everyone Can Contribute

A teenager getting his or her first job is a rite of passage in most families, but for Amy Julia Becker's daughter Penny, who has Down syndrome, it was even more meaningful. Society doesn't always accept that people with Down syndrome can live rich, fulfilling lives, but the fact remains that they can absolutely do so when given opportunities like everyone else.

Writing on her Facebook page, Becker explained that Penny started working at a local café and bakery for four hours a day, three days a week. It is part of a jobs program in the state of Connecticut, which involves coordinating "with local businesses to find summer jobs. The local business pays minimum wage. The state provides a job coach. Everyone wins."

When Becker dropped Penny off on her first day of work, Penny told her, "Mom, this is a dream come true." Later, a happy Penny returned home with traces of flour, sugar, and chocolate on her clothing. Becker concluded, "This is what it looks like to assume that everyone can contribute, everyone belongs, and everyone can find ways to make their dreams come true."

I know the plans I have for you, says the Lord... to give you a future with hope. (Jeremiah 29:11)

Creator, may society welcome the contributions of all.

Breathe Deep the Oxygen of Life

"In the unlikely event of an emergency, if you are traveling with children, place your own oxygen mask on first." Jennifer Hubbard had heard that announcement numerous times when traveling by plane with her young son. But now that her son was off attending college, she viewed it from the perspective of an empty nester.

Writing at *Aleteia,* Hubbard reflected, "In not breathing deep the oxygen of life intended for me, I had starved my heart enough to make it barely recognizable." Hubbard chose to focus on herself for the following year. She trained for and ran a half marathon, and became a patron at a local art museum.

The primary lesson she learned, however, was not about herself, but about God. That's because she carved quiet time into her daily routine and "discovered that the oxygen my identity desperately required was from the One who breathed it into my lungs in the first place. Instead of searching for me, I should seek Him. Perhaps if I can understand His love for me, if I can claim myself as He sees me, if I can comprehend how He loves me, my heart will respond in kind."

**The breath came into them...they lived.
(Ezekiel 37:10)**

Father, breathe life into our bodies and spirits.

Grandma Hosts Unique Birthday Parties

A birthday party is supposed to be a joyous occasion, but for kids with special needs, it could be devastating if no one shows up. That's what happened to Ronie Williams's grandson Jakob, who is on the autism spectrum. This inspired her to create unique parties for children with special needs.

Ronie told Michigan's *WPBN* that children with special needs sometimes don't get invitations to birthday parties, let alone have guests show up to their own. Therefore, she "decided to get together and throw big parties, and celebrate everybody's birthday, not just Jakob's, but everybody's birthday."

The community parties are held at local parks and have themes such as Spider-Man, with the superhero himself sometimes making an appearance. They've seen anywhere from 25 to 50 kids show up, and Jakob was all smiles at his own unique party.

Williams says that each of these children is unique, just like the parties she creates to spread joy to all children on their birthday.

I praise You, for I am fearfully and wonderfully made. (Psalm 139:14)

God, thank You for creating us all unique and loved.

Shoplifter Makes Good

Many years ago, the mayor of Boulder, Colorado, received a letter containing an apology and four hundred dollars.

The anonymous note came from a shoplifter, who was hoping to compensate the city for several items he had stolen in the past for his children.

The letter also contained a list of various shopkeepers, a description of the items taken from each merchant, and the money to cover reimbursements.

Referring to this honest admission, the mayor said, "It's a good day in Boulder when something like this happens."

It's a good day anywhere when you make amends for the mistakes you made. That will not only help you deal with guilt, it will brighten our world with hope in the goodness of human nature.

First be reconciled to your brother or sister, and then come and offer your gift. (Matthew 5:24)

Give me the strength to admit and rectify my mistakes, Father, and believe in Your forgiveness.

Teacher Makes Every Child Feel Loved

Julie Guenther feels like she has two families: one that she lives with at home, and one that grows larger at the start of every school year. Having worked as a teacher for more than three decades, she has taught more than 900 six-year-olds and continues to share her faith with them.

In 2023, Guenther received the Archdiocesan Elementary School Teacher of the Year award. As an educator at School of the Incarnation in Gambrills, Maryland, she is blessed to be able to share her life and faith with her students, and believes strongly in the Catholic education system.

One key part of her teaching curriculum is sharing the importance of prayer. As she observes students throughout the year, she says that they come to "understand what it is to pray for somebody."

"I have opportunities every single day to strengthen my own faith with the children I teach, and with my colleagues," Guenther told Sharon Crews Hare of the *Catholic Review.* "I see God as being part of everything we do."

Lord, teach us to pray, just as John taught his disciples. (Luke 11:1)

Loving Father, I give thanks for all teachers. May You continue to lead them as they guide our children.

Baseball Manager Motivates High Schooler

After two seasons managing Major League Baseball's New York Mets, Buck Showalter was let go from the team, much to the dismay of many of his players. Journalist and radio personality Tony Paige also lamented Buck's loss, especially since he experienced firsthand the baseball veteran's kindness.

Writing in New York's *Daily News,* Paige recalled interviewing Buck in 1995 when he was managing the Yankees. Buck asked Paige if he had any kids, and Paige responded that he did, but that his oldest son, Dante, who was in high school, "wasn't pushing himself to succeed."

To Paige's surprise, Buck invited him to bring Dante to the Stadium, so he could have a talk with him. Naturally, Dante agreed, and after his conversation with Buck, the youngster gained the motivation he needed to focus on his studies.

When Paige talked to Buck again during his Mets' tenure, he reported that Dante had become "an IT wunderkind," now working for major companies. Buck was pleased that the young man's story had a happy ending. Paige concluded, "[Buck] will always be special to me for what he offered."

I will counsel you with My eye upon you. (Psalm 32:8)

Help me offer guidance to those who need it, Paraclete.

**Your steadfast love,
O Lord,
extends to the heavens.**

(Psalm 36:5)

Edith Bunker's Jesus Connection

Writer/producer Norman Lear died in 2023, leaving behind a television legacy that includes the iconic characters Archie and Edith Bunker from the series *All in the Family*. Inspired by Lear's father, Carroll O'Connor's Archie became known for his bluster and bigoted attitudes in the 1970's series. However, Archie could also be a three-dimensional human being with major flaws, as well as virtues.

His wife, Edith, brilliantly portrayed by Jean Stapleton, was Archie's opposite, a warm and loving person who embraced everybody, regardless of color or religion. Their differences were so extreme that Oprah Winfrey once asked Lear why Edith stayed with Archie.

Lear explained that when it came to that relationship, the writers always asked themselves, "What would Jesus do?" In essence, Edith saw through Archie's sins and understood the fearful, but decent man he could be underneath the bluster. Edith's love, like God's love, was meant to bring out the best in him and be his voice of conscience. So, the next time you watch an *All in the Family* rerun, try to see Jesus's presence in Edith.

Live in love, as Christ loved us. (Ephesians 5:2)

Creator, help me to bring out the best in those I love.

The Spirituality of Spring Cleaning

As the weather gets warmer and the flowers and trees begin to bloom, our minds can turn to spring cleaning. But going through all the items we've accumulated can take a lot of time, while also being an emotional experience. Writing at *Aleteia*, Daniel Esparza brings a spiritual perspective to this topic.

"Think of spring cleaning as an exercise in detachment," he said. "As you sort through your belongings, be thankful for the abundance in your life and then ask yourself: Does this serve a real purpose? Can someone else benefit more from this?"

Items that hold precious memories should be kept and given due respect. Say a prayer of gratitude for whatever blessings a specific item brought you. Then, consider what items can be donated and possibly bring joy to others.

"The act of cleaning itself can also be a spiritual practice," Esparza noted. "Think of dusting off cobwebs as clearing away distractions that cloud your connection to God. Washing windows allows you to see the world with new clarity. Offer each action as a prayer, a small act of service in gratitude for God's blessings."

**Create in me a clean heart, O God.
(Psalm 51:10)**

Help me find the spiritual side of spring cleaning, Creator.

St. John's Bread & Life

For more than 40 years, St. John's Bread & Life, located in Bedford-Stuyvesant, Brooklyn, has provided Catholics with the perfect charitable outlet for almsgiving throughout the year, but especially during the Lenten season.

Established in 1982, this nonprofit distributes "hot nutritious meals" to "1,500 people a day," as of 2024. It also houses a food pantry which operates like a grocery store, allowing "guests" to pick whatever fresh fruits, vegetables, and canned goods they want to bring home to their families.

In addition, for the past four years, St. John's Bread & Life has successfully hosted an annual fundraiser, with the dual goal of collecting $40,000 and serving at least 40,000 meals during the 40 days of Lent.

Associate executive director Sister Marie Sorenson told *The Tablet's* Paula Katinas, "It really struck a chord with people, and we find great success running this campaign. People really...feel like their little bit is adding to making the world better for people in need."

I am the living bread...from heaven. (John 6:51)

God, may we value physical and spiritual nourishment.

Matthew Perry's Spiritual Road, Part 1

When Matthew Perry drowned in 2023, his death came as a shock. The actor, who had battled addiction for decades, finally seemed to be in a good place and had even established a new connection with God.

In Perry's memoir, *Friends, Lovers, and the Big Terrible Thing,* he explored the roots of his addictions. Non-celebrities looking at his story might be inclined to think, "He's on top of the world. What does he need drugs to feel good for?" Yet in Perry's mind—even at the height of his success—he struggled with feelings of inferiority and not being good enough.

Perry also noted that he endured "a lifelong feeling of abandonment," partially brought on by his parents not always having enough time for him—and by his father actually abandoning his family. Without his dad around, Perry took it upon himself to be a soothing, entertaining presence for his mother, trying to make her laugh and becoming a "people pleaser." He went on to have decent relationships with both his parents, but that scared little boy inside him never disappeared.

Pray for one another, so that you may be healed. (James 5:16)

Remind me that I am loved and "good enough," Lord.

Matthew Perry's Spiritual Road, Part 2

As he got older, actor Matthew Perry kept trying to fill the emptiness inside him with sex and alcohol. He wrote in his memoir, "Whatever holes you're filling seem to keep opening back up... Maybe it's because I was always trying to fill a spiritual hole with a material thing."

Perry believed fame would solve his problems, so one day, he got on his knees and prayed, "God, You can do whatever You want to me. Just please make me famous." Soon after, Perry was cast as Chandler Bing on the TV series *Friends*. He reflected, "You have to get famous to know that it's not the answer. And nobody who is not famous will ever truly believe that."

While shooting the movie *Fools Rush In*, Perry hurt his neck, so a doctor prescribed a painkiller for him so he could get through his scenes. Perry described that pill as leaving him "in complete and pure euphoria...I shook hands with God that morning. Was it God, or someone else?"

Less than two years later, Perry was taking 55 of those pills a day, so it wasn't God's presence he had experienced.

All human toil is for the mouth, yet the appetite is not satisfied. (Ecclesiastes 6:7)

Guide me towards true spiritual fulfillment, Creator.

Matthew Perry's Spiritual Road, Part 3

Actor Matthew Perry struggled with addiction for decades, and went through many treatment centers and recoveries. One in particular moved him towards a stronger spiritual life. While detoxing, Perry felt both physically and emotionally awful. He wrote in his memoir, "I frantically began to pray… 'God, please help me…Show me that You are here.'"

Perry then noticed a "small, golden light" in the air growing bigger and bigger. "I was starting to feel better," he recalled. "The light engendered a feeling more perfect than the most perfect quantity of drugs I had ever taken. Feeling euphoric now, I did get scared and tried to shake it off. But there was no shaking this off. It was way, way bigger than me. My only choice was to surrender to it.

"For the first time in my life, I was in the presence of love and acceptance and filled with an overwhelming feeling that everything was going to be OK. I knew now that my prayer had been answered. I was in the presence of God. Bill Wilson, who created AA, was saved by a lightning-bolt-through-the-window experience where he felt he was meeting God. This was mine."

In Your presence there is fullness of joy. (Psalm 16:11)

Help addicts surrender to Your healing power, God.

Matthew Perry's Spiritual Road, Part 4

After experiencing that golden light moment, actor Matthew Perry stayed sober for two years. In his memoir, *Friends, Lovers, and the Big Terrible Thing,* he recalled:

"God had shown me a sliver of what life could be. He had saved me that day, and for all days, no matter what. He had turned me into a seeker, not only of sobriety, and truth, but also of Him. He had opened a window, and closed it, as if to say, 'Now go earn this.'"

"Nowadays, when a particular darkness hits me, I find myself wondering if [that experience] was just Xanax insanity...But quickly I return to the truth of the golden light. When I am sober, I can still see it, remember what it did for me...I was there, and it was God."

"When I am connected, God shows me that it was real, little hints like when the sunlight hits the ocean and turns it into this golden color...And I feel it when I help someone get sober, the way it hits my heart when they say thank you. Because they don't know yet that I should really be thanking them."

Come to Me, all you that are weary...I will give you rest. (Matthew 11:28)

May addicts experience Your healing love, Savior.

Matthew Perry's Spiritual Road, Part 5

Addicts never say they're cured, but rather that they're in recovery because they know that falling off the wagon is always a possibility. And so it was for actor Matthew Perry, who went on to suffer more personal and professional ups and downs. That doesn't diminish the epiphanies he experienced, though, nor the people he helped make their own way through recovery.

In an interview with Tom Power, Perry stated, "The best thing about me, bar none, is that if somebody comes to me and says, 'I can't stop drinking, can you help me?' I can say 'yes' and follow up and do it. When I die, I don't want *Friends* to be the first thing that's mentioned. I want [helping addicts] to be the first thing that's mentioned."

Perry's story of addiction is both a cautionary tale and, despite his sad ending, a story of hope because he fought the good fight and gained the wisdom he needed. Hopefully, in the next life, Perry is experiencing the unconditional love and acceptance he craved all his earthly life.

I have fought the good fight, I have finished the race. (2 Timothy 4:7)

Help those struggling with addiction find fulfillment in serving others, Holy Spirit.

Superman Helping the Hungry

Everybody knows that Superman's alter ego is Clark Kent. But in Wallington, New Jersey, Superman has a different identity because Phil Stafford dons the iconic red cape with the "S" logo. Although Phil can't fly or leap over tall buildings in a single bound, he offers a lifeline to many people in need.

Ten years ago, Phil and his wife, Renay, founded a charity called N.J. Food & Clothing Rescue in cooperation with the food pantry of Most Sacred Heart of Jesus Catholic Church. Phil spends about 100 hours per week driving to various stores that donate food for the group to distribute to those in need.

The seeds of the Staffords' mission were planted in 1999 when they lost everything to the floods of Hurricane Floyd. They realized they wanted to help others in any way possible.

Phil told *The Tablet's* Alicia Venter that he puts on the Superman cape when making his rounds to lighten the mood of his serious work. But he never sees himself as Superman. He noted, "I have always believed in helping people. The Church has always taught to help people, so it aligns."

He has filled the hungry with good things. (Luke 1:53)

May my efforts to help others be super, Messiah, while still keeping me humble.

Priests Serving Youth in Wartime

The war in Syria has led to hundreds of thousands of Christians fleeing the country, reports Azré Khodr for the Catholic Near East Welfare Association (CNEWA). Those who remain, however, have numerous clergy and nuns supporting their practical and spiritual needs.

Salesian priest Father Georges Fattal helps run a center for 850 youth in Aleppo, which is supported by CNEWA. He said, "Despite the risks, war, and death, we will never leave [Syria] because we have chosen to serve the youth."

During his childhood, Srour Ibrahim found faith and companionship at the center. Now, he volunteers there, teaching catechism classes. He notes, "It's the only place where we feel physically and psychologically safe, while everything around us is falling apart."

Father Fattal concluded, "Some will always remain here because we are the yeast with which the dough is leavened...May God grant us the strength to persevere and remain in this land."

Even though I walk through the darkest valley, I fear no evil; for You are with me. (Psalm 23:4)

Protect those serving You in war zones, Prince of Peace.

'God Moved Her Over'

When 46-year-old Elizabeth Ursin started attending St. Peter Claver Church in New Orleans, she found a true spiritual home. "I really felt the Holy Spirit here," she told Christine Bordelon of the *Clarion Herald*.

St. Peter's is also where Ursin got to know Willie and Faye Harrison, an older African American couple whose three granddaughters were altar servers there. Elizabeth soon made it a point to sit next to the Harrisons because she saw them as her "church family." Willie believes that "God moved her over."

The reason? When Faye mentioned that her son, Darren, was suffering with end-stage renal failure and needed a kidney transplant, Elizabeth volunteered to be tested—even though she had never met Darren. She was a match, so the transplant took place at Tulane University Medical Center. Darren said, "I definitely have love for Elizabeth...She is like a sister to me."

Elizabeth concluded, "I am blessed that I was able to do this. God brought me to it and will get me through it. And He did."

As you did it to one of the...members of My family, you did it to Me. (Matthew 25:40)

Dear Lord, bring me to it, and get me through it.

The Happiest Guy

At age 69, Michael has trouble getting around due to nerve pain and numbness in his legs. Though he receives physical therapy for the problem, walking more than a block or two in his Kips Bay, New York neighborhood requires him to use a walker. That makes grocery shopping extra difficult.

Thankfully, Michael is a recipient of deliveries from Citymeals on Wheels, which brings delicious food right to his door. In fact, when Michael heard that his older neighbors couldn't leave their apartments, he contacted Citymeals on Wheels to request deliveries for them, too. Today, they all enjoy and appreciate the marvelous food and service they receive from this indispensable nonprofit.

As Michael told the newsletter *Special Delivery,* he particularly relishes the holiday boxes he receives for Passover. And despite his medical issues, Michael does not give in to self-pity. Instead, he keeps his attitude positive and grateful, noting, "I'm the happiest guy you're going to meet!"

A cheerful heart is a good medicine, but a downcast spirit dries up the bones. (Proverbs 17:22)

Help me find joy, even in difficult circumstances, Creator.

God's Path of Totality

In April 2024, people around the country became fascinated by the solar eclipse and following its "path of totality," traveling to places where they could see it in full. Writing in the Diocese of Albany's *The Evangelist*, Mary DeTurris Poust noted she found the event both "hopeful and fascinating" because it brought many different people together to appreciate the beauty of the natural world.

DeTurris Poust also reminded readers that we don't need to wait for events like an eclipse to treasure nature. St. Francis of Assisi, for instance, saw "daily reminders of God's magnificence. Water and earth, air and fire, even death itself—all of it called Francis back to the Creator, gave him pause, and filled him with gratitude and a sense of belonging to something greater than himself, something Divine."

"What if we chased beauty right where we are?" DeTurris Poust added. "What if we looked at our daily lives not through special glasses that darken everything except the sun, but through the truth of a faith that lights everything it touches?"

The heavens are telling the glory of God; and the firmament proclaims His handiwork. (Psalm 19:1)

Today, I open my eyes to Your glorious creation, Lord.

A Sign of True Faith

In 2019, Archbishop Molloy High School sophomore Ryan Curran was disappointed at his school's lack of a club for students who were "hard of hearing," like himself. He wrote about this dilemma in his high school newspaper, *The Stanner.*

Curran's story was then picked up by Dana McMenamin and Henry Ventura, two teachers who work at the Lexington School for the Deaf in Queens, New York. As Molloy graduates themselves, they were happy to assist Ryan in establishing an American Sign Language (ASL) club at their alma mater. This organization now boasts over 100 members and has hosted numerous events and volunteer opportunities.

"I always wanted to learn ASL in middle school," Molloy junior and club member Laila Gulino told *The Tablet,* "but my old school didn't have any opportunities to learn it. When I came to Molloy, I saw there was an ASL club and joined… Jesus teaches us to love one another and to treat others the way we want to be treated. Learning ASL has helped me follow those teachings."

Let the wise…gain in learning, and the discerning acquire skill. (Proverbs 1:5)

Lord, may we remember Your Word crosses all barriers.

Author's Journey Through Cancer, Part 1

Lisa Hendey was treated for breast cancer 15 years ago and has done self-exams every month since then. While doing one a couple of years ago, she didn't feel any lumps, but noticed that something looked amiss. Her instincts told her to check it out.

Lisa's doctor was reluctant at first, but agreed to her request for a mammogram, which didn't reveal any problems. But Lisa kept following her instincts, which led to her getting an MRI, which led to a diagnosis of stage three breast cancer.

During a *Christopher Closeup* interview, Lisa explained, "I was diagnosed with invasive lobular cancer, and it's a little tricky. Most women know that we typically look for lumps in our breasts. [Invasive lobular cancer] spreads in a way that's cellular, so it doesn't create a mass. It can be missed on mammograms."

"The doctor told me that this had probably been growing for at least a year, if not longer. By the point that we intervened, it was quite large, and I ended up having a double mastectomy, reconstruction, and radiation...It was really good that I listened to my gut on this."

Who has put wisdom in the inward parts, or given understanding to the mind? (Job 38:36)

Holy Spirit, help me trust my instincts.

Author's Journey Through Cancer, Part 2

Author Lisa Hendey's recovery from stage three breast cancer was more painful and slow than she had anticipated. She is on medication for the next several years, but finally feels like her old self again. Thankfully, she had support throughout her ordeal. Her husband, a physician, tended to her needs in the best way possible. She was also surrounded by spiritual support.

"If you're facing anything like this," Lisa noted, "I'd encourage you to ask for anointing of the sick. I'm at a parish with the Paulist Fathers here in Los Angeles...They surrounded me with beautiful spiritual care, both in offering anointing, hearing my Confession before I went in for surgery, and coming to visit me in the hospital."

"One of the most beautiful moments following surgery was my husband [Greg], who is a convert to the faith...brought the Eucharist home to me. He was commissioned as an Extraordinary Minister of Holy Communion. I cried big, fat, happy tears to have my husband bring me the body of Christ. That was a great gift. Our parish community was cooking meals for me...Mass was offered, and all kinds of things lifted me up."

The Lord sustains them on their sickbed. (Psalm 41:3)

Send me spiritual support in times of illness, Jesus.

Author's Journey Through Cancer, Part 3

During the times when she was feeling terribly sick, Lisa Hendey could barely muster the strength to pray. But she said she felt the intercessory prayers of others giving her strength. And when she was able to pray herself, the rosary was the prayer she turned to the most.

Lisa said, "If you're undergoing the kind of radiation treatment that I had, which was five and a half weeks, every day you're in the same place surrounded by people who are very ill."

"I decided I'm not taking my phone in there. I'm going to try to focus on praying. If I have to wait, which inevitably you do when you're in a medical care situation, I'm going to use that time to be praying for my fellow patients.

"I started praying what I would call a 'waiting rosary.' I would count 10 heads in the waiting room and intentionally try to, without looking like I'm staring at them, look at the people that were in the room with me and pray in that moment for their intentions. Then, that waiting time went by so quickly."

Pray in the Spirit at all times in every prayer and supplication. (Ephesians 6:18)

Help me block out distractions and focus on praying for those in need, Savior.

The Healing Power of Prayer

Elizabeth Scalia acknowledges that following Jesus's command to love our enemies and pray for those who persecute us isn't easy. It is, however, effective, which she knows from personal experience.

Writing for *OSV News*, Scalia noted that when praying the Divine Mercy chaplet for family and friends, she started to include individuals that she has pulled away from: "One day while praying, I realized that all my resentments had seemed to melt away. Jesus nailed it; it's nearly impossible to feel bitter toward someone when you're praying for their good—and praying 'mercy' for anyone is an unqualified good."

Scalia recently ran into someone against whom she had harbored resentment. After talking a while, she realized this person had endured some difficult times, and was now wiser and more humble than she recalled. Scalia continues to pray for her "because prayer is good. But now the supplication is joined to thanksgiving, because praying for the good of my 'enemy'—for the love of God—had cleansed away all the ache."

Love your enemies and pray for those who persecute you. (Matthew 5:44)

Give me the strength to pray for my enemies, Jesus.

Jesus Conquered Hatred with Love

Jesus told us that we should love one another the way that He loves us. So, how can we carry out that command? Father Paul Kim, pastor of St. Raphael Church in Queens, New York, offered this reflection in his church bulletin:

"Jesus tells us that it is easier to change a man's soul with kindness and love than to retaliate with anger or hatred. Remember, Jesus on the cross, after suffering through His Passion and nailing on the cross. People were still insulting Him and speaking ill of Him. But instead of showing hatred, He says, 'Father, forgive them for they do not know what they do.'"

"I'm sure many of us, myself included," Father Paul continued, "would use a few choice words to these people. I'm sure Christ would like to do the same, but He shows the world how we can break the cycle of hatred and conquer with love. He did during His ministry, on the cross, and even during the Easter season. Let us conquer the darkness in the world by showing the world we are not just any human beings, but as disciples of Christ, we are loving always to all God's creatures."

By this everyone will know that you are My disciples, if you have love for one another. (John 13:35)

Holy Spirit, give me the strength to choose love over hate.

The Power of Easter Hope

Though we celebrate the Resurrection of Jesus on Easter Sunday, it can be easy to forget the life-changing implications of this unique event in human history. Writing at *Busted Halo,* Caitlin Kennell Kim offers these thoughts: "Jesus did not come to give us vague hope…He lives. Really and truly lives. Not figuratively. Not in some hyper-spiritualized, otherworldly sense. He is alive.

"In the days following the Resurrection, the disciples see Him, touch Him, and eat with Him. His body—the same body knit together in the womb of His mother and nourished lovingly at her breast. The same body slick and gritty with hard work at the side of His foster father. The same body constantly reaching out to touch, heal, forgive, comfort, and feed. The same body subject to torture, degradation, and death has been raised from the dead. Jesus has conquered death."

"Jesus came to give us hope that is resplendent. He knows intimately the depth of the darkness we face. If we are brave enough and trusting enough and reckless enough to hope in Him, it cannot overcome us."

He is not here, but has risen. (Luke 24:5)

Help me to hope in You, Jesus.

A Teacher's Heart

It was a typical Friday afternoon basketball game at Oak Park High School in Detroit, Michigan. Suddenly, the physical education teacher and coach, Alfred Kattola, collapsed due to cardiac arrest. Fortunately, high school juniors, Isreal DuBose and Correy Coleman, who had recently completed CPR training at school, were seated in the bleachers and sprang into action.

"I just knew I had to do something," DuBose told *Fox 2 Detroit News*. "I began compressions... around two and a half rounds of compressions, the AED [automated external defibrillator] was brought, and Correy placed the AED pads."

Thankfully, the two girls were able to restore Alfred's heartbeat before the paramedics arrived. Both juniors have medical aspirations, which Kattola intends to help financially support.

"What more can a teacher say?" Alfred told his students during their emotional reunion the following week. "You've always been strong-minded...Keep that confidence...if you've got a backbone like that, and you've got skill to back it up, nobody can stop you. I love you. Thank you so much."

The...breath of the Almighty gives me life. (Job 33:4)

God, help us to be schooled in life-saving skills.

An Earth Friendly Wardrobe

The next time you're looking for a soft, comfortable piece of clothing, consider wearing a tree. Okay, you wouldn't be wearing the actual tree, but rather a fiber called TENCEL, which is made from the wood pulp of trees grown in sustainable forests.

Produced by a company called Lenzing, TENCEL is mainly derived from eucalyptus trees, "but can also include wood from beech, spruce, birch, and pine trees," reports *Costco Connection* magazine. Because the resulting material is soft and breathable with anti-bacterial properties, it can be used for clothing, as well as more sensitive items such as baby wipes.

In addition, TENCEL's fibers are "fully biodegradable," meaning that if they are disposed of properly, they will decompose within 65 days, as opposed to plastic which can take up to 500 years to break down.

God calls us to care for His creation. Now, human ingenuity is allowing us to better do so, using parts of that creation. After all, as poet Joyce Kilmer wrote, "Only God can make a tree."

Then shall the trees of the forest sing for joy before the Lord. (1 Chronicles 16:33)

Father, guide us in the caring and keeping of Your creation.

Writing for Better Health

Some therapists suggest that their clients keep a journal since research shows that the act of writing down thoughts and feelings can be good for your health.

Time magazine's Angela Haupt quotes therapist and author Alison McKleroy as saying journaling is "a beautiful radical act of caring for yourself."

It can lead you to discover if you're too hard on yourself in "self-talk." It can also help you think through problems and review past actions. Of course, the trick is to get started. Some motivational strategies:

- Name why you're doing it: for health, joy, personal growth?
- Make an appointment with yourself: tie writing to an established habit like during coffee or after a shower.
- Set easy goals to begin with: even writing just five minutes a day.
- Try different formats and tools: pen and paper, Notes app in your phone, audio journal, etc.

Do not let loyalty and faithfulness forsake you...write them on the tablet of your heart. (Proverbs 3:3)

Lord, support us in our attempts to improve our lives.

Waiter's Spontaneous Act of Kindness

As a result of his cerebral palsy, 51-year-old Lee Bondurant of Raleigh, North Carolina, isn't able to use his hands. So, when he went out to dinner at 42nd St. Oyster Bar with his mother, Linda, she began feeding him. That's when an unexpected act of kindness made both their days.

A waiter named Five noticed that Linda was attempting to feed both herself and her son during the dinner. Five "casually came over and asked Lee if he had ever had oysters," Linda recalled to *ABC News*. Lee told him he had not, so Five asked if he could serve him first, then proceeded to feed Lee himself.

In a Facebook post about the encounter, Linda shared that she was grateful to Five for treating Lee "with respect and kindness, not pity." She was also happy to see her son's faith in the goodness of humanity affirmed.

Hunter Correll, general manager of 42nd St. Oyster Bar, said, "We are beyond fortunate to have so many loyal and caring staff members." Regarding Five's actions, Linda added, "You don't find it every day."

The fruit of the Spirit is love, joy, peace, forbearance, kindness. (Galatians 5:22)

Gracious Lord, help me do an act of kindness today.

AcompañARTE

From the time he was a child, Claretian Brother Manuel Benavides felt drawn to the arts, especially sacred art which he felt added beauty to the world. In pursuing his religious vocation, he studied mosaic and stained-glass techniques to "bring those who are far from the Church closer to God," reported *Living Hope*, the newsletter of the National Shrine of St. Jude.

In 2014, Brother Manuel founded the AcompañARTE Cultural Center in Springfield, Missouri. AcompañARTE is a Spanish term, which translates to mean "accompany you." The Center develops and preserves Hispanic arts, ranging from the visual to dancing to cooking. In addition, Brother Manuel teaches art classes and continues to produce his own mosaics, depicting images such as the Sacred Heart of Jesus and St. Jude.

Father Javier Reyes said this about his friend: "Manuel is the type of brother who brings joy and laughter, bringing people together, even during the most difficult times. He is a bridge between the Hispanic and Anglo communities of Springfield by offering many opportunities to come together and celebrate."

He has filled him with divine spirit...to devise artistic designs. (Exodus 35:31-32)

May the beauties of art lead me to You, Holy Spirit.

Doctor Treats Body and Soul

Dr. Youngjee Choi of Johns Hopkins Medicine was near the end of a visit with a longtime patient who had chronic health issues. Though doctor and patient knew each other well enough to have discussed their religious faith before, this was the first time her patient said to her, "Please pray for me."

Recalling the incident on the website *Closler,* Dr. Choi wrote, "I'm glad she felt comfortable asking me to pray for her. In hindsight, my response, 'Yes, I'll be praying for you,' may have been the most helpful thing I gave her that day."

"In the medical profession," Dr. Choi continued, "we often think we should keep our personal lives, including faith, out of conversations with patients. Of course, there are appropriate boundaries...However, in our work as healers, being prepared for emotional or spiritual requests may be one of the greatest gifts we can offer patients. This is perhaps especially true when there are limited medical treatments available. Being ready to respond when patients express an emotional or spiritual need can be an important part of the care we give to patients."

I pray...that you may be in good health, just as it is well with your soul. (3 John 1:2)

Jesus, may my prayers bring comfort to those who need it.

The Work of Forgiveness

John and Sharon Echaniz endured an agonizing grief after their 23-year-old son Michael's murder. His killer was soon arrested and sentenced to 40 years in prison. John and Sharon found some comfort in justice being served, but they also recalled their Catholic faith's teachings about forgiveness. As John said in his court statement, he could not ignore "those pesky words near the end [of the Lord's Prayer]—forgive us our trespasses as we forgive those who trespass against us."

As such, the Echanizes told the murderer at his sentencing that they hope his heart becomes opened "to the unconditional love of the Almighty." At the same time, they acknowledge that true forgiveness is a process. They have not arrived there yet, but they are working toward it.

"Anger begets anger. Misery begets more misery; violence begets more violence," John told *OSV News's* Gina Christian. "That cycle can only stop one person at a time, one heart at a time. And each of us can only start with ourselves."

In Him we have...forgiveness of our trespasses, according to the riches of His grace. (Ephesians 1:7)

Guide me through the difficult process of forgiveness, Jesus.

Down by the Old Mill

Many years ago, members of the Hellertown, Pennsylvania Historical Society decided to restore a local 18th-century gristmill that had been neglected for years. But they had a big problem.

Most of the society's members were older. While they could handle the planning and skilled work, they couldn't take on the heavy labor. So, the town's mayor turned to a group that had helped the community before: the Chi Phi fraternity of Lehigh University.

The 40 young men painted, laid brick and drainage pipes, shingled the roof, and fixed the floor and stairs. The mill was restored to such good shape that it became the site of the town's anniversary celebration.

But the cooperative effort did more. One student remarked, "At college, you don't interact with elderly people at all. But we like them, and they treat us with respect."

Respect is vital to people of every age.

You shall rise before the aged, and defer to the old. (Leviticus 19:32)

God, help us to respect our elders, our youth, and all people.

Sickness Didn't Limit Her Love

In 1952, Alberta Saar was told that despite an operation for cancer, she had only one year to live.

She decided to make the most of her time by visiting cancer patients every day to cheer them up. Sometimes, she phoned them at night to ease their fears.

Cancer had claimed Saar's own mother, father, sister, and brother, but somehow she carried on, not letting these personal tragedies keep her from her work.

More than three decades later, Alberta Saar was still visiting cancer patients. She had become a symbol of hope to the patients because she refused to give in to cancer even though she required treatment for the rest of her life.

When sickness comes, accept the physical limitations it imposes. But if at all possible, try not to let sickness dictate your attitude towards life.

He took our infirmities and bore our diseases. (Matthew 8:17)

Help me to use my pains and struggles to bring comfort to others, Lord.

Soap Actor Models Leadership

Many people knew actor Bill Hayes from his long-running role as Doug Williams on the *NBC* soap opera *Days of Our Lives.* Upon Hayes' death in 2024, actor Bryan Cranston (*Malcolm in the Middle, Breaking Bad*) shared a personal memory of him with *Deadline.com.*

In 1980, Cranston was just starting his acting career when he landed a three-day job on *Days.* His first day, he recalled, was "a disaster." Cranston had failed to set his alarm clock correctly, so he got to the studio two hours late and missed rehearsal for two scenes, which held up production.

During a break, Cranston retreated to his dressing room, feeling ashamed. Just then, Bill Hayes knocked on his door. Cranston assumed the veteran actor was there to chew him out.

"Instead," Cranston recalled, "he said some comforting words, commiserating with my situation, and asked if I wanted to know the backstory to the character and the scene. I was shocked. He spent 20 minutes helping a stranger to feel a little less humiliated...I will never forget his kindness and patience."

His mercy is as welcome in time of distress as clouds of rain in time of drought. (Sirach 35:26)

Help me be merciful when responding to mistakes, Lord.

Pop-Up Food Bank at Bermondsey Home

After the food bank at her local church shut down, Henrietta Onyema, 63, from Bermondsey in South London knew she had to help the people in her neighborhood who were struggling to make ends meet. This prompted her to start her own pop-up food bank outside her house.

At first, Onyema used her own money to buy food and other supplies for her neighbors, especially to assist the elderly who were in most need of help. Then, word spread, and Onyema was met with an outpouring of support from local people and even supermarkets who offered donations.

"It pleases your heart when you do something good for people, but everybody should help each other," Onyema told the *BBC*.

The local priest from St. Peter & the Guardian Angels church, Father Tesfamichael Negusse, described Onyema as "incredible," observing that "she has her heart in the need of people. She's always concerned with the neighborhood."

A generous person will be enriched, and one who gives water will get water.
(Proverbs 11:25)

Merciful Father, what can I do to help my community today?

Science and a Miracle

Though they already had two biological children, Clint and Alissa Finlayson of Kalispell, Montana, felt God calling them to adopt a child as well. As reported by Lisa M. Krieger in *The Mercury News,* they wound up adopting two daughters, Lily and Ada, from an orphanage in China, despite the fact that the girls were suffering from a hereditary red blood cell disease, which required them to get six-hour-long transfusions every 21 days.

When the Finlaysons learned that UCSF Benioff Children's Hospital in Oakland, California, was offering a cutting-edge gene therapy for the disease, they applied for Ada and Lily to receive treatment. The girls were accepted, so the family moved to Oakland for several months.

Ada was the first to receive the four-month treatment that involved collecting stem cells from her blood, enduring chemo to kill off "the bad stem cells," then have the new re-engineered cells infused into her body. The process proved to be a success. Alissa noted, "It's science, and it's a miracle…We believe that God has paved a way for us to be here."

Honor physicians for their services, for the Lord created them. (Sirach 38:1)

Lord, pave a way towards healing for all who are sick.

Perfection is Impossible

Though he is now retired, Roger Federer remains one of the greatest tennis players in the history of the game. Yet, in a commencement speech to the graduates at Dartmouth College in 2024, he pointed out to them that "perfection is impossible."

Federer explained that despite earning victories in 80 percent of the 1,500+ singles matches he played, he only won his points 54 percent of the time: "In other words, even top-ranked tennis players win barely more than half of the points they play."

That fact taught him to treat each point as important while he was playing it, but to put it behind him once it was over so he could focus on the next point. That approach can also be applied to life, Federer said, because everyone will face losses.

"Negative energy is wasted energy," Federer concluded. "The best in the world are not the best because they win every point...It's because they know they'll lose...again and again...and have learned how to deal with it. You accept it. Cry it out if you need to...then force a smile. You move on. Be relentless. Adapt and grow."

Do not remember the former things...I am about to do a new thing. (Isaiah 43:18-19)

Help me learn from the past without dwelling on it, Jesus.

My Life with the Jedi, Part 1

Two of Eric Clayton's great passions are Ignatian Spirituality and *Star Wars*. He has found his faith nurtured by St. Ignatius of Loyola's ideal of seeing God in everything—and by the heroic moral and spiritual journeys of the characters from a galaxy far, far away. As such, Eric wrote a book titled *My Life with the Jedi: The Spirituality of Star Wars.*

A key aspect of Jesuit spirituality is being "a man (or woman) for others." One of the main elements of *Star Wars* is how the heroes are people who live for others. Han Solo, for instance, begins the series as someone looking out only for himself.

When Eric watched *Star Wars: A New Hope* with his daughter for the first time recently, he was shocked to discover she thought Han was the villain because he seemed selfish. It made Han's turn to selflessness and friendship at the end of the film that much more powerful for both Eric and his daughter.

Look not to your own interests, but to the interests of others. Let the same mind be in you that was in Christ Jesus. (Philippians 2:4-5)

Allow me to be a "person for others," Jesus.

My Life with the Jedi, Part 2

My Life with the Jedi author Eric Clayton believes that one way to grow in knowledge of ourselves and our world is to become "contemplatives in action," another Ignatian tradition.

During a *Christopher Closeup* interview, Eric explained, "The term comes from Jerome Nadal, who was one of the early Jesuits with Ignatius...At that time, [the] 1540s, your common form of religious life was to be in the monastery. So, this idea of a religious order that was out in the world was very uncommon.

"Nadal says, 'The world is our monastery. We are called to take that form of prayer and experience of God—discovering how God wants to shower us with love—and bring it into the world...then allow the world to affect us and keep doing it.'

"What are the Jedi? They reflect, they meditate, but then they go back into the world and keep serving peace [and justice]...[So you need to] bring all these moments of suffering and challenge from the real world into your prayer, let [them] inform how you act. Then, you go into the world and do what you uniquely are able to do."

Prepare your minds for action. (1 Peter 1:13)

Lead me to put my prayers into action, Creator.

From Foster Care to Adoptive Dad

There are over 390,000 children living within the U.S. foster care system, according to the Department of Health and Human Services. One of those children was Robert Carter.

Though he was never adopted, Carter, now 33, turned his pain into purpose and went on to adopt five children—all siblings—who had been separated in the foster care system.

"I feel like I just used my trauma and my hurting stuff to be my fuel, to keep going and... want to help people and do better in life," Carter told *CBS News.*

Carter entered the Cincinnati, Ohio foster care system at age 13. He persevered through that tough time to graduate high school and open his own business. He became a foster dad of three young brothers in 2018, and when he discovered they had two sisters, it struck a chord in him to reunite this family.

Carter worked passionately to bring all five siblings together. When the adoption became finalized, it was a blessed day. Now, Carter is giving his kids the life he always dreamed of.

The testing of your faith produces perseverance. (James 1:2-3)

Merciful Jesus, open people's hearts to adoption.

Florence Nightingale's Legacy, Part 1

Florence Nightingale, considered the founder of modern nursing, was born to a wealthy British family in 1820. Early on, she developed a passion for caring for those who were sick or in poverty, and she believed God was calling her to become a nurse. Her parents forbade it, however, since upper class young women in that era were expected to marry wealthy men, not take jobs that involved "menial labor," reported *History.com*.

Nightingale eventually defied her parents' wishes and traveled to Germany to enroll in nursing school. Upon completion, she returned to London to work at a hospital during the city's cholera outbreak. Because of unsanitary conditions in the hospital, the disease spread quickly. So, Nightingale improved hygiene practices in the facility, which lowered the death rate considerably.

Nightingale's next mission would be the challenge of her career. British soldiers were fighting Russia in Crimea over control of the Ottoman Empire. Thousands of soldiers there were in military hospitals with few nurses to care for them. Nightingale answered the call. More tomorrow...

Rescue the weak and the needy. (Psalm 82:4)

Guide me in being a healer, Divine Physician.

Florence Nightingale's Legacy, Part 2

Florence Nightingale organized a group of nurses to travel to Crimea and care for British soldiers in military hospitals, reaching out to nuns from various religious orders to accompany her. A few days later, they were on their way.

Upon arrival in Constantinople, Nightingale's team was met by the worst conditions any of them had ever encountered. As reported by *History.com,* the hospital was built on a cesspool, which contaminated the water; patients often lay in their own waste; and rodents and bugs ran around everywhere.

Nightingale ordered her team to both sanitize the facility and compassionately care for the soldiers. At night, she would walk through the hospital with a lamp, personally checking each patient. Because of this, they dubbed her "the Angel of Crimea."

When Nightingale returned to England after the war, she received a hero's welcome. She had also changed the perception of nursing among the upper classes, who now deemed it a worthy profession. Despite being bedridden from illness from age 38 on, she advocated for better health care until her death at age 90.

If you...satisfy the needs of the afflicted, then your light shall rise in the darkness. (Isaiah 58:10)

God, bless compassionate nurses.

The Rookie Shepherd

Taking part in birthing a sheep was not something Kerry Weber had done before, but it was the situation in which she found herself at an educational farm many years ago. With the baby stuck in the birth canal, Weber helped pull it free, after which the little lamb began frolicking in the field, oblivious to the help it had received from a "rookie shepherd."

Writing for *America* magazine, Weber then recalled Jesus' words, "My sheep hear My voice; I know them, and they follow Me." She reflected, "It takes time for a lamb or sheep to follow a shepherd. It is a learned behavior, not instinctual."

"As a modern-day member of Jesus' flock," Weber continued, "I have faith that my shepherd knows me...I also know that...sometimes I forget to listen for God's voice. Other times I hear it and ignore it. Sometimes I find myself like that little lamb, frolicking about the earth oblivious to the shepherd who over and over again pulls me out of darkness and sets me free...But also, I know that even as I wander, I will not be lost for good. I take heart in the knowledge that, for all my mistakes, 'no one can take [me] out of [God's] hand.'"

Be their shepherd, and carry them forever. (Psalm 28:9)

Keep watch over me and guide me, Divine Shepherd.

Cooking with Nonna

When she was a student at St. John's University in Queens, New York, Rossella Rago lived with her grandmother, Romana Sciddurlo, in a basement apartment in Brooklyn. The two spent a lot of time together, so Rago absorbed lots of cooking lessons from her beloved "nonna" (Italian for "grandmother").

When Rago's father asked her what career she wanted to pursue, she jokingly responded that she'd like her own cooking show. Though initially meant in jest, they developed the idea together, and came up with a show titled *Cooking with Nonna,* in which Rago would join her own grandmother, as well as others, in the kitchen. As reported by *St. John's Magazine,* they soon shot some episodes, and the program became increasingly popular, leading to cookbooks and more.

Rago has cooked with about 50 different nonnas throughout the years, but notes the show is not just about food. She explained, "These nonnas are part of the greatest generation that ever lived, and it's so important to document them. They are the ones who really deserve all the attention and accolades."

I am reminded of your sincere faith, a faith that lived first in your grandmother. (2 Timothy 1:5)

May we revere our grandparents, Father.

A Mother's Love

It was a reunion 34 years in the making. In March 2023, 34-year-old Rachel Ruiz shared a heartwarming TikTok video, showing her long-awaited meeting with her birth mother, Angie Howard.

While few words were spoken by the two women, the love and gratitude between them was clear, especially after they were joined by Ruiz's adoptive parents, Brent and Marian Haslam.

More than 10 years ago, the Haslams gave Rachel a letter from her birth mother, in which she wrote that she hoped the two could connect in person someday. That led Rachel to start searching for Angie. Not only did the two finally connect, but their families also got to know each other. Rachel was even able to meet her biological grandmother just three days before her death.

"My mom thanked Angie, as my parents couldn't have biological children," Rachel told *Today.com*. "Angie said she was grateful that I was raised by such loving parents. She always prayed for that."

Can a mother forget...the child of her womb? (Isaiah 49:15)

Abba, we thank You for the unconditional love of mothers.

Yogi and Scooter: Friends for Life

Baseball Hall of Famers Lawrence "Yogi" Berra and Phil "Scooter" Rizzuto became great friends when they played for the New York Yankees during the 1940s and 50s. That relationship extended decades beyond their days on the diamond.

Yankees broadcaster Michael Kay recalled, "When Phil Rizzuto became ill towards the end of his life, he was put in an assisted living facility, 30 minutes away from where Yogi lived. Every single day, because teammates were important to him, Yogi would drive there and play cards with Phil. When Phil would start to fall asleep, Yogi would hold his hand." Phil died in 2007, and Yogi remembered him as "a hell of a guy."

When Yogi passed away in 2015, many of his acts of kindness came to light. They were celebrated even more in the 2023 Christopher Award-winning documentary *It Ain't Over*, which highlighted not only his massive baseball accomplishments and unforgettable "Yogi-isms," but the humble and loving man that he remained all his life.

A true friend sticks closer than one's nearest kin. (Proverbs 18:24)

Lord, give me the heart and strength to be a good friend until life's end.

Deacon's Mental Health Mission, Part 1

Shame, stigma, and misconceptions surround the topic of mental illness, even in church circles. For instance, there are some Christians who believe that mental illness can be healed or avoided solely by improving your spiritual life. But this is simply not the case. Mental illness and suicide can happen in "good Catholic families," just as they do in less religious homes.

That doesn't mean religious faith has no role to play in navigating these situations. In fact, the opposite is true. In conjunction with professional counseling and sometimes medication, the light of Christ can serve as a guide and a strength to patients and their families navigating mental illness.

Following the suicide of his 29-year-old daughter Katie, who had bipolar disorder, Deacon Ed Shoener made it his mission to reduce the stigma around mental illness in the Church, to encourage compassion for those dealing with mental illness, and to guide parishes in creating their own mental health ministries. Deacon Ed joined us on *Christopher Closeup* to share his story and mission. More tomorrow…

When the righteous cry for help, the Lord hears. (Psalm 34:17)

Help us reduce the stigma around mental illness, Savior.

Deacon's Mental Health Mission, Part 2

Katie Shoener's mental illness first manifested itself when she was in high school, though she hid it well from her parents. Their introduction to the problem occurred after she attempted to commit suicide. It was extra shocking because, outwardly, Katie appeared to be thriving.

"We had no idea what was going on," Deacon Ed recalled. "We knew very little about mental illness. Me, in particular, I attributed it to other things. I thought, 'You're being a drama queen. You're drinking,' that sort of thing. [I] got off on the wrong foot with this, but eventually came to learn what mental illness is, and that she was living with bipolar disorder."

"My heart goes out to so many people I've ministered to since that, whose child actually died in their first suicide attempt in their late teens. It comes out of the blue, and [the parents] are so wracked with guilt that they didn't see it coming... Fortunately for us, Katie survived that first suicide attempt, and eventually got into mental health care and treatment."

The wisdom from above is...willing to yield, full of mercy and good fruits. (James 3:17)

Make us humble enough to explore mental illness honestly, Lord.

Deacon's Mental Health Mission, Part 3

Katie Shoener's bipolar disorder manifested itself mainly as depression and mania. Counseling and medication stabilized her most of the time, but every once in a while, she would fall prey to a bipolar episode.

Deacon Ed Shoener observed, "I'd literally be talking to her, and a half hour later...she'd be almost catatonic. She'd be so depressed...But most of the time, she was good, and she took it very seriously. She took all the meds. She saw a therapist and psychiatrist, and she understood it was an illness and tried to manage it as best she could as an illness.

"But mental health care is still not where it needs to be. It's not like you can take a blood sample and say, 'Okay, well, such-and-such levels are off. We need to act quickly.'...It's more trying to understand your feelings and symptoms. So, it's a more difficult illness to manage at this stage."

Katie managed her bipolar for more than a decade and was building a good life. Deacon Ed believes her suicide was an impulsive choice made during a major depressive episode.

Precious in the sight of the Lord is the death of His faithful ones. (Psalm 116:15)

Comfort parents who lose a child to suicide, Jesus.

Deacon's Mental Health Mission, Part 4

In the aftermath of his daughter Katie's suicide, Deacon Ed Shoener wrote an obituary about her and what happened so that there wouldn't be any "gossip or speculating" in their parish or small town of Scranton, Pennsylvania. That obituary went viral, shocking Deacon Ed, but also teaching him a vital lesson.

During a *Christopher Closeup* interview, he said, "Apparently, it spoke to what so many people with mental illness live with. The stigma, the discrimination, being defined by their illness...I was open that [Katie] had this illness, but she wasn't defined by [it], and she's a beautiful child of God, loved by Jesus Christ. This clearly resonated with people."

"This viral response, for me, was almost a mystical experience, of so many people around the world saying that the Church needs to step up and...start ministering to people that live with these illnesses and their families and their caregivers, because I'm absolutely convinced that Christ wants to be in the middle of all of this... Christ wants to be there, and He sends His Church to do that."

Let each of you look not to your own interests, but to the interests of others. (Philippians 2:4)

Christ, help us bring Your presence to the mentally ill.

Deacon's Mental Health Mission, Part 5

Deacon Ed Shoener emphasizes that mental illness cannot be prayed away with a stronger spiritual life, as some people suggest. He explained, "This outdated notion that they have a mental illness because they don't pray enough, that's harmful."

"People, often, with depression and anxiety, already [feel] they're not good enough. The illness tells them they're not worth living, that they're a terrible mistake. So, to have someone heap on top of that by saying, 'You're thinking that way because you don't pray enough,' that makes things worse. So, I hope people stop thinking that way. Mental illness is an illness, like every other illness. We have to understand it and treat it that way."

Deacon Ed continued. "I'd add that people living with mental illnesses have very deep spiritual lives...We can pray with people with these illnesses, we can support them...I live with depression. Twenty percent of people in this country live with some sort of diagnosable mental illness at the moment...So, we're all in this together."

The Spirit helps us in our weakness; for we do not know how to pray as we ought. (Romans 8:26)

Support me in my mental struggles, Holy Spirit.

Deacon's Mental Health Mission, Part 6

After losing his daughter to suicide, Deacon Ed Shoener co-founded the Association of Catholic Mental Health Ministers in 2018, along with Bishop John Dolan from the Diocese of Phoenix, Arizona. They offer resources to parishes on ways to begin their own mental health ministries, as well as resources to individuals looking for prayers, community, books, liturgy, films, and more.

"When Katie first experienced bipolar disorder," recalled Deacon Ed on *Christopher Closeup*, "we had no one to talk to. And to be honest with you, the last place I thought to go was the Church to talk about mental illness and what happened. Now, we encourage parishes to have support groups for the parents and caregivers, where they can come in and talk about this.

"So often, people are isolated. They think they're bad parents, [that] they did something wrong [because] their child had a mental illness... So, we offer this online training program...It's free...I would encourage people, go to our website (*catholicmhm.org*), take the training courses, and it'll give you the confidence to start this type of ministry."

Bear one another's burdens. (Galatians 6:2)

Inspire parishes to start mental health ministries, Abba.

Deacon's Mental Health Mission, Part 7

Though his daughter Katie is no longer physically present in Deacon Ed Shoener's life, his faith affirms his belief that she is still with him in some way. He said, "The communion with the saints is not just the saints who are painted on a wall...We all hope to be a saint one day, to live eternally with God. So, our loved ones, we're still in communion with them. And yes, absolutely...I pray for Katie all the time."

"The other thing I want to add on death and judgment, particularly for suicide," Deacon Ed added, "is that there's still people out there that think the Church teaches that someone who died by suicide goes to hell."

"That's not what the Church teaches. The Church teaches that our loved ones who died by suicide have the opportunity for what the catechism calls 'salutary repentance,' and that we pray for the souls of our loved ones who have died by suicide. That old teaching was a misunderstanding of the psychology of suicide. The Church has a better informed understanding of what brings people to suicide now than it did 50 years ago."

The free gift of God is eternal life in Christ Jesus our Lord. (Romans 6:23)

Welcome those who have died by suicide into Your heavenly Kingdom, Lord.

Deacon's Mental Health Mission, Part 8

The death of a child is the darkest experience any parent can go through. Having survived the most intense pain and grief he's ever experienced, Deacon Ed Shoener is now focused on the light.

At the end of his *Christopher Closeup* interview, he concluded, "I've always thought that this ministry is bringing the light of Christ into very dark places. So, my assurance is that I'm carrying the light of Christ. It's not me. It's not Ed Shoener. It's not anybody else that's in ministry that's doing this. It's Christ that's bringing His light into these lives. That's the solace I take. I know Christ is with me in this ministry.

"Admittedly, it can be a difficult ministry at times. I have someone I have to call this afternoon whose best friend died by suicide yesterday. It's a tough ministry at times, but it's joyful in the sense that you know you're doing the will of God, that God wants to be there and wants to send His ministers into these dark places. So, that's where I find joy."

In all your ways acknowledge Him, and He will make straight your paths. (Proverbs 3:6)

Guide me in bringing Your light into people's lives, Jesus.

The 72-Year-Old Graduate

At age 72, Sam Kaplan never dreamed he would be walking across the stage wearing a cap and gown. Yet in May of 2023, more than 50 years after graduating high school, Kaplan earned his bachelor's degree in Cinema and Media Arts. His decision to enroll was essentially a whim.

"I was riding down 316 and heard on the radio that Georgia Gwinnett College [in Lawrenceville] was offering a degree that involved script writing," Kaplan told NBC affiliate *WWBT*. "My car seemed to have developed automatic steering...Five minutes later, I was registering for the Fall [semester]."

Sam, who grew up as one of seven children and worked many odd jobs throughout his life, made fast friends with both his younger fellow students and professors alike. "Sam was always willing to share photos and stories of his interesting life and family," Associate Professor Kate Balsley added. "We're so proud to see him graduate...We will miss him."

The proudest person in the audience on Kaplan's graduation day? His 99-year-old mother! It just goes to show, no matter your age, it is never too late to fulfill a long-held dream.

Let the wise...gain in learning. (Proverbs 1:5)

Savior, may we always seek to further our education.

Prayer for Families

One could argue there is no greater wealth than that of a loving, devoted family. Like all of life's precious gifts that come from above, we should strive to give thanks to our Heavenly Father for this priceless blessing every day, as it is a blessing far too often taken for granted. The United States Conference of Catholic Bishops offers this prayer for families everywhere:

"We bless Your name, O Lord, for sending Your own Incarnate Son, to become part of a family, so that, as He lived its life, He would experience its worries and its joys.

"We ask You, Lord, to protect and watch over this family, so that, in the strength of Your grace, its members may enjoy prosperity, possess the priceless gift of Your peace, and, as the Church alive in the home, bear witness in this world to Your glory...Amen."

May the love, strength, and wisdom of our families, near and far, immediate and spiritual, continue to guide and sustain us through all of life's beautiful triumphs and sorrows.

I am reminded of your sincere faith, a faith that lived first in your grandmother...and your mother...and now, I am sure lives in you. (2 Timothy 1:5)

Abba, may we always strive to maintain a legacy of faith.

Blessing in a Bag

More than 10 years ago, Chicago high school sophomore Jahkil Naeem Jackson came up with the idea of handing out Blessing Bags, as a means of alleviating the plight of the homeless. Now, after learning about the concept from a Facebook post, P.S. 204 crossing guard Sandy Irrera has adopted the practice in her Brooklyn, New York neighborhood as a way of living out her Catholic faith.

Irrera's Blessing Bags contain several of life's everyday essentials (i.e. soap, snacks, etc.), along with her own special addition: a five dollar bill. "I want each bag to have the same things, things I think they could use," Sandy told *The Tablet's* Paula Katinas. "I always keep at least three Blessing Bags in my car, so that if I see someone, I can jump out and give them one."

With the encouragement of P.S. 204 principal Ursula Annio, students at the school have already donated items towards their crossing guard's philanthropic efforts. "It's like we're part of a movement," Sandy concluded. "It's not a big, orchestrated thing...I want to prove to people that it doesn't take much to help."

Kindness is like a garden of blessings. (Sirach 40:17)

God, may we cherish all life's blessings, big and small.

Brooks Robinson Found Hope in Faith

During the 1960s and 70s, Baltimore Orioles third baseman Brooks Robinson was known as "the Human Vacuum Cleaner" because he was so good at catching balls hit toward him. On the occasion of Robinson's death in 2023, he was also remembered as a kind, decent, charitable man whose faith was key to his life.

Though he was raised Methodist, his wife, Connie, was Catholic. Robinson told the *Catholic Review* newspaper that once they had children, he thought it was important that they go to church together, so he converted to Catholicism.

As recounted by George Matysek Jr., Robinson relied on his faith to get through health challenges, including prostate cancer. Robinson said, "It's...been an outpouring of love which I've never seen before. I've compiled a lot of [religious] medals that people sent me. I really think that was a big part of it."

As he got older, Robinson noted, "I think more about my Catholic faith now than I ever did. It seems like the older you get, the more you think about Jesus Christ and how you're living." Surely, heaven gained an All Star upon Robinson's passing.

Abide in My love. (John 15:9)

Remind me to think about Your love, Jesus.

A Country United

Last Memorial Day, former *WWL-TV* News anchor Karen Swensen was at her local Winn Dixie supermarket in Metairie, Louisiana, when she saw 90-year-old Dillon McCormick in the parking lot, collecting shopping carts. Swensen told *CBS News* that she wondered, "How can someone who's clearly lived a long time and worked so hard be out here in this heat, pushing carts?"

Swensen approached McCormick to make further inquiries. A veteran of the Air Force, he explained that he had been working at Winn Dixie for the last 23 years to bridge the gap in his monthly bills, which his Social Security checks did not cover.

Moved by McCormick's plight, Swensen shared his story on social media, along with a *GoFundMe* page. Within 24 hours, the retired newswoman had raised a whopping $244,000 to gift to the grateful McCormick.

"We take care of our own, not only in Louisiana," Karen concluded proudly, "but this entire nation banded together. I looked at who was donating...it's the left, it's the right, it's everything in between. We united for the right reason."

Be united in the same...purpose.
(1 Corinthians 1:10)

Messiah, may we strive to unite for all the right reasons.

We Will Remember

Connor Nicol comes from a military family, so the teen Eagle Scout is inclined to respect those who serve their country. In 2020, he created a special nonprofit, named We Will Remember, to honor Americans who lost their lives in combat overseas.

As reported by Sheniece Chapell of *Scouting Magazine,* Connor combed through the national archives to collect the names of every fallen veteran. Then, he began making memorial dog tags with each veteran's name, along with listing some background information about the person on a piece of paper.

Connor invites people to adopt each dog tag and remember the fallen veteran every day in their thoughts and prayers. To date, he has created 36,000 dog tags for those lost in the Korean War. He is now making more for those who died in Vietnam.

Connor said, "I want to create a personal connection so there is at least one person who is remembering that service member's name—keeping their memory alive...It also increases awareness and appreciation for the dedication and sacrifice of those who gave everything for our country to be safe."

Precious in the sight of the Lord is the death of His faithful ones. (Psalm 116:15)

Welcome our fallen military members into Your kingdom, Lord.

Professor's Baby Friendly Policy

Jerusalem psychology professor Sydney Engelberg gained Internet fame for a simple gesture: holding a student's fussy baby while continuing to teach class.

When a student was in a bind and asked if she could bring her baby to class, Engelberg agreed, even volunteering to hold the baby so that the student could concentrate on her group exercise. Another student snapped the photo of Engelberg comforting the baby, sharing it on social media.

This may not seem like a lot, but this simple gesture gained admiration from parents around the world. As reported by *CNN*, one commenter wrote, "Good for him for understanding how hard it is for her to be a student and a mother and that she's trying to better herself for her son."

This is just one example of many in which Engelberg is helping those students who are unable to find alternative childcare arrangements—and doing so "in a way which enables them to remain engaged, [and] shows respect for their situation."

Those who respect their mother are like those who lay up treasure. (Sirach 3:4)

Help me, dear Jesus, show respect for others, no matter their situation.

Staying the Course with Courtesy

It might surprise you, but the late Mario Andretti, a champion auto racer, once said that he felt "safer on the racecourse than I do on the streets."

Not only do professional drivers keep their minds on their driving, Andretti explained, but the pros are "exceedingly courteous to one another on the track."

The reason is simple. Courtesy saves lives. Once, A.J. Foyt saw sparks flying from the back of Andretti's car and signaled him to pull over. He could have done nothing and allowed his rival to break down. Instead, Foyt's courtesy prevented a potential pile-up.

If these sportsmen can make time for courtesy, even in the heat of a race, why can't the rest of us? Small, ordinary acts of thoughtfulness add up to a life well lived.

Speak evil of no one...avoid quarreling...be gentle...and show every courtesy to everyone. (Titus 3:2)

Give me a grateful heart and a thoughtful manner, Holy Spirit.

Fantastic Voyage

At age 29, Cole Brauer made history, becoming the first American woman to race around the world by herself in her 40-foot boat, First Light. The only woman and the youngest competitor in the grueling, four-month-long, 30,000-mile Global Solo Challenge, Brauer placed second out of 16 sailors.

"It would be amazing if there was just one girl that saw me and said, 'Oh, I can do that too,'" Brauer told *NBC News*. It's likely that far more than one girl saw her. Although sailing alone, Brauer was buoyed by the support of other team members, family, friends, and 450,000 Instagram followers.

In addition to stormy seas, dangerous icebergs and 30-foot waves, Brauer faced challenges even before she set foot in her boat. Potential sponsors didn't think the 5-foot 2-inch woman could do it. But telling her she couldn't do something just made Brauer even more motivated to complete the task. The race's organizer, Marco Nannini, observed, "The biggest asset is your mental strength. Cole is showing everyone that."

You have given it a path in the sea, and a safe way through the waves. (Wisdom 14:3)

Holy Spirit, help us inspire young people to live life to the fullest.

Watch Out for Money Scams

According to AARP, a lot of older people have lost significant amounts of money to investment scams. Here are some of the steps they advise you to consider before investing in anything:

- **Check credentials.** Most scams involve unregistered groups. Check at *adviserinfo.sec.gov.*

- **Look for transparency.** "Be wary if you can't independently verify financial statements."

- **Take your time.** "If it's a legitimate investment, it's going to be available tomorrow," says Claire McHenry, president of the North American Securities Administrators Association.

- **Get a reality check.** Ask someone not involved with the suggested investment for their thoughts.

- **Know your limitations.** Can you afford to lose the money? Do you understand the proposed opportunity?

The plans of the diligent lead surely to abundance. (Proverbs 21:5)

Guide us to make wise choices, Lord.

A Prayer Group's Call to Action

As the parishioners of St. Anthony Catholic Church in Davenport, Iowa, were holding a prayer vigil one evening, groups of rattled and upset strangers began arriving. A nearby six-story apartment building had partially collapsed, leaving these people without homes.

Father Rudolph Juarez and his parish team quickly stepped in to help. As reported by Barb Arland-Frye for *OSV News*, "St. Anthony's is well known for its service to the most vulnerable and marginalized people." Volunteers came together to serve "homemade deli sandwiches and picked up boxes of Little Caesars Pizza, which was a big hit with the guests."

Lorena Pérez, who attended the prayer vigil, shared the story on social media, noting the displaced people "had nowhere to go...Thank God a very small group (of us) were in prayer, and by the grace of God the church was open. Now, it's a haven for them...Now, San Antonio is a sanctuary for them. Thank God they found a place to go."

If you offer your food to the hungry and satisfy the needs of the afflicted, then your light shall rise in the darkness. (Isaiah 58:10)

May I be a comfort to those who need help, Father.

**Teach me Your way,
O Lord, that I may
walk in Your truth.**

(Psalm 86:11)

Memories of the Ice Cream Truck

Were you lucky enough to grow up on a street visited by an ice cream truck? If so, you must remember the thrill of hearing those chimes or bells and realizing it was time for a delicious, sweet treat during the sweltering heat of summer!

You may not know that ice cream used to be primarily enjoyed only by people from wealthy households because it was so expensive to make. Technological advances changed that, but the advent of the ice cream truck made the frozen delicacy more accessible to everyone.

As reported by *CBS News,* it started 100 years ago with refrigerated trucks being used to transport ice cream to stores. Ice cream parlor owner Harry Burt got the idea to paint one of those trucks white and use it to sell chocolate-coated ice cream on a stick around town. He dubbed the treats Good Humor Ice Cream Suckers, and they proved so popular, they gave birth to a new industry.

Manish Vora, co-founder and co-CEO of the Museum of Ice Cream, observed, "What started as a simple idea back in the 20s has become a worldwide phenomenon."

Taste and see that the Lord is good. (Psalm 34:8)

Thank You for life's simple pleasures, Creator.

TV Food for the Soul, Part 1

If you need a break from the cynical stories that make up much of our media landscape today, take a trip to Hope Valley, the fictional town at the center of the popular, Christopher Award-winning *Hallmark Channel* series *When Calls the Heart*. Set in a Canadian frontier town in the 1920s, the show celebrates the better angels of our nature and what we can achieve when a community works together for the common good.

During a *Christopher Closeup* interview, creator and executive producer Brian Bird noted that TV programs in recent years often focus on the dark side of humanity. *When Calls the Heart* offers viewers the opposite.

He said, "There's not a cynical bone in the body of this show. It reminds people that they need to be part of something bigger than themselves...I believe we're put here by a Creator, and there is a purpose for our life. At a time when not too many people are talking about those kinds of subjects on television, we are. I actually think that's why we've resonated so well with people is that they're starved to death for these values."

Everything has been created for its own purpose. (Sirach 39:21)

Nurture the better angels of my nature, Holy Spirit.

TV Food for the Soul, Part 2

Providence and faith in God are recurring themes in *When Calls the Heart*. In a season 11 episode, for instance, Pastor Joseph mediates a dispute between his son and daughter. When they reconcile, he looks up to heaven and mouths the words, "Thank You." It is a subtle expression of faith in a show that incorporates spirituality without thumping you over the head.

"I've never believed personally in creating content that was just a sermon on film," executive producer Brian Bird said. "What's important to me is that whatever we stir up on the screen stirs up something that pulls people together into conversation, into community, so they can help each other out."

As the son of a preacher turned radio DJ, Brian grew up spending a lot of time in church and came to faith at age seven. This faith was "sorely tested" in his college years, while attending journalism school. Brian recalled, "I was now being confronted with a much broader world... and a lot of questions. Journalists are naturally skeptics, right?...You want to find out the real reasons for things. You want to get to the truth."

How did Brian do that? That story tomorrow...

Send out Your light and Your truth. (Psalm 43:3)

Lead me to seek the light of Your truth, Lord.

TV Food for the Soul, Part 3

After finding his faith challenged when he started attending journalism school, TV writer and executive producer Brian Bird sought guidance from one of his professors, asking him, "How do I reconcile who I have been and who I've been raised to be...with this much bigger, more complex, messy worldview that I'm now seeing as a journalist and in college?"

The professor responded, "Here's how I reconciled it. I'm also a believer. My advice to you is, don't be afraid of the marketplace of ideas because, in the marketplace of ideas, truth will always show up. Ultimately, truth will rise to the top. But if you're afraid of the questions, you're going to be afraid of the answer. So, don't ever be afraid of the questions."

Brian explained, "For me, as an adult Christian, who reaffirmed my faith and my relationship with God and with Christ all those years ago in college, I'm now not afraid of questions...The Bible is full of questions, lots of existential doubt on display all across the Bible. And yet, there's a harmony of truth there that is as right-side up as the world is upside-down. Truth emerges despite the questions."

The truth will make you free. (John 8:32)

Teach me not to be afraid of questions, Creator.

TV Food for the Soul, Part 4

The Christopher Award-winning *Hallmark Channel* series *When Calls the Heart* is in its 12th season, and executive producer Brian Bird believes the show has plenty of story potential to go on for many more years. He also reflected on the show's loyal fans, who have dubbed themselves "Hearties."

Brian said, "The best legacy of *When Calls the Heart* [is that it] has fostered friendships all over the world between people who didn't know each other until they started watching the show. The show became a catalyst for them to have a friendship."

"Community is king in a show like this," Brian added. "We need to...have a sense of community in our lives when we've grown so isolated in our own silos in our culture...I think that it's a way to survive the brokenness that we see all around us, when politics and other aspects of culture seem to be in a mess."

"[*When Calls the Heart*] can show a community that figures out how to get along together. They're not all perfect people, but at the end of the day, they do the right thing...There's something profoundly comforting about that."

We, who are many, are one body in Christ, and...we are members one of another. (Romans 12:5)

Help us build stronger communities, Lord.

The Sands of Omaha Beach

Each June 6th marks the anniversary of the D-Day invasion of Normandy, France, in 1944, when American soldiers began their final efforts to defeat the Nazis in Europe. More than 9,000 Americans died that day and were buried in the Normandy American Cemetery nearby.

During the 1950s, the names of the dead on the white headstones began to fade, making them hard to read. As reported by Komal Banchhor at *Upworthy*, "[French gardeners] came up with the idea of using sand from [Omaha Beach] to fill in the letters, making them more legible and creating a poignant connection between the soldiers buried in the cemetery and the place where they had fought and died."

The local population eventually took over this tradition, which continues to take place every year on the eve of the June 6th anniversary and commemorations. Banchhor concluded, "Filling in the letters on the tombstones is a small but powerful way to show gratitude for [the soldiers'] sacrifice and ensure that their memory lives on for generations to come."

I thank my God every time I remember you. (Philippians 1:3)

Bless all those who sacrificed their lives for freedom, Lord.

To Sir, with Love

What is the most generous gift you ever gave to an educator you appreciated? In 2023, Clayton Guy, a government and economics teacher at Arcadia High School in Phoenix, Arizona, received nearly $10,000 from his graduating class. This sum was raised through a *GoFundMe* page, which these young people created to help pay for their teacher's wife's upcoming heart surgery.

Parker Bond, one of Guy's pupils, told *Fox News Digital* that Mr. Guy was always an unfailingly enthusiastic and upbeat individual. But he underwent a stark personality change about halfway through the school year. When Guy revealed the cause of his anxiety to them, Bond and his fellow classmates knew immediately what they needed to do.

While initially shocked when they first ran their plan by him, Guy was deeply "honored" that his students would go to such lengths. Thankfully, Guy's wife, Angel, has since had a successful procedure. "We just need more kind acts," Bond said. "A teacher like Mr. Guy…who gave so much to us when he was down…was able to receive back because of his kindness."

The one who sows…will also reap.
(2 Corinthians 9:6)

Abba, we thank You for the gift of good teachers.

Andrea Bocelli on Silence and Generosity

As someone who has sold 90 million records and continually travels around the world to perform concerts, Italian singer Andrea Bocelli is a busy man. So perhaps it is the hectic pace of his life that makes him appreciate the value of silence.

In an interview with George P. Matysek Jr. for the *Catholic Review,* Bocelli said, "Silence, I believe, hides true treasures, because it leads to reflection, while it is also an essential space in which to collect one's thoughts in prayer. Whenever I can, I try to escape the clamor and confusion of cities and go to the country and nature that are a haven for the spirit, ideal for finding the right dimension for reflection."

Another aspect of life that Bocelli makes time for is his charitable foundation, which supports arts education for children, and humanitarian causes, such as poverty relief. He said, "Doing good for others, I believe, is a natural desire. Being a philanthropist...does not simply mean being generous, and it is not only a moral duty. It's an act of intelligence, a path that all of us—each as much as we can—should perceive as the only path to follow."

Be rich in good works. (1 Timothy 6:18)

Father, help me build on my desire to do good for others.

City Helps Teen's Thriving Business

At age 13, Jaequan Faulkner wanted to earn some money over the summer, so he started a hot dog stand right outside his house. Despite a major setback, the teen's entrepreneurial spirit and business acumen produced positive results.

Business at Jaequan's old-fashioned hot dog stand in north Minneapolis was thriving when a neighbor reported him to the health department for operating without a license. Instead of simply shutting him down, the city of Minneapolis, along with the nonprofit NEON, stepped up to help him rectify that issue. Health inspectors taught him about proper food handling and even paid the fee for his permit when he passed inspection.

"My hope...is to be an inspiration," Jaequan told *NBC* affiliate *KARE 11*. "I want to inspire other young teens that live in north Minneapolis." Jaequan also appeared on *The Steve Harvey Show* after his story gained national recognition. Harvey said of his situation: "They didn't shut [Jaequan] down. They showed him how to be bigger."

Doers who act — they will be blessed in their doing. (James 1:25)

Lord, despite the obstacles I face, I know I can trust in You to help me reach my full potential.

From TV Career to House of Mercy

In her 20s and 30s, Liz Buckley climbed the corporate ladder, building a successful career for herself in TV post production. But in 2022, she chose to dramatically shift her path to one of "radical hospitality" instead, becoming Executive Director of the Williamsburg House of Mercy in Virginia.

The nonprofit provides: respite and services to the area's homeless and works towards ending their homelessness; support for those struggling to maintain housing; a food pantry to assist the hungry; and a pregnancy center that makes it more financially feasible for women to choose life for their babies.

Buckley told the *Williamsburg Yorktown Daily* that she doesn't regret her TV career, but wishes she had found a better work-life balance. When asked how she now defines success, she noted, "I subscribe to the Ralph Waldo Emerson quote: 'To know even one life has breathed easier because you have lived. This is to have succeeded.' Success isn't about you the individual, but rather the individuals impacted by your choices and actions… Every day brings an opportunity for success."

Commit your work to the Lord, and your plans will be established. (Proverbs 16:3)

Make me successful in extending love and hospitality, Lord.

A Gift for Charles Bronson

Actor Charles Bronson conveyed a tough guy image in his movie roles, but he was also that way off camera early in his career. In an interview with Jimmy Kimmel, actor Kurt Russell recalled working with Bronson on a TV series in 1963.

Russell, only 12 at the time, heard it was Bronson's birthday, so he bought him a remote-controlled airplane as a gift. When Russell gave it to him and wished him a happy birthday, Bronson accepted it without saying a word or smiling, then walked away. Russell wasn't sure what to make of this response.

A few minutes later, Bronson called Russell to his dressing room for a private conversation. A slightly emotional Bronson, who had grown up very poor, told him, "Nobody ever really got me a present before for my birthday. Thanks."

A few months later, when Russell's birthday came around, Bronson bought him a skateboard—and got one for himself as well. The two pals began skateboarding around the studio lot together. The moral of this story? Sometimes tough guys just need to experience kindness to soften up a little.

He will keep a person's kindness like the apple of His eye. (Sirach 17:22)

May troubled souls receive the kindness they need, Lord.

Growing an Artist

Working with his father when he was young led John Parra to write and illustrate a Christopher Award-winning children's book about the experience. Titled *Growing an Artist*, it tells the tale of a boy named Juanito, who helps out with his Papi's landscaping business, while also drawing pictures in his sketchbook about the beauty he observes in nature.

Parra told *QNS.com* that he started accompanying his dad to jobs at age seven, then worked for him part-time between the ages of 12 and 24. Parra wanted the book to highlight the dignity of manual labor and taking pride in who you are. He added, "The book is also a celebration of workers who contribute to creating a better, more beautiful world, but sometimes go unseen."

Regarding his Christopher Award for a work he deems a love letter from sons to fathers, Parra said, "I love the motto written on the award—'It's better to light one candle than to curse the darkness'—and deeply connect with this and its connection to my purpose in art."

A wise child makes a glad father. (Proverbs 10:1)

Lord, strengthen and deepen the bonds between fathers and their children.

A Nine-Year-Old Superman

Wayne and Lindy Baker, and their nine-year-old son Branson, were driving to Dickson, Oklahoma, to avoid the devastating storms headed in their direction. But they were too late. They crossed paths with a tornado, which threw their truck into a tree.

As reported by *CBS News,* Wayne and Lindy both suffered broken backs and necks. Branson, however, escaped unscathed and ran to get help. The youngster begged his parents, "Mom, Dad, please don't die. I will be back."

Branson "ran over a mile in the dark, through downed power lines and debris to get help. He made it to the house of a neighbor and friend and brought him back to help his parents." The boy's uncle, Johnny Baker, explained, "The only way he found his way back was with lightning strikes that lit the road."

The couple's serious injuries will take time to heal, but they are expected to recover. A GoFundMe was established to help cover their medical bills. Regarding Branson, Baker concluded, "He had to become his parents' Superman."

A little child shall lead them. (Isaiah 11:6)

Give me divine courage in challenging situations, Father.

Man with Down Syndrome is Proud Father

There are many misconceptions when it comes to genetic disorders, such as Down syndrome. One fallacy is that people with Down's cannot have children. Though it is more difficult, one man has overcome this obstacle and is a proud husband and father whose son is on the path to becoming a dentist.

Jad Issa, a Syrian man with Down syndrome, faced many prejudices, but he was determined to not let his condition prevent him from living a full life. He met his wife after he started working in a local wheat mill, and they had a child named Sader, who does not have Down syndrome. Sader, now grown up, is becoming a dentist, as reported by *My Modern Met*. Jad couldn't be prouder, exclaiming, "My son is a doctor!"

Sader said that having a father with Down syndrome inspired him to achieve his dreams: "Personally, I think I would've been much less excited about life and much less passionate with what I do if I didn't have my special father."

The father of the righteous will greatly rejoice; he who begets a wise son will be glad in him. (Proverbs 23:24)

Loving Lord, bless all the fathers in the world!

A Father's Work and Example

When retired *MAD Magazine* editor John Ficarra was growing up in the 1960s, he witnessed his father doing chores that would be described as "women's work" at the time: washing laundry, scrubbing dishes, vacuuming rugs. He didn't do these tasks in the name of gender equality, however. He simply wanted to help his wife.

Writing in New York's *Daily News*, Ficarra recalled that his mother helped him with his homework and handled all the cooking (a task at which his father was terrible). But everything else was fair game:

"My father was the son of an Italian immigrant who found dignity in any kind of work...He just saw things that needed to be done to help his family and alleviate some of the daily stress on his wife...In his mind, there was no chromosome test that needed to be given before a particular task could be undertaken."

"[My father] taught me through example about life, responsibilities, and commitment...His work ethic and basic decency provided the syllabus on what it means to be a real man, a devoted husband, and an exemplary father."

Hear, my child, your father's instruction. (Proverbs 1:8)

Guide fathers in being role models for their children, Lord.

Tilly and the Tsunami

It's a good thing that 10-year-old Tilly Smith pays attention in school. Her education helped save lives.

Tilly and her parents, who hail from Surrey, England, were on vacation at a beach in Thailand in 2004, when the girl noticed unusual bubbles in the ocean. In addition, the water kept encroaching on more and more of the beach.

Suddenly, Tilly remembered a lesson from school a few weeks prior and told her parents, "We should get off the beach. I think there may be a tsunami coming...They are strong waves caused by undersea earthquakes. And they travel very fast."

Tilly and her parents quickly made their way back to their hotel and explained to the staff what she had seen. When the staff went to check themselves, they confirmed that Tilly's instincts were correct, so they called everyone in off the beach.

A few minutes later, a tsunami crashed onto the beach with a force so strong that the water hit the hotel and went miles beyond as well. Everyone inside the hotel remained safe, thanks to Tilly.

When you pass through the waters, I will be with you. (Isaiah 43:2)

Creator, guide us to safety in natural disasters.

The Cristo Rey Way

In 2020, Cristo Rey High School opened in San Diego to offer financially disadvantaged students the opportunity to both learn in a private school environment and gain work experience in the real world. Four years later, those initial students became the school's first graduating class.

A unique aspect of Cristo Rey schools is that they offset tuition costs through a work-study program. Students attend classes four days a week, and work offsite on a fifth day. Alexa Jasso, for instance, expressed interest in a nursing career as a freshman, so she interned at Rady Children's Hospital. She is now slated to attend San Diego State's nursing program.

Jasso told *ABC 10's* Marie Coronel, "Seeing the compassion [nurses] had for the patients...and seeing the compassion they had towards me, and I had towards them, it made me want to do it even more."

Why is Cristo Rey's approach so successful? Student Citlali Pina observed, "Everyone supports us...There's just so much love, and everyone is here for one another."

Wisdom gives life to the one who possesses it. (Ecclesiastes 7:12)

Help young people gain an excellent education, Lord.

Horticultural Therapy for Dementia

People with dementia become disengaged from the world due to the deterioration of their brains, but horticultural therapy might make a difference. As reported by the website *Being Patient*, a small study discovered that dementia patients who worked with plants had "improved cognitive function" and were slightly more engaged with their surroundings.

Horticultural therapist Joel Flagler observed, "Any time a person reconnects with nature, good feelings and healing can come." He added that giving a person responsibility for another living thing can give them a sense of accomplishment and purpose, especially when they see a flower they planted bloom.

Flagler said, "I will ask people: 'What does a plant need to survive?' They'll answer: 'Water, sunshine and love'...In a nursing facility or something of the sort, these individuals are always on the receiving end of care. Now, we're making them a caretaker, and we're bringing out their nurturing skills. Now, we're talking about real empowerment."

He took a seed from the land, placed it in fertile soil. (Ezekiel 17:5)

Guide caregivers for dementia patients, Divine Physician.

Ironman with Down Syndrome

Chris Nikic of Maitland, Florida, began making history in 2020 when he became the first person with Down syndrome to finish an Ironman triathlon. In addition to running 26.2 miles, he swam 2.4 miles in the Gulf of Mexico and bicycled 112 miles through Panama City Beach.

By 2024, Chris had achieved a Guinness World Record for being the first person with Down syndrome to complete all six of the World Marathon Major races. His father, Nik, praised his goal of getting "one percent better every day."

Both Chris and Nik aim to inspire others with Down syndrome to push themselves beyond the limits the world might set for them. They also hope to promote more inclusivity in sports, reports *Guinness World Records.*

When Chris first wanted to sign up for marathons, he wasn't allowed to because there was no category for those with intellectual challenges. That has since changed, but it was a battle every step of the way. Next up, father and son are opening an academy so high school grads with intellectual challenges can continue their education and play sports as well.

I have finished the race...kept the faith.
(2 Timothy 4:7)

Help those with Down syndrome reach their potential, Lord.

Willie Mays Throws a Kids Party

Following the death of baseball icon Willie Mays in 2024, many recalled his accomplishments on the field. But Peter Hartlaub of *The San Francisco Chronicle* found some old clippings that highlighted the Say Hey Kid's personal generosity.

In 1963, when Mays was playing with the Giants, he threw a party for some neighborhood children at his house in Forest Hill. Kids from the three surrounding blocks were invited for cake, ice cream, bubble gum, chips, and more.

As other children passed by the house, they looked longingly inside, wishing they could be part of the fun. Mays told one parent, "Not invited? Bring them over. They're probably hungry. These kids didn't come to see me. They came to eat."

One boy named Jimmy, not at all intimidated by the baseball great's fame, looked at Mays' beautiful home and told him, "Not a bad pad you got here, Willie."

What started as a party for around 25 became a gathering of 100. It was only one instance in a life in which Mays repeatedly demonstrated his kindheartedness to children.

Clothe yourselves with compassion, kindness, humility, meekness, and patience.
(Colossians 3:12)

May I be hospitable to all, Lord.

A Hobby's Rewards

Many years ago, Ernest Perry of Armuchee, Georgia, gave his work away. When he retired from carpentry, he began to handcraft exquisite wooden canes and give them to people who needed them.

In working and shaping each cane, he gave attention to the knurls, the grain, and the shape of the limb.

In all, he gave away more than 400 canes before he had to give up the work because he was growing too old to hike through the mountains searching for proper wood.

"It was my hobby," he once told an interviewer. "It's given me a lot of pleasure just to give somebody something they can use."

If you are looking for a rewarding hobby, try making something others can really use. You and the recipient will be twice blessed.

Blessed are the people...who walk, O Lord, in the light of Your countenance. (Psalm 89:15)

Help me to find a fulfilling hobby that also brings joy to others, Divine Savior.

'We Have Samurais in the Family'

"Have a positive attitude, be thankful, try to help others," is former Olympian Peter Westbrook's philosophy.

Westbrook, 72, grew up in Newark, New Jersey's housing projects with his mother and sister. When he was 14, his mother encouraged him to take up fencing. She was originally from Japan and told him, "We have Samurais in the family."

Skeptical at first, Westbrook got hooked and eventually attended college on a fencing scholarship. Later, he became a six-time Olympian.

"My father was Black, and I became the first Black man to ever win an Olympic medal in fencing," he told Jennifer E. Mabry for *AARP Magazine*.

Westbrook began a foundation to teach underserved kids about fencing and life. He said, "We talk about emotions, and how to keep going even when faced with the most dire of circumstances."

Whenever we have an opportunity, let us work for the good of all. (Galatians 6:10)

May I remember to share my God-given talents with others.

You Are a Tree, Part 1

When she was growing up, Joy Marie Clarkson's family moved 16 times. After college, she pursued graduate studies and worked in various universities internationally, which led to her moving once a year for 10 years. As she was packing up her apartment for yet another new season of life, she noticed a plant that had gotten scraggly because it had grown too large for the small pot that contained it.

Joy realized, "Oh my gosh, I'm a potted plant! I've grown too much to fit into my little portable life. If I'm going to grow any more, then I need to be able to be in a place where I can have roots and sunshine."

Joy's mind turned to tree imagery from Hebrew and Christian Scriptures, reminding her that "as human beings, we need to be rooted somewhere: to people, to a particular place; that we need sources of nourishment; and even that we're not the same in every year or even every month of our life, that there are seasons when we are fruitful and there's abundance of harvest—but there are also seasons of winter."

They are like trees planted by streams of water, which yield their fruit in its season. (Psalm 1:3)

Help me to grow roots and flourish, Creator.

You Are a Tree, Part 2

Joy Marie Clarkson's interest in the Bible's tree imagery led her to write a book titled *You Are a Tree: And Other Metaphors to Nourish Life, Thought, and Prayer.* In her research, she learned that trees can teach us a lot about community.

For instance, while trees seem to be isolated, individual entities, their roots below the surface reach far beyond what the eye can see and intermingle with the roots of other trees. If one tree is lacking in nourishment, the other trees sustain it by passing along some of theirs. When a person is facing difficult times, he or she can also receive nourishment if enough people reach out to build that person back up.

These ideas are more compatible with human beings than the computer imagery we often use about ourselves. When we think of ourselves as machines, we are denigrating an essential part of our humanity. Computers, for instance, are designed for a functional purpose. If a computer stops working, you get rid of it. Humans, on the other hand, reflect the image and likeness of God, so we should never think of ourselves as disposable.

I praise You, for I am fearfully and wonderfully made. (Psalm 139:14)

May I embrace the inherent dignity of all people, Abba.

You Are a Tree, Part 3

During a *Christopher Closeup* interview about her book *You Are a Tree,* Joy Marie Clarkson noted that metaphors are crucial to our spiritual lives: "[They] allow us to speak about God, but they keep us in that posture of wonder and humility, knowing that we can't contain Him in words." And Jesus is a metaphor master who refers to Himself as "the way, the truth, and the life" and the "light of the world," among other things.

In fact, the imagery of light as wisdom—and darkness as ignorance—is common throughout the Bible and in our everyday language. You might describe a person as "dim," for instance, or as "brilliant."

Joy added, "Especially in Proverbs and in the wisdom literature...God is characterized as both light and the source of wisdom... That gives us...a sense that wisdom is...a source of illumination that allows us to proceed in a wise way...It means being oriented towards the source of wisdom, oriented towards God, and also having a sense of clear perspective on things."

God is light and in Him there is no darkness at all. (1 John 1:5)

Illuminate my mind and heart with Your wisdom, Jesus.

You Are a Tree, Part 4

Another metaphor that Joy Marie Clarkson addresses in her book *You are a Tree* is that of sadness being heavy or a burden. In Matthew 11, Jesus says, "Come to Me, all you who are weary and burdened, and I will give you rest...For My yoke is easy and My burden is light."

Joy observed, "[Jesus] doesn't say you will have no burdens...He says that the burden you'll carry will be light, that I can carry it with you... For life to be meaningful, we have to carry burdens. To love somebody, to have children, that comes with burdens...But that creates what Augustine describes as the weight of love.

"These burdens [of love] keep us on the path of life. They give us a gravity to life that moves us forward. But we, in the Christian life, need to know that we don't bear those burdens alone. There's the sense that Christ bears our burdens...So, just like Christ bore our burden of sin and of death, we get to image Him when we bear each other's burdens and help each other carry things that are too heavy for us."

Bear one another's burdens, and in this way you will fulfill the law of Christ. (Galatians 6:2)

Savior, may our burdens serve to bring us closer to You and each other.

Seacrest Studio Helps Hospitalized Kids

Ryan Seacrest is no stranger to the TV industry, from *American Idol* to TV talk shows. And since 2011, the Ryan Seacrest Foundation has opened broadcast studios in hospitals across the country. They launched their newest facility and closed-circuit channel inside Cohen Children's Medical Center in New Hyde Park, New York, in 2023.

The studio is designed to educate and entertain adolescent patients, helping them develop media skills by producing their own shows to be broadcast throughout the hospital. Seacrest told *QNS*, "We've really discovered what makes a difference and moves the needle in terms of having patients, hopefully for a little bit, forget about what they're going through."

Seacrest added, "These patients are missing important things in their lives: their friends, their birthdays and proms. To have something to look forward to—and a place to go and connect— helps with the healing. Laughter is great medicine, too. When you see a patient laughing or realizing they've got a special talent, I think that helps."

I do not despair of my condition, for I have good hope of recovering from my illness. (2 Maccabees 9:22)

Father, send hope and healing to sick children.

Nothing Short of a Miracle

In June 2022, just days before his 18th birthday, Anthony Mercado endured life-saving brain surgery following a fiery car crash. Dr. Jonathan Rasouli, the neurosurgeon at Staten Island University Hospital who operated on Mercado, told *silive.com* that the young man's recovery was "nothing short of a miracle."

Mercado—saved from the wrecked car by a good Samaritan—arrived at the hospital in critical condition and was placed in a medically induced coma. He had to undergo a five hour surgery, with little chance of success. Mercado's mother, along with his sisters, never lost hope and were there by his side. After two more grueling weeks in a coma, Mercado finally woke up and managed to utter his first word: "Mom."

After a tough, yearlong recovery, Mercado is now walking, planning a career, and grateful for this second chance. And it couldn't have been accomplished without the unwavering optimism, hope, and support of Mercado's family, who wouldn't give up on him.

Rejoice in hope, be patient in suffering, persevere in prayer. (Romans 12:12)

Be with me, Lord, especially in my weakest moments.

Reaching Out to a Stranger

Following his retirement, Scott Kuczmarski traveled from his home in Rhode Island to Palo Alto, California. The reason? He wanted to be with his son, who was beginning "a medical school rotation at Stanford," Scott told *AARP: The Magazine*.

While walking his dog one morning, Scott spotted a man riding a bike that seemingly held all of his possessions. This man was obviously homeless, yet he still had a big smile on his face. Scott engaged him in conversation and learned his name was Robert Pineda. The two men ate breakfast together that day—and almost every day after that for the next three weeks.

As Scott listened to Robert's life story, he deduced that he was suffering from mental illness and worked to get him an official diagnosis. Robert then learned he had schizophrenia and began taking medication to treat it.

To get Robert off the streets after 30 years, Scott found an old cabin near his home in Rhode Island and bought it. He and Robert fixed it up together, and Robert finally has a home again. He feels grateful that Scott has given him "a second chance."

You shall also love the stranger. (Deuteronomy 10:19)

Guide me in showing kindness to strangers, Prince of Peace.

An Impossible Proof

Do you remember studying the Pythagorean Theorem in high school math class? Well, two recent graduates of St. Mary's Academy in New Orleans, Louisiana, did more than study it. They came up with an "impossible" proof that revolutionized the way it is taught.

Calcea Johnson and Ne'Kiya Jackson appeared on *60 Minutes* in 2024 to discuss their remarkable achievement. *The Black Catholic Messenger* reported, "The two classmates were seniors when they discovered a new trigonometric proof for the Pythagorean Theorem, sparking discourse on the history of the formula and its enduring conundrums."

Johnson and Jackson credited St. Mary's rigorous standards with encouraging them—and all students—to pursue excellence. The school was founded in 1867 by Venerable Henriette DeLille and the Sisters of the Holy Family. This African American order of nuns dedicated their lives to educating Black children, who were poor and disadvantaged. Today, they have a 100 percent graduation rate and 100 percent college acceptance rate.

An intelligent mind acquires knowledge. (Proverbs 18:15)

Help all young people value education, Creator.

Engage in Productive Boredom

Boredom is often viewed in a negative way. For instance, there's the old adage that "an idle mind is the devil's workshop." But sometimes, boredom can be God's workshop instead.

At *Aleteia,* Daniel Esparza notes that "productive boredom" can be a good thing from a Catholic perspective. It allows us to slow down, look inward, and contemplate our lives and the world around us. Isaac Newton discovered the law of gravity, for instance, not when he was actively looking for it, but when an apple fell on his head. For him, stillness led to discovery.

Esparza writes, "Allowing oneself time for unstructured exploration, even unstructured prayer, or simply gazing at the clouds affirms this fundamental truth. It is in these moments of seemingly unproductive time that we can reconnect with ourselves, with God, and rediscover the value in the ordinary.

"When faced with a seemingly unproductive stretch of time, it is advisable to embrace it. Allow your mind to wander, be present in the moment, and trust that even in the quiet, something positive might emerge."

Be still, and know that I am God! (Psalm 46:10)

Help me find moments of quiet contemplation, Lord, and may they lead to the discovery of important truths.

A Safe Haven for Kids

"A safe haven for kids to stay off the streets and out of trouble." That's how *CBS New York* describes New Jersey's Salvation Army Newark Westside Corps Books and Basketball Program. Run by Muhammad Oliver, the program provides young people with opportunities for tutoring, learning, and fun.

Oliver explained, "Programs like this save lives. If you give a kid an option and let them know what they could be doing, it keeps them off the streets. The more kids we keep off the streets, keep active and in positive situations and positive environments, the more kids we can save."

Malachi Thomas, age 18, finds that Books and Basketball offers a sheltering and nurturing environment. He said, "Newark is not really safe. You come and play basketball, and you just get a lot off your mind."

The program runs on donations, and no child is turned away. Oliver concluded, "I was a kid who needed help growing up, and a lot of people were a part of...my story, so I just try to be that helping hand for anybody who needs it."

He brought them to their desired haven. Let them thank the Lord for His steadfast love. (Psalm 107:30-31)

Guide children toward havens of love and safety, Lord.

To Do Some Good for Someone Else

Jim Cava, a Vietnam veteran, was badly injured when his helicopter was shot down. He lost an arm, his legs were crushed, and his back was fractured in three places. He spent eight months in a hospital.

It took four years of therapy before he was able to walk. Yet he was so determined that he constantly pushed himself. He began jogging and got to the point where he could run in the New York City Marathon. But he didn't run for himself.

Cava obtained hundreds of sponsors so he could raise funds for a residence for homeless youngsters. He did it, he said, "to do some good for someone else."

Cava learned an important lesson in all this: namely, that thinking of others is what makes life worthwhile. Good advice for all of us.

Of how much more value is a human being!... So it is lawful to do good. (Matthew 12:12)

Jesus, how can we do good to those who need our caring?

The House I Live In

In 1945, after World War II had ended, a short film titled *The House I Live In* was released to combat antisemitism in the U.S. Starring Frank Sinatra, it showed the singer coming out of a recording session and witnessing 10 kids chasing one boy in order to beat him up.

Sinatra intervenes and asks what's going on. "We don't like his religion," one boy answers, suggesting their intended victim is Jewish. Sinatra is appalled, but decides to take a more tactful approach with the kids.

"People all over the world worship God in many different ways," Sinatra explains. "God created everybody. He didn't create one people better than another. Your blood's the same as mine, and mine's the same as his."

Sinatra goes on to sing the film's title song, which begins: "What is America to me?/A name, a map, or a flag I see./A certain word: democracy./ What is America to me?/The house I live in./A plot of earth, a street, the grocer and the butcher, and the people that I meet,/The children in the playground, the faces that I see,/All races and religions, that's America to me."

**God created humankind in His image.
(Genesis 1:27)**

God, continue shedding Your grace on these United States.

A Plant Assassin's Hope and Prayer, Part 1

Simcha Fisher calls herself a "plant assassin." As much as she loves house plants, she rarely succeeds at keeping them alive. As an example, she pointed to her "little fig tree," which she forgot to bring inside before the first frost.

Writing at *Our Sunday Visitor*, Fisher explained, "The poor thing turned brown, all the leaves fell off, and it went from a luxurious, broad-leafed beauty to a dry stick in a pot."

After plants had died in the past, Fisher would simply throw them out. But she had grown attached to this fig tree, so she took a different approach.

She wrote, "I kept watering it and letting it get some sunlight and warm air, and after a week or two, lo and behold! It wasn't dead after all. It wasn't in great shape, but it was very willing to make an effort. So I kept caring for it, and there are now eight little tender baby leaves budding out of the dry stem, and it is a delight to see."

While this seems like a lesson on plant care, Fisher relates it to a withered prayer life. That part of the story tomorrow.

From the fig tree learn its lesson. (Matthew 24:32)

God, remind us all good things are worth the effort.

A Plant Assassin's Hope and Prayer, Part 2

Simcha Fisher succeeded in nurturing her seemingly dead fig tree back to life. She noted that metaphorically watering and nurturing your prayer life—or rather, lack of a prayer life if that's the case—can also restore you spiritually.

If you haven't prayed for a while, you might start by sticking with the basics, Fisher advised in *Our Sunday Visitor*: "There's a reason people like the Rosary or grace before meals or the Angelus or the mercy chaplet. They're basic and achievable, and it's really pretty easy to keep them going."

Fisher also recommended establishing a routine based on your strengths and weaknesses. Since her phone is her weakness, she makes it a point not to turn it on until she says her morning prayers. In addition, people should put reminders to pray where they will be most noticed, depending on their daily lives.

Finally, if your attempts at prayer are initially unsuccessful, just start over. God is a great granter of second (and third and fourth) chances because He wants you to bloom to your full potential.

They are like trees planted by streams of water, which yield their fruit in its season. (Psalm 1:3)

Guide me in building a spiritually fruitful life, Holy Spirit.

A Blue Sky Attitude

Our attitudes and outlook can affect the atmosphere around us. We might compare the situation to the way the earth's atmosphere colors the sunlight. Sunlight is made up of all colors. But the particles of the air scatter the blue light waves (which are short) more than the red and other colors (which are longer). And since it is mostly blue light waves that bounce off the particles and reach our eyes, the sky looks blue.

In somewhat the same way, everyday events impact our lives and bounce off in the way we react to them, coloring other people's views of life. Have you ever noticed how individuals who show enthusiasm have an encouraging effect on those around them, just as those who react with pessimism tend to dishearten others?

Psychologists have observed that kind, loving parents produce an atmosphere conducive to trust, affection, and self-confidence. Those who are harsh or uncaring produce an atmosphere that stunts the emotional growth of their children. So, let's try to reflect positive, constructive attitudes that will help others see life's blue skies.

A cheerful heart is a good medicine.
(Proverbs 17:22)

May I be a source of light and kindness to others, Lord.

Black Belts Save the Day

It was a typical summer afternoon at the family-owned Yong-In Tae Kwon Do Academy, located in Katy, Texas. Han and Hong An, and their children, Hannah, Simon, and Christian, were going about their business when they heard a woman's piercing scream coming from the adjacent cell phone store.

Simon, age 21, and his father, an "eighth-degree black belt...and veteran of the South Korean military," raced next door to find a man assaulting a woman.

Using their taekwondo skills, Simon and Grandmaster Han were able to subdue and hold the perpetrator for 10 minutes until the police arrived. In the meantime, Hong and her daughter took the woman to the safety of their dojo to recover.

The media called them heroes, but Simon just hoped, along with his parents, that "anyone—regardless of their black belt status," would do the same to "help the person in need."

"My life is taekwondo," patriarch Han An humbly concluded to *KHOU News*. "I'm very proud of my family."

Defend...the...needy. (Proverbs 31:9)

Abba, inspire our youth to stand up for those in need.

Catch of the Day

When 14-year-old Connor Halsa felt a giant tug on his fishing pole in the middle of Minnesota's Lake of the Woods, his first thought was that he had hooked one massive fish. Instead, with his cousin's help, Connor proved to have netted a thick billfold with an even tidier haul: $2,000, to be exact. "My dad said we should give it to the person [who lost it]," Halsa told *WDAY TV News,* "and I said we should, too."

As it happened, there was a business card uncovered with this stack of money, identifying the owner of the wallet as "Jim Denney, a farmer from Iowa who had done fishing on the lake a year before." Denney had intended to use this money as the final payment for his stay at a local resort, but while he was out on the water, it slipped out of the pocket of his overalls.

Connor refused the cash reward Denney offered him, so the farmer gifted the teen with a customized cooler and family dinner to show his gratitude. "I would take Connor as a grandson any day," Denney declared.

"We didn't work hard for the money," Connor humbly concluded, "[Mr. Denney] did. Be nice to everyone and give back."

Give, and it will be given to you. (Luke 6:38)

Abba, may we remember a good deed is its own reward.

Community Clean Up a Family Affair

"About five years ago, I was in a really dark place, and...about to take my own life at a riverside," 33-year-old Scottish father of three Mike Scotland told *The Mirror.* "I was saved by a phone call that stopped me then and there—but after that, whenever I'd walk past that area where I'd wanted to end my life, I felt like a dark shadow was haunting me."

To vanquish his gloomy feeling, Mike started doing something positive by the riverside: picking up litter. One day, he and a helpful bystander collected "three full black bags of litter together." Their joint efforts ended with Mike telling his new friend he "was going to start a litter-picking group."

He dubbed his organization Community Clean Up, and after meeting on a weekly basis for a few months, the group had "collected over 13,500 kg [29,762 lbs.] and a whopping 2,500 kg [5,511.5 lbs.] of metal from the river itself." Six years later, they are still going strong. In addition, Mike and his six-year-old son, Lucio, sometimes dress up as Batman to go out and "fight the litter" together. Mike noted that he is excited to see all his children so willing to "make a difference."

Let us work for the good of all. (Galatians 6:10)

Lord, may we remember that in unity, there is strength.

Tell Me a Story

CBS News sent correspondent David Begnaud to San Antonio, Texas, to find a story. So, Begnaud sat himself down in Pearl Park with a sign that read, "I'm looking for a story." People were more than willing to share.

A woman named Denise approached him and revealed she was on vacation from Minnesota, accompanied by her husband, who has Alzheimer's, and their grandchildren. Though her husband was a little more confused than usual, being with his grandchildren was a balm. Denise said, "We went to a doctor, and we talked about meds. And [the doctor] said, 'I cannot prescribe for you a medication that will do anymore for him than being with the family'…And it's true because he lights up."

Beganud also met Bethany, who runs a local business providing virtual homeschooling for kids. She noted a lesson she has learned the last few years that would apply to anyone: "There's more than just work, sleep, repeat. There's more to life than that. You only have 24 hours in a day. Your family, your spiritual health—that's the most important thing."

Teach us to count our days that we may gain a wise heart. (Psalm 90:12)

Help me cherish life's most important elements, Paraclete.

A TV Legend's Kindness

Dick Van Dyke is a legendary entertainer and comedian. He is also known for having a kind heart. Consider this story shared on social media by actor Mark Hamill, best known for playing Luke Skywalker in the *Star Wars* series.

In 1974, several years before making *Star Wars*, Hamill was at CBS Television Studios working on a series. One day, his mother came to visit him, and they went for lunch in the commissary. That's when they spotted Van Dyke eating alone at a nearby table.

Hamill wrote, "He had no idea who I was, but when I went to his table to ask if I could bring [my mom] over to meet him because we were both longtime fans, I got a real shock. He asked me to point her out, and when I did, without asking, he immediately walked over to our table, sat down & proceeded to charm the socks off the both of us for almost 20 minutes, until I was due back on set. Needless to say, it was an experience we both treasured forever!"

Clothe yourselves with compassion, kindness, humility. (Colossians 3:12)

Help me go out of my way to show kindness to others, Paraclete.

Sawyer Swims for St. Jude

In 2016, five-year-old Sawyer Hansen was sitting on his parents' bed, watching TV with them. Suddenly, a commercial for St. Jude Children's Research Hospital appeared onscreen. Sawyer innocently asked if children really did "die from cancer," as the announcer on the television said.

Determined to be honest with their children, Sawyer's mother, Rebecca, answered, "Yes." From that moment on, Sawyer was inspired to help the kids at St. Jude. And on the advice of his parents, he decided to use his "talent for swimming" to do so, reported *stjudeinspire.org*. Thus, the Sawyer Swims for St. Jude fundraising page was born.

"It started off as, 'I want to raise $500 and swim 100 lengths of the pool," Sawyer's father, Jay, recalled. "And he ended up that year at $3,400, and swimming 100 lengths."

Since then, Sawyer has made it an ongoing goal to swim farther every year for the sake of these youngsters. "These kids, they deserve a life like I have," he concluded, "and that's what just sparked me to do this. I just believe that everyone deserves an equal chance."

I have finished the race...kept the faith. (2 Timothy 4:7)

Lord, may we be motivated by the selflessness of our youth.

What We Remember Will Be Saved, Part 1

In 2004, Texas-born Stephanie Saldaña moved to Syria to study as a Fulbright Scholar. She learned Arabic, met the man who would become her husband, and made many Christian and Muslim friends.

When Syria's civil war broke out in 2011, Stephanie was no longer living in the country, but knew many people who were.

"It was not a story about strangers," she explained during a *Christopher Closeup* interview. "It was a story about my friends, former neighbors, and former teachers, so I was personally invested."

"I'm also a member of the Syriac Catholic Church. And so, when Daesh, what we call ISIS, moved into northern Iraq [in 2014], and hundreds of thousands of people were displaced, many of them were from my church community... [I] wanted to figure out how to share some of those stories with the world."

Stephanie has now shared those stories in the Christopher Award-winning book *What We Remember Will Be Saved*. More tomorrow...

You shall not wrong or oppress a resident alien, for you were aliens in the land of Egypt. (Exodus 22:21)

Open my heart to the plight of refugees, Creator.

What We Remember Will Be Saved, Part 2

In order to escape the terrorist group ISIS, Syriac Catholics from Iraq's city of Qaraqosh (also known as Baghdeda) fled to Amman, Jordan, to resettle. Author Stephanie Saldaña traveled there to meet them and learn about their experiences as refugees.

She met Father Elian, the priest from Qaraqosh, who now ministered to his flock in this new country. Stephanie also attended the Mass he celebrated and was moved by the beauty of the choir singing in their homeland's language of Syriac, "a liturgical form of Aramaic."

During an interview about her Christopher Award-winning book *What We Remember Will Be Saved,* Stephanie described the Mass this way: "It was as if the space began to slowly be lit from the inside. One person after another began to sing along in Aramaic, first softly and then with more confidence, until the church was alive with the song of a people who—for a very brief moment—were home again."

By the rivers of Babylon—there we sat down and there we wept when we remembered Zion. (Psalm 137:1)

Lord, may displaced people around the world find comfort and strength in Your presence and love.

What We Remember Will Be Saved, Part 3

Following the Syriac Catholic Mass in Amman, Jordan, Stephanie Saldaña met many refugees from Iraq, including Hana, who had created a dress unlike any that Stephanie had ever seen.

With bright colors, Hana had extensively embroidered her home city of Qaraqosh's history, traditions, and people into an article of clothing that could have hung in a museum as a work of art. It was her way of keeping her town's history alive for herself and others.

Stephanie explained, "So many people I'm writing about, they see themselves as part of a community. They're realizing that their communities are fragmenting, and so they're trying to find ways of holding their communities together. For [Hana], this is a dress for her, but also somehow for everyone she knows, for her town, for her family. It's an act of memory.

"ISIS was engaged in the project of destroying memory, targeting religious shrines of Muslims, of Christians, of Yazidis. And so, the people who were affected also set out on this incredible act of...resistance...saying, 'You don't have the power of destroying our memories, of destroying our pasts.'"

May their memory be blessed! (Sirach 46:11)

Help us find ways to keep good memories alive, Creator.

What We Remember Will Be Saved, Part 4

Another aspect of Middle Eastern life featured in Stephanie Saldaña's Christopher Award-winning book about refugees, *What We Remember Will Be Saved*, is the prominence of interfaith friendships. Stephanie noted, "When people were displaced, one of the things they spoke to me the most often about was their devastation at losing their interfaith friendships."

"I have lived in the Middle East for nearly two decades, and that's certainly a deep part of my life: my relationships with people of other faiths, how we take care of each other during holidays, how we give each other gifts [and] greetings."

Stephanie recalled meeting Munir in the refugee camp Moria in Greece. He had lived in a Muslim and Christian neighborhood in Mosul, and protected his Christian neighbors when they were targeted for persecution in 2003.

"By putting these stories next to each other in one book," Stephanie said, "I wanted to preserve the feeling of what it was for us to be neighbors. Unfortunately, this migration that's happening means many of those friendships are now dispersed."

Love your neighbor as yourself. (Matthew 19:19)

God, may we seek to mend the fabric of broken friendships.

What We Remember Will Be Saved, Part 5

Despite the hardships and the horrors of war and genocide depicted in *What We Remember Will Be Saved,* author Stephanie Saldaña believes it is ultimately a hopeful book filled with "extraordinary human beings" who have managed "to remain good, and to remain kind, and to love."

"I often think about the Dorothy Day quote," Stephanie continued, "where she says... something about a single act of grace is more powerful than a cobalt bomb."

Stephanie hopes the book helps readers put a human face on the stories of displaced people all over the world. She concluded, "I hope that they'll come to understand this issue better. I hope that they'll come to see refugees not as victims or as threats, but as gifts, as people who have a lot to teach us.

"Migration is really the issue of our times. I think a lot of people don't want to talk about it, don't want to think about it, and I hope that these people with their beautiful stories are offering a way in."

Show kindness and mercy to one another; do not oppress the widow, the orphan, the alien, or the poor. (Zechariah 7:9-10)

Lord, guide refugees on their journeys to belonging.

Camp No Limits

Santino Iamunno feels hesitant about meeting new people. It's not because the 11-year-old is antisocial, but rather because he always has to explain the noticeable fact that he was born without the majority of his right hand. At Camp No Limits, however, Santino feels comfortable because he fits right in.

As reported by Pat Eaton-Robb for the *Associated Press*, Camp No Limits was founded by physical therapist Mary Leighton in 2004 for children dealing "with limb loss or limb differences." Though these kinds of programs exist in many states, Connecticut's group uses physical and occupational therapy students from Quinnipiac University as counselors.

Eaton-Robb writes, "[Campers] attend physical therapy sessions, learn about prosthetics and other equipment, and are taught life hacks such as how to tie their shoes, put their hair in a ponytail or climb stairs." Campers—and their parents—also get to meet other families who are dealing with similar issues, making them feel like part of a greater community. Parent Rosanne Keep observed, "It's just good mentally."

I can do all things through Him who strengthens me. (Philippians 4:13)

Father, may children with limb differences find acceptance.

Sports Can Offer Religious Lessons

Sports and religion have numerous things in common. For instance, there's chanting, praying, and singing in stadiums, as well as churches. In an article for *Columbia Magazine,* Paul Hond writes about alumnus Gotham Chopra and his belief in the "power and profundity of sports."

Chopra, a writer and documentary maker, developed a project called Religion of Sports. He has interviewed top athletes and elicited their thoughts about their high achievements. They share what sports teach about life, such as the value of discipline and how to cope with loss.

Consider tennis icon Serena Williams, who has won 23 Grand Slam finals in her career. When Chopra asked her what quality most contributed to her success, she replied, "Showing up and doing the work. I can't tell you how many times I woke up and didn't want to go to the court to practice. But I did—I showed up, and I did the ritual even when I didn't want to."

Religion can be approached the same way. Even when we don't feel like praying or attending Mass or a church service, we can do it anyway because it strengthens our foundation of faith.

The hand of the diligent will rule.
(Proverbs 12:24)

Increase my commitment to practicing my faith, Yahweh.

A Model of Grit, Humor, and Loyalty

John, a longtime supporter of The Christophers from Valhalla, New York, recently sent a copy of an obituary to our office because the story behind it touched him.

The obit from *LoHud* briefly chronicled the life of George Berridge Jr., who had spent 49 years as a quadriplegic after suffering a diving accident at age 19. His injury might suggest George had a sad life, but this perception would be way off the mark. In fact, he is described as "displaying a remarkable combination of grit, humor, and loyalty," and always entertaining those around him.

Professionally, George developed his skills as a writer and became a published humorist. On the personal front, family, friends, and strangers were drawn to his positive nature. His siblings, stepdaughter, and step-grandchildren relished his presence, as did his caregivers.

Alfred Attram was George's caregiver every weeknight for 25 years. He noted in admiration, "George was just an amazing human being...We would all benefit by following his advice to 'enjoy every sandwich.'"

A cheerful heart is a good medicine. (Proverbs 17:22)

Help me endure challenges with grace, Savior.

Student Adopted by Principal

When Jason Smith, a Kentucky school principal, stepped outside his office in 2015, he saw 11-year-old Raven, who had just been suspended from the sixth grade for misbehaving. Little did he know that this encounter would change both of their lives.

"She was just this sweet looking, little innocent child sitting there, kind of defeated," Smith told *Good Morning America*.

Smith uncovered that Raven was living in a group home after being bounced around in the foster care system for most of her life. Smith and his wife, Marybeth, agreed to foster Raven, and despite a rocky beginning, they grew into a loving family. They adopted Raven as their daughter in 2017.

Now, at age 20, Raven is a student at the University of Kentucky, where she is studying social work, a passion inspired by her own life. And Smith is so proud of the woman Raven has become. He said, "Given the proper support, love and affection, all children can be successful."

Whenever we have an opportunity, let us work for the good of all, and especially for those of the family of faith. (Galatians 6:10)

Jesus, watch over all children in the foster care system and provide them with love and support.

A Real Lifesaver

Because Andrew Dibner remembered an incident from his youth, shut-ins and the aged can live a more independent life today.

Dibner once knew an elderly woman who lived alone. She had a stroke, but no one knew it, and she was left unattended for four days. Dibner couldn't forget what happened to her.

So, as a psychologist with an interest in electronics, he devised a system that automatically dials a hospital or other agency when a shut-in is unable to reset a small timing device they carry with them. It meant no one had to fear a blackout or accident anymore.

These are the medical alert systems that have become so well-known today. If you've ever seen the "I've fallen, and I can't get up" commercial, you know Dibner's legacy.

Independence is important for the aged and convalescent. Is there a way you can help one person feel more independent?

The Lord is compassionate and merciful; He... saves in time of affliction. (Sirach 2:11)

May we reflect Your compassion and mercy, Lord, and help the afflicted.

Loose Ends: A Good Thing

Masey Kaplan and Jennifer Simonic were visiting a grieving friend who asked them if they could finish crocheting the two blankets her late mother had started, but never finished.

Kaplan and Simonic were knitters, however, not crocheters, so they tried to think of another solution.

One idea led to another, and they started a website and nonprofit named Loose Ends, "that matches unfinished craft projects with volunteer finishers." It's not only for bereaved families but for crafters themselves, who are no longer able to finish their projects.

During a joint interview, the women told Robin Westen of AARP that they now have 18,000 volunteers in every state and 61 different countries signed up for a project.

Flyers go up in places such as yarn shops, nursing homes, and libraries. Kaplan said, "For me, helping complete someone's gesture of love is a way to spread that love even farther."

The God of all consolation...consoles us in all our affliction, so that we may be able to console those who are in any affliction. (2 Corinthians 1:3-4)

Encourage us, Jesus, to be generous with our time.

Retiree Helps Feed the Hungry

Five years ago, Mark Moreland moved to New York post-retirement and wanted to give back to the community. He never expected he would find himself in the middle of a pandemic, but through his volunteerism at Fifth Avenue Presbyterian Church, he helped launch the house of God's food distributions in 2020.

Now, years later, the need hasn't diminished, and Moreland continues to help his fellow New Yorkers by handing out food and clothing—and even setting up medical and social services at the church. "It feels like I'm doing something important, very important in their lives, too, to really make a difference for them," Moreland told *NY1 News*.

Moreland is estimated to have helped tens of thousands of New Yorkers. Scott Black Johnston, the senior pastor at Fifth Avenue Presbyterian, said, "He's an exemplary human being who gives and gives and gives back to the community where he lives."

I would feed you with the finest of wheat, and with honey from the rock I would satisfy you. (Psalm 81:16)

Loving Lord, bless all those who hunger and thirst, and show me the way to help those less fortunate.

America's Cobbler, Part 1

Nowadays, you might associate the word "cobbler" more with a pie-like dessert than the profession of mending shoes. But Jim McFarland, a fourth-generation cobbler in Lakeland, Florida, is hoping to change this perception.

In an interview with *NBC News's* Sam Brock, McFarland recalled that he had no plans of following in his father's footsteps and running his shoe repair shop. But when his father's health declined, he stepped in to help and eventually took over the business in 1986 when his dad passed away.

The year 2025 marks the 125th anniversary of McFarland's Shoe Repair. In order to promote the shop and highlight the work that cobblers do, Jim's daughter, Tori, started creating videos of him on the job and posting them on TikTok under the handle "America's Cobbler."

The videos garnered millions of views from people fascinated by this disappearing craft. Some viewers even expressed interest in learning to cobble themselves. But perhaps most important to Jim is the emotional connection his work produces with his customers. That part of the story tomorrow.

I have given skill to all the skillful. (Exodus 31:6)

May we appreciate the skills of craftspeople, Lord.

America's Cobbler, Part 2

In an era when everything seems disposable, cobbler Jim McFarland knows that some items are irreplaceable. When he receives footwear for repair at his Lakeland, Florida shop, it is often accompanied by a letter explaining its importance.

During an interview with *NBC News's* Sam Brock, McFarland recalled getting a pair of boots from a father whose 16-year-old son had recently died. The boots had belonged to his son, so the father, who wore the same size, wanted to get them repaired so he could wear them himself in memory of his boy.

Tearfully, McFarland reflected, "You read the whole letter, and you grab the boots, and you take every ounce of love you have inside, and you put them into those boots, and you ship them back. And you hope that when he puts those on, it gives him some kind of band aid on his heart."

"You have no idea how valuable this shoe may be," McFarland explained about the emotional connection. "And it's not about money. To hold that shoe can be like holding that person one more time."

You will walk on your way securely and your foot will not stumble. (Proverbs 3:23)

May my work bring comfort to others, Father.

The Ties that Bind

World Youth Day is described in *The Tablet* as an "international celebration of faith," a universal reminder by Pope Francis for young adult Catholic Christians everywhere to band together to "pray for one another...in fellowship."

In 2023, at St. Bernard of Clairvaux Church in Bergen Beach, Brooklyn, more than 60 young people gathered, along with other parishioners, to make 400 friendship bracelets that also serve as prayer aids. The volunteers were not able to attend World Youth Day themselves, held in Lisbon, Portugal that year, but their beaded creations were donated to the Pontifical Mission Societies of the United States and distributed at their fair booth.

Isabella Wagner, a St. Bernard's parishioner and Pontifical Mission Societies member, said, "We really, truly hope that we are inspiring these young people that there are people out there in the missions...that need our help...and...support."

"The bracelets are representative of so much more than the people who made them," Danielle Zito, a St. John's University senior and fellow St. Bernard's parishioner, concurred. "Through the bracelets, you...show...a sign of faith."

**We are...created...for good works.
(Ephesians 2:10)**

Abba, may we seek to establish an eternal legacy of faith.

Front Yard Becomes Field of Dreams

Eleven-year-old Blake Foley loves playing catch in the front yard of his Houston, Texas home with his mom, Hope. But he never expected a player from Major League Baseball's Houston Astros to pull up next to his house and ask to play, too!

That's exactly what happened to Blake when Astros relief pitcher Ryan Pressly, who lives nearby, pulled over and asked if he could borrow Hope's glove to play catch with her son.

Blake told *ABC 13* that he was in shock that the All-Star and top relief pitcher wanted to play catch with him, thinking, "Holy cow, this is crazy!"

Pressly stayed for a few minutes not only to catch, but also to give Blake a chance to try to hit a whiffle ball off him. Hope is beyond grateful to Pressly for taking the time to do that for her son: "The whole city should know how amazing Ryan Pressly is and what he did to spend time with a huge Astros fan."

It truly was a "Field of Dreams" moment that Blake will never forget.

Whoever pursues righteousness and kindness will find life and honor. (Proverbs 21:21)

Lord God, what can I do to help brighten someone's day today?

The Blessed Doorkeeper

Beatified in 2017, Father Solanus Casey's spiritual path during his life included some interesting twists. Casey was born in Wisconsin in 1870, the son of Irish immigrants. At age 26, he entered a seminary in Detroit and joined the Franciscan order. His superiors didn't think he understood theology well, so they made him a simplex priest, meaning he couldn't hear confessions or preach homilies.

While working at parishes in New York, Father Casey was assigned the job of doorkeeper. As recounted by Catherine Odell for *OSV News,* "Parishioners were soon drawn to Father Solanus—finding that the doorkeeper was compassionate, wise and patient—and sought his pastoral care… Within a year or two, the lines of visitors wanting to talk with the doorkeeper about their family, medical and financial problems were long."

Upon his death in 1957, thousands attended Father Casey's wake and funeral. Odell concluded, "Today, people come from all over the world to see his tomb…He is a model for the value of caring and continues to teach us the power of listening."

When you call upon Me…I will hear you. (Jeremiah 29:12)

Teach me to listen with compassion, Savior.

Praying with the Imagination

In writing his book *Meditations at Midnight: Poetry and Prose*, author Gary Jansen imagined what was going through the mind of Jesus during His Passion. He then composed 14 exquisite poems that correspond to the Stations of the Cross.

This kind of exercise, explained Gary during a *Christopher Closeup* interview, is a regular part of the Ignatian spirituality he has practiced for years: "[It involves] praying with the imagination, and allowing yourself to read a passage of Scripture, and use your imagination to get into the scene."

"When you think about all the movies that have come out over the years—whether it's *Passion of the Christ* or TV shows like *The Chosen* or *Jesus of Nazareth*—if you think about it… they're taking this Ignatian approach: let me imagine what this scene would be like. Let me imagine what Jesus would be like. How would He react? How does Judas react?…I wanted to engage in that and to use…a little bit of creativity to create something that was artistic but also approachable."

Hear and see these things being narrated, as though you were hearing with your own ears and seeing with your own eyes.
(Ludolph of Saxony)

Guide my imagination to deeper prayer, Christ.

**Lord, You have been
our dwelling place
in all generations.**

(Psalm 90:1)

Meals Full of Love at NYC Church

Thirty-five years ago, a church secretary at Christ and St. Stephen's Episcopal Church in New York City offered her lunch to a hungry individual looking for something to eat. That was the beginning of the church's Brown Bag Program, which provides "Grab & Go" lunches to anyone who asks.

Today, Eddie Mouzon is helping to carry out that legacy. He starts his day at 4:00 a.m., so he can walk 40 city blocks to help pack and distribute meals for those in need.

Mouzon has been volunteering for the program for the past 13 years because he knows what it's like to be on the other side of the table. He used to be the one to pick up a Brown Bag lunch at the church between work shifts.

Now, he is paying it forward by handing out the sack lunches, while also making friends with those he meets. He told *NY1 News,* "A lot of homeless, they really just want someone to talk to."

I remember with affection your esteem and goodwill. (2 Maccabees 9:21)

Lord, I know that anyone can be on the other side of the table. Help me treat those less fortunate as You would: with love and kindness.

Age No Barrier to Achievement

Georgiana McMenamin had a special place in the hearts of New York City's Bravest. In 1991, she retired after serving 54 years as firehouse matron for Engine Co. 40 and Ladder Co. 35.

Being close to the firefighters came naturally to Mrs. McMenamin. She became a widow when her young firefighter husband, James, perished while fighting a blaze in 1930. She was invited to join the ranks of those widows who supplemented their $50 a month pensions by acting as housekeepers. She began her daily sojourn from her home in Hell's Kitchen to the firehouse, and kept going until she was nearly 90.

Mrs. McMenamin was the last of the matrons. She credited her longevity to "God's help and the nice attitudes of all my boys." Among the people attending her farewell party were her nine grandchildren and 10 great-grandchildren.

Even the toughest troubles in life don't have to stop us from success, if we define success by the way we serve God's people.

Be strong and of good courage; be not frightened, neither be dismayed...for the Lord your God is with you wherever you go. (Joshua 1:9)

Help me achieve my highest goals, Creator.

Independent Living for Those with Autism

Children and teens who have autism generally receive the education and services they need. But once they reach young adulthood, that support system ends, leaving parents greatly concerned about their child's future. Enter ArchCare, a continuing care initiative from the Archdiocese of New York.

As reported by Christopher Parker in *America* magazine, ArchCare converted a former convent (St. Teresa's) in Staten Island, New York, into an apartment complex for autistic adults between the ages of 24 and 35. The facility only holds eight to 10 people, so residents must be high functioning in order to live there independently.

Kristin Thatcher, one of the residents, loves being able to have her own apartment and make her own choices. She has also bonded with the other tenants and their families. Millie Mazzone, whose son Vincent resides at the facility, noted, "I've gotten to know a lot of the kids' siblings and their parents. We do favors for each other. It's nice to know you can count on more than just your family...[The project is] a godsend."

**Love one another with mutual affection.
(Romans 12:10)**

Guide those with autism to lead fulfilling lives, Holy Spirit.

Father Wright's Path to the Priesthood

Father Jack Wright's path to the priesthood has been paved with lessons that had a profound impact on his journey.

As a student chaplain at Ascension St. Vincent Hospital Indianapolis, Wright learned the gifts of compassion and presence when a young couple's daughter passed away. He told *The Criterion* that he realized Jesus needed him "to be able to be present with them, pray with them, and just be with them."

Father Wright also received the gift of divine patience since he initially felt opposed to God's calling. In 2009, as a teenager, he felt a powerful awareness that God wanted him to become a priest. It wasn't until seven years later, however, that he opened his mind and heart to that possibility.

"I think our Lord wants me to surrender myself to Him," he said, "and that's what I want to do...I know He's leading me. I know He loves me. And I know He will support me in my priesthood."

For God's gifts and His call are irrevocable. (Romans 11:29)

Jesus, bless all those who hear the call to follow in Your footsteps.

A Family's Heartaches and Joys, Part 1

In many ways, Meg Kissinger's childhood was idyllic. Growing up Irish Catholic in late 1950s/early 1960s Chicago with her mom, dad, and seven brothers and sisters, there were fun times aplenty. But behind closed doors, there simmered a largely unacknowledged darkness: mental illness. She shares that story in her memoir, *While You Were Out: An Intimate Family Portrait of Mental Illness in an Era of Silence.*

Nobody knew much about mental health at the time, and they certainly didn't talk about this problem which evoked feelings of shame. During a *Christopher Closeup* interview, Meg noted that her childhood "was really a blast," but adds there were also periods of "great heartache and sorrow."

She now knows the Kissingers' troubles stemmed from severe bipolar disorder, a mental illness she dubs "the family curse...The point that I was trying to underscore," Meg explained, "is that both of those things can be true at once. There can be heartache and sorrow and mental illness, but also great joy and warmth and love."

For everything there is a season...a time to weep, and a time to laugh. (Ecclesiastes 3:1,4)

Help me deal with the complexities of life, Creator.

A Family's Heartaches and Joys, Part 2

For Meg Kissinger's parents, the practice of their Catholic faith was an important part of their lives. During a *Christopher Closeup* interview about her memoir *While You Were Out,* she recalled, "It was expressed in different ways, which matched their personalities.

"My mother was quieter, but I would say her faith was bedrock to everything about her. I have a scene in the book where I talk about her wrangling all of us to bed, these eight little kids... I can remember so clearly she was exhausted, but every night—and I mean every night, no matter what shape she was in—she always knelt by the side of the bed and prayed. That left a big impression on me.

"My dad was more outgoing, more vocal. He wrestled with his faith a lot. He was a lector at church. They were both avid Mass attendees. We went, of course, every Sunday, hell or high water, and often during the week...I'm glad for that gift of their expression of faith because it stuck with me and has proved to be quite a life raft."

Set the believers an example in speech and conduct. (1 Timothy 4:12)

Aid parents in modeling faith for their children, Father.

A Family's Heartaches and Joys, Part 3

As years passed, Meg Kissinger's sister, Nancy, began acting erratically due to her mental illness: cutting class, drinking, and shoplifting. The worst, however, was when Nancy swallowed a bottle full of aspirin and said she wanted to die.

Though she survived, her behavior kept getting worse. Despite that, her grandmother believed Nancy's problems were "all in her head." Her parents supported her as best they could, but Nancy eventually committed suicide at age 24. Meg said, "It was a great sorrow to us, but not at all a surprise. We were left reeling without the resources or the ways to talk about it."

In addition, her father told the family to tell people Nancy's death was an accident: "He was afraid that our family would not be able to have a funeral Mass for her. This is 1978, and the prevailing dictates were that if somebody dies by suicide, that's a mortal sin, and you are not to be given a Catholic Mass or a burial...As it turns out, that was not the case in our family...I think there were at least three or four priests up on the altar, which was a great comfort to my mom and dad."

**The Lord is near to the brokenhearted.
(Psalm 34:18)**

Jesus, bring Your healing to families dealing with the tragic aftermath of suicide.

A Family's Heartaches and Joys, Part 4

Never talking about Nancy's suicide produced negative consequences for the Kissingers. During a *Christopher Closeup* interview about her memoir, *While You Were Out,* Meg said, "We felt ashamed, we felt responsible, many of us, scared. We began to show the effects of that, which was turning to the bottle too much ourselves or acting out."

Another one of Meg's siblings, Danny, ended up taking his life in 1997. She said, "[We wondered], why couldn't we have seen this coming and done more to help him? I believe now it's because we didn't properly mourn Nancy's death, and so we didn't have the skill set to be able to have those conversations."

By the time of Danny's death, the Catholic Church's attitude toward those who committed suicide had thankfully evolved to a more compassionate approach. The family received "so much outreach, love, support, and comfort from the parish," Meg noted. In addition, her father and her brother, Jake, took part in an Archdiocese of Chicago program called Loving Outreach to Survivors of Suicide, which brought them healing.

Blessed are those who mourn, for they will be comforted. (Matthew 5:4)

Move Your Church to comfort all who mourn, Savior.

A Family's Heartaches and Joys, Part 5

Prior to his suicide, Danny sent Meg a letter acknowledging his bipolar disorder after years of being in denial, and apologized for his actions in the past. At the end, he wrote, "Only love and understanding can conquer this disease." Meg wrote those words on an index card, taped it to the side of her work computer, and adopted them as her guiding light.

As a journalist with the *Old Milwaukee Journal,* Meg wrote about her siblings' suicides during an era when these topics were not yet publicly discussed. She received such a positive response from readers, who wrote in to share stories of their own, that Meg covered mental illness in America for years, asking, "Why aren't people with mental illness given the same kind of care that we give people suffering from other illnesses? What can we do to make their lives better?"

Meg concluded, "I want readers to understand that shame is toxic. Shame kills...So, if you're suffering, you need to have the courage and the humility to say that...[And] if someone you love is going through something difficult, find the compassion and the care to be with them."

If they fall, one will lift up the other. (Ecclesiastes 4:10)

Give me a better understanding of mental illness, Lord.

Lemonade for Lahaina

Most kids open lemonade stands to pass the time on a hot summer day or make some extra cash. Five-year-old Edison Juel of Seattle, Washington, however, had a specific and selfless reason for setting up his lemonade stand in August 2023.

Earlier in the year, Edison and his family had enjoyed a visit to Lahaina, Hawaii. The boy was troubled when he heard about the wildfires that devastated Lahaina in August. His mother, Ami, said on Instagram, "He kept asking questions... On our walk Thursday night, he suggested a lemonade stand so that he could make money to give to the kids in Lahaina."

"I hoped for his sake he would sell a couple of pitchers of lemonade, maybe make $100...He made that much from Venmo donations before starting...Throughout the day, people just kept sending money."

In the end, reported *USA Today,* Edison earned a whopping $17,000, with both his mom and her husband's companies matching her son's profits. "Generosity begets generosity," Ami said. "Thanks to everyone, from the bottom of this sweet little five-year-old's heart and mine."

Look...to the interests of others.
(Philippians 2:4)

Father, open our hands and hearts to those in need.

A Lifesaving Breath

When Jason Aussin went golfing with his father and grandfather, he never imagined his newly acquired CPR skills would end up saving the life of his beloved *abuelo,* Jose. But he was grateful to have been in the right place at the right time.

"My grandpa had a great shot onto the green," Aussin, a student at Piedmont University in Georgia, recalled to *Fox 5 Atlanta News.* "[My dad and I] thought he was celebrating, looked over, [and my grandfather] collapsed...Checked his breathing, checked for a pulse, nothing."

Jason had recently been schooled in CPR before being certified as a lifeguard. So, with the grateful assistance of his father, he immediately provided both the instructions and know-how to revive his grandfather, who had gone into cardiac arrest. "Incredibly proud of him," Jason's father, Tony, added. "If he wasn't there, my dad wouldn't be here."

Jason's parents are already planning on getting lessons in CPR, and Aussin urges every person he knows to do the same. "If you learn it... you can save countless lives," Jason said. "Who knows? I was not expecting to save my grandpa."

The breath of the Almighty gives...life. (Job 33:4)

Lord, may we seek to increase our lifesaving skills.

I Am Earth's Keeper, Part 1

Author Lisa Hendey loves the outdoors, so she found inspiration in Pope Francis's call for us to care for God's creation in his encyclical *Laudato Si*—and also in St. Francis of Assisi's spiritual classic *Canticle of Brother Sun and Sister Moon*. As a result, she wrote the children's book *I Am Earth's Keeper*.

During a *Christopher Closeup* interview, Lisa explained, "The entire inspiration for this book was a photo that was taken by a dear friend of mine who lives in Mississippi, near where my parents used to live. One morning, [he] was out on the pond near his house…It was at a moment of sunrise, he took this beautiful photo where the sky was reflected in the stillness of the water."

"He shared it on Facebook, and he said, is the sky up or down? Something about that photo and the majesty of that moment jumped into my heart. That day, I sat and wrote the poem that would eventually become this book. I just could not get it out of my head."

The heavens are telling the glory of God; and the firmament proclaims His handiwork. (Psalm 19:1)

Open my eyes to the beauty of Your creation, Father.

I Am Earth's Keeper, Part 2

Lisa Hendey's *I Am Earth's Keeper* is a rhyming book for children, with lavish illustrations by Giuliano Ferri. It only takes around five to 10 minutes to read. Lisa hopes that families or classrooms that read it together have conversations about what they can do to be better stewards of God's creation.

In light of Lisa's long and difficult recent journey through breast cancer (detailed earlier in this volume of *Three Minutes a Day*), she noted that she now has an even deeper appreciation for St. Francis of Assisi's view of the world.

During a *Christopher Closeup* interview, Lisa concluded, "St. Francis...reminds us that the natural creation around us is not just put there for us to use at our will, but really that we're called to live in union with everything around us. I think one of the gifts of being called to slow down because of illness is that it caused me to stop and to see the little details that, perhaps in my haste, I may have been missing before this."

Bless the Lord, all that grows in the ground; sing praise to Him and highly exalt Him forever. (Daniel 3:76)

Remind us to be good stewards of this beautiful world that You have entrusted to our care, Abba.

Peace Prayer

There is a Children's Monument in Hiroshima's Peace Park to honor Sadako Sasaki and all the children who were victims of the atomic bomb.

Sadako was two when the bomb hit, and age 10 when she contracted leukemia and fought valiantly for her life. Her classmates, inspired by her struggle, started a national campaign to honor her—and all other children like her.

Before she died, Sadako, in her own appeal for peace, folded almost a thousand paper cranes. In Japan, the crane is a bird which symbolizes life.

At the monument, there is a place for the thousands of paper cranes that were made by the children of Japan in the cause of peace. And at the base of the monument, there are these words: "This is our cry, this is our prayer: Let there be peace in the world."

All of us should join the prayer of these children. Work and pray for peace in our world, our cities, our homes, ourselves.

Be at peace with one another. (Mark 9:50)

Lord of all, turn our swords into plowshares.

Pray the Rosary

Five years ago, two mothers at Our Lady of Hope Catholic Academy, located in Middle Village, New York, established the Children of Hope Rosary Club. Their goal was to remind students that devotion to Jesus' mother Mary can move us closer to Jesus Himself. The club started with just a small group of youngsters gathering in front of the shrine dedicated to the Blessed Mother.

"This was during the pandemic," Rosemarie Laspisa, one of the co-founding mothers, recalled to *The Tablet*, "and we thought it would help the children cope...I think the rosary is getting lost in the new generation. It was important to us to have as many kids dedicated to it as possible and to keep it going."

As of 2023, the Children of Hope Rosary Club boasted 47 members, ranging in age "from pre-K to eighth grade." These Catholic youngsters continue to meet every month, and in both spiritual and recreational activities, regularly celebrate the beautiful mother and constant intercessor we have in Mary.

As a mother comforts her child, so I will comfort you. (Isaiah 66:13)

Holy Mary, Mother of God, pray for us, now and always.

Everyone is Somebody Special

Peggy Flanagan, who ran the Christopher Awards program many years ago, once shared with us this story about her childhood.

During the Depression of the 1930s, Peggy's father was one of the lucky people who had a steady job. The Flanagans were thankful for their good fortune and quick to share with those who were out of work. Strangers often came to ask for food at the family's apartment, a fifth floor walk-up in a Bronx tenement.

Peggy's mother always set an extra place at the table so that anybody who happened to come in at mealtime could join the family without being embarrassed. One day, Peggy walked in on a stranger eating a bowl of soup in the kitchen. When he finished, he thanked her and left.

When Peggy's mother returned to the room, she was disappointed the man had left without her giving him a piece of cake. Many such incidents in Peggy's childhood made her aware that each person is important and deserves to be helped.

Give, and it will be given to you. (Luke 6:38)

Divine Giver, inspire parents to be good examples for their children.

Bolivian Llama Party Blessings

When he was coming up with a name for the restaurant he was starting in Queens, New York, David Oropeza decided on something unique to celebrate his heritage: Bolivian Llama Party. And when he achieved success, he made sure to give back to those who, like his family at one time, struggled with hunger.

Oropeza's restaurant in Sunnyside is located two blocks away from St. Teresa Catholic Church, which hosts a weekly food pantry. One day, the restaurateur noticed the long lines of people waiting to get into the pantry, so he started donating $400 worth of groceries a week.

Oropeza told the diocesan newspaper *The Tablet* that when his parents came to the U.S. more than three decades ago, they were helped by food pantries in Catholic churches.

In addition, Oropeza and his brothers attended a Catholic school, where they learned lessons about aiding the less fortunate. He said, "God helped me a lot in my life, and I think the best way to show appreciation to God is to help people."

Those who are generous are blessed, for they share their bread with the poor. (Proverbs 22:9)

Remind me, Father, to pay forward my blessings.

World's Greatest Godfather

It was a mother's worst nightmare. Nikki Huckaby was in a movie theater in New Haven, Connecticut, with her three-month-old baby, Tooka, when suddenly, her infant stopped breathing. As it happened, Huckaby noticed Mike Harton, a police officer, standing nearby, and ran up to him for help.

"[Tooka] curled back and tried to take a breath, and then she went completely limp on me," Harton recalled to *Local 12 News*. "All I could think in my head was, not on my watch."

Thankfully, after about 30 seconds of Harton applying the correct chest compressions and back blows for resuscitation, Tooka began to cry, indicating she could breathe once more.

"That cry was the best cry ever," Harton said. "I literally watched a miracle happen...That day, an angel came down...My life changed that day. Our family got extended."

Indeed, six years after this harrowing incident, Harton, now a Detective, is still in close touch with the Huckabys, and is the proud godfather of Tooka, who, like her guardian angel, aspires to be a police officer when she grows up.

A father's blessing strengthens...children. (Sirach 3:9)

Abba, we thank You for the strangers who become family.

The Gift of Aging, Part 1

Several years ago, while rushing from the Kroger's parking lot towards the supermarket's entrance, Marcy Cottrell Houle tripped on a drainage gate and broke both her arms. This left her virtually helpless for several months, unable to do even simple tasks, such as cutting her food or tying her shoelaces.

Thankfully, Marcy's husband was able to take time off from work to care for her, but the experience left her depressed and feeling like a burden. That led her to contemplate the infirmities and medical conditions many people face as they grow older—and whether there are ways to stay healthy.

Marcy had won a Christopher Award in 2016 for her book *The Gift of Caring*, which was inspired by her caregiving experience with her parents. She now approached her co-author on that book, Dr. Elizabeth Eckstrom, to see if she would like to explore what it means to age well, with joy.

Dr. Eckstrom responded positively, so the two friends embarked on a journey that led to their latest book, *The Gift of Aging*.

Do not cast me off in the time of old age. (Psalm 71:9)

Remind me that aging is a gift, Creator.

The Gift of Aging, Part 2

The Gift of Aging co-author Marcy Cottrell Houle cited a Yale study which showed that people who have a positive view of aging tend to live 7.5 years longer than people who don't.

During a *Christopher Closeup* interview, she noted, "Many of us have a very negative idea about aging. It's just going to be loss, frailty, dementia...The people I interviewed did lose significant people in their lives, some had real health problems, some lost children...Yet, they could say they loved life, it had meaning, it was joyful. How?...There are things we can do to make life have joy until the end."

One of the key factors to aging well is having a sense of purpose. While retirement and having fun sound appealing to many, human beings need more in order to thrive. "People who are doing the best," Marcy said, "they're the ones who are not just living for themselves. They're living for the people coming after us...You can find such joy if you get out of yourself, get out of your aches and pains and say, 'How can I make life a little better for someone else?' That can make a big difference."

Each of us must please our neighbor for the good purpose of building up the neighbor. (Romans 15:2)

Jesus, guide me towards a joyful sense of purpose.

The Gift of Aging, Part 3

One of Marcy Cottrell Houle's interview subjects for *The Gift of Aging* was 97-year-old Rabbi Josh Stampfer. When she met him, he was in a wheelchair, accompanied by a caregiver. Marcy expected his handshake to be frail, but he had quite a grip, as well as a personality that conveyed "dynamism."

Rabbi Stampfer had spent his life helping Jewish people suffering in countries such as Russia and China. He had also lost his wife in recent years. Yet he still worked as a teacher and gave sermons on the radio. How did he accomplish all this at 97? He said he had learned that life needs a higher goal than joy.

Quoting Rabbi Stampfer, Marcy said, "In all of us, there is an innate need for happiness, but happiness is not just based on good health. Not everyone has that...What I have found—and suggest to others—[is that] the way to be happy is to be good. When people do a good deed for others, they enjoy life more. It's nice to have wonderful thoughts, but it's also important to translate those thoughts either into deeds or into words. Bringing happiness to others is the quickest way to have it yourself."

Trust in the Lord, and do good. (Psalm 37:3)

Regardless of my age or condition, Father, help me to be of service to others in some way.

The Gift of Aging, Part 4

Another important element in healthy aging is community. One person whom Marcy Cottrell Houle interviewed, Eleanore, is thriving in this respect, even though she is 106 years old.

Eleanore still makes time to volunteer and order food to be delivered to homebound seniors, who she sometimes visits herself. She has also become friendly with her grandchildren's and great-grandchildren's friends. Unfortunately, this is not the norm for many seniors in the U.S.

During a *Christopher Closeup* interview, Marcy said, "Social isolation is an epidemic in our country, especially as you get older...The studies show that being isolated socially is as bad for you as smoking 15 cigarettes a day in terms of death and causing dementia...But our society is set up that people get isolated, [so recognize] you need to do something."

In essence, if no one—be it individuals, churches, or community organizations—is reaching out to seniors, perhaps they need to take the first step and reach out to others, like Eleanore is doing.

Love one another with mutual affection. (Romans 12:10)

Guide me in finding a supportive community, Holy Spirit.

The Gift of Aging, Part 5

Another factor shared by many of Marcy Cottrell Houle's interview subjects in *The Gift of Aging* is the practice of faith, which offers guidance to people in general—and helps them move through the difficult seasons that life brings to everybody.

As an example, Marcy quotes the words of 102-year-old Lucille, who offered this bit of wisdom: "Each phase of life has its blessings, as well as its trials, so enjoy what you can now. As far as I know, this is the only chance we get. Old age isn't so frightening. Do all you can to stay healthy, keep active both mentally and physically, then recognize that all things eventually wear out—and you will, too.

"It helps to be able to laugh at yourself. Remember, death itself is just another phase of life. I've been lucky. I've enjoyed a long-lasting faith that provides a supportive community and a guide. I'm not sure what follows this precious life on earth, but my faith gives me, not fear, but a grand sense of wonder about it. In life and death, we have only to do one thing: simply let love in."

Faith is the assurance of things hoped for, the conviction of things not seen. (Hebrews 11:1)

Jesus, may love and faith guide me in this life and the next.

The Gift of Aging, Part 6

Marcy Cottrell Houle's *The Gift of Aging* co-author, Dr. Elizabeth Eckstrom, traveled to "blue zones" in different countries where people often live into their 100s in good shape. Exercise, a healthy diet, community, and a sense of purpose are a few common factors there that Americans can try to emulate.

Marcy hopes that readers of the book are left with both practical and inspirational advice that will help them get older with improved health and a positive attitude. During a *Christopher Closeup* interview, she concluded:

"Bill McKibben, an author, wrote the Foreword...He talked about the legacy we leave. What kind of world are we leaving for those we love? And if you want to not be thought of as elderly, then act as an elder.

"It made me realize, these people [I interviewed] were given a gift of aging. They have made it into their 80s, 90s, and 100s, but they've made this time count. I want to make this time count, too, not just living for me, but to make a difference. We have that opportunity. I think the world needs us."

Live, not as unwise people but as wise, making the most of the time. (Ephesians 5:15-16)

Help me fill my senior years with meaning, Father.

School for the Blind Makes a Difference

Born with a birth defect that left her blind, Ana Centeno of Jersey City, New Jersey, remains a young woman filled with hope and possibility. This optimistic attitude is largely thanks to the care and education she has received at St. Joseph's School for the Blind for the last 16 years.

As reported by Evan Wyno for *Good Morning America,* Ana's classes are "thoughtfully adapted to her needs, allowing her to engage in hands-on experiments and utilize assistive technology such as a refreshable braille display." As a result, she became proficient in reading, writing, and math.

Diana Lao, one of Ana's teachers who has known her since she was three years old, noted that she is motivated to excel. She thinks, "If I can do this, I can do more."

In return, Ana loves St. Joseph's. She said, "As I started growing up, I'm like...I have to accept myself the way I am. When I came [to St. Joseph's], a lot of people treated me like a normal person... Even though we have a disability, we're perfect the way we are. No matter what, just support us in any way."

I will lead the blind by a road they do not know...I will turn the darkness before them into light. (Isaiah 42:16)

God, may we accept others for who they are.

Sew Creative by Malia

Malia Martinez of Westport, Massachusetts, is helping cats and dogs in shelters find their "furever" homes, one stitch at a time. Last Christmas, the 12-year-old received a gift certificate for sewing lessons, and she took to the craft right away. Every week, Malia also visits her grandmother, who is adept with a sewing needle, to sharpen this skill. A few months into her sessions, Malia got the idea to make bandanas to give to local animal shelters.

"When I go see [cats and dogs] in the animal shelter, it's kind of sad," Martinez told *WJAR News*. "I thought if we maybe got them a bandana, they would look cute...and they would get a home." This was also a way for Martinez to deal with the grief of losing her own dog, Jada, last year.

Malia has started selling her wares at pop-up events, gifting all her "proceeds to the animals." She even created an online business, named "Sew Creative by Malia," to help "as many animals as possible in every way possible."

"When it has anything to do with caring and helping," Malia's mother, Crystal, concluded, "she...puts her heart into it."

Let all...you do be done in love.
(1 Corinthians 16:14)

Father, may I put my heart into every task, big or small.

Not a Typical Saturday Night

After enjoying themselves on a Saturday night, teens Freddie Corbett and Harley Hollingworth arrived at the train station in South Yorkshire, England, intending to get home before their parents' curfew. As the train approached, however, a man who had been sleeping on the platform jumped onto the tracks and said he wanted to kill himself.

Despite the danger of being struck by the oncoming train themselves, Freddie and Harley jumped down after him and wrestled him back to the platform. They pinned him down and talked to him calmly about his troubles until police arrived.

Network Rail employee Gary Robinson posted on social media, "Called out tonight to a male with intent to self-harm on the railway. These two lads were his angels! Dragged him off the railway...sat with him talking 'til I got there and make no mistake, saved his life!"

Freddie's father told *Sky News*, "[It's] not every day you can say your son is a hero." Harley's dad added that he is "proud as punch" of the boys.

Be strong and courageous...The Lord your God is with you. (Joshua 1:9)

Jesus, help me be courageous in times of trouble.

Painting as a Holy Endeavor

Painting is a holy endeavor for Warren, Michigan's Mary Zabawski. Her passion and talent for art were nurtured by her grandmother, and though she has a job in the insurance industry to pay her bills, she experiences God's presence when working on her oil paintings—and aims to make God present to others through them as well.

As a lifelong member of St. Anne parish, Zabawski has found inspiration for her paintings in common scenes around the church, from the entrance to the chapel to a peaceful spot in the church garden. She donated her works to a St. Anne's fundraiser and was thrilled when people liked them enough to buy them.

Zabawski told *Detroit Catholic's* Gabriella Patti, "You could paint incredible vistas or European cathedrals, but I have always just been fascinated by the stuff in your own neighborhood; there are so many incredible things if you look for them. Regardless of what I am painting, I feel the same way about them—I am (just) the hands, and I just try to find the beauty in every day, and that beauty comes from God."

From the greatness and beauty of created things comes a...perception of their Creator. (Wisdom 13:5)

May I observe Your beauty all around me, Creator.

Free Blockbuster

If you're of a certain age, you may have a collection of VHS tapes and DVDs that seem outdated in an age of online streaming. But hold on! There is a small renaissance underway for these classic forms of media.

As reported by Livia Albeck-Ripka and Aimee Ortiz in *The New York Times,* producer and former Blockbuster Video employee Brian Morrison created a project in 2019 called "Free Blockbuster." He painted an old newspaper box on the street in the Blockbuster colors, added the words "Take a movie, Leave a movie," then filled the box with his own VHS tapes and DVDs for people to borrow and watch.

Since then, 200 other community boxes have been created around the country. Morrison believes nostalgia factors into the appeal, as well as getting to physically hold something and even getting to chat with neighbors while you're at the box. "We are social animals; we want to go out into the world and engage with each other," Morrison concluded.

Stand at the crossroads, and look, and ask for the ancient paths. (Jeremiah 6:16)

Remind me to treasure good traditions from the past, Abba.

Remember Your Role as Healers

Anyone who has ever spent time in a hospital knows how important nurses are to providing quality healthcare. Patients rely on them not just for medical basics, but for compassion and understanding. That's why training the next generation of nurses is a vital task. Thankfully, St. John's University's new nursing program is up to the task.

In 2023, the program's first cohort celebrated the Nurses Pledge ceremony. Joanna Villamayor, New York-Presbyterian Queens' Director of Nursing Professional Development, served as keynote speaker, noting, "Nurses are the last line of defense before an error—which is paramount. That's how valuable our role is. So please be curious, and always speak up."

Associate Dean Cathleen A. Murphy added, "Remember that the patients in front of you have families. They are people who are loved and love others, and whose lives may be in your hands. Let your stethoscopes remind you of their hearts and the love that fills them. Remember to be empathetic and sympathetic. Patients will be nervous and need you to comfort them. Remember your role as healers."

We were gentle...like a nurse.
(1 Thessalonians 2:7)

Bless all compassionate nurses, Savior.

Franciscan Sisters Welcome All

Only four Sisters remain at the convent of The Franciscan Missionaries of Mary in Aleppo, Syria. Though they are few in number, their impact has been great, reports Azré Khodr for the Catholic Near East Welfare Association (CNEWA).

During Syria's civil war, the Sisters welcomed and fed many displaced people, most of whom were Muslim. Sister Silham Zgheib explained, "After the emergency kitchen closed, we realized how their vision of us had changed. They really appreciated that we opened the convent for them."

The Sisters not only organized support groups for the Muslim women, but also held sewing classes so these ladies could earn money to support their families. Sister Antoinette Battikh observed, "The Muslim women used to be afraid of us, but when they saw that we didn't discriminate between Muslims and Christians, they were surprised."

Muslims now support much of the Sisters' work. Sister Renée Koussa said, "This is our role: to be a sign of the presence of Christ where Christ is not known."

**Live in harmony with one another.
(Romans 12:16)**

Prince of Peace, may we learn to love our neighbors, not fear them.

**May you be blessed
by the Lord,
who made heaven and earth.**

(Psalm 115:15)

Employer Made a Difference

The late Harry Granader ran a string of McDonald's restaurants in Michigan. That made him a large employer of teenagers, and he took a personal interest in all of them. He even asked the youngsters to bring in a copy of their report cards.

Those who showed scholastic improvement based on grade point averages were given a higher hourly wage. He also had a college tuition plan. In addition to their pay, workers were given college tuition credits payable to the college they attend.

When Granader found out that more and more of his older employees had entered the work force to help a grandchild or relative with college costs, he extended the tuition credit plan to them.

For more than 30 years, Granader was active in civic and educational affairs. An admirer said he provided "another example of what one person can do to light a candle." Granader himself simply said, "It gives me a great feeling when they come back to one of the restaurants to let me know how successful they've become."

Bear one another's burdens, and so fulfill the law of Christ. (Galatians 6:2)

Inspire those who care for young people, Paraclete.

The Countercultural Mister Rogers, Part 1

Marybeth Baggett relishes the time she has spent at The Fred Rogers Institute in Latrobe, Pennsylvania. Yes, it is named after the late host of the children's show *Mister Rogers' Neighborhood,* and it is dedicated to preserving the ideals he stood for: "love and genuine respect for persons, serious devotion to play and other humane endeavors, protection and care for children and the vulnerable."

Writing at the website *Moral Apologetics,* Baggett recalled telling some friends and colleagues she was taking part in a conference there. They chuckled, not thinking Rogers was worthy of "meaningful scholarship."

Baggett disagreed, noting, "It's true that Fred's ideas are in no way complex. Even still, they are profound. In a world quick to discard those on the margins, to drain life of the sacred, to commodify and diminish the humanity of others, the legacy Fred offers is thoroughly countercultural."

More tomorrow…

Keep your heart with all vigilance, for from it flow the springs of life. (Proverbs 4:23)

Jesus, help me treasure the sacred humanity of others.

The Countercultural Mister Rogers, Part 2

As an admirer of Fred Rogers, Marybeth Baggett knows his mission was centered on "Jesus' command to love God and neighbor." Writing at the website *Moral Apologetics,* she noted that Rogers, a Presbyterian minister, "affirmed and practiced that ethic in all he did, seeing his calling as cultivating a neighborhood in which all are welcomed and treasured. Kindhearted and soft-spoken as Fred was, he is easy to underestimate and underappreciate."

Rogers landed on TV in the 1960s and recognized that the medium could be used in a positive or negative way. When executives at *NBC* tried to get him to compromise his principles for financial gain, he refused and ended his contract with them.

Baggett wrote, "Where most television programs sought to get something from their audience, Fred was...only concerned about what he could offer his. This intentionality and commitment to his convictions provides a powerful testimony for Christians devoted to the public good."

Take thought for what is noble in the sight of all. (Romans 12:17)

Increase my commitment to the public good, Father.

The Countercultural Mister Rogers, Part 3

When Fred Rogers began hosting *Mister Rogers' Neighborhood* on PBS in 1968, he brought an air of calm, humility, and wisdom to an era of "political and social chaos," wrote Marybeth Baggett at *Moral Apologetics*. In one episode, she recalled, "Fred helped children and parents alike navigate the challenges raised by Bobby Kennedy's assassination."

Rogers also focused on empowering others, especially vulnerable children. For instance, he engaged in conversation with Jeffrey Erlanger, a 10-year-old in a wheelchair due to a spinal tumor. "Fred uses his social clout to elevate Jeffrey," Baggett observed, "recognizing as valuable his experience and providing him a platform from which to educate others about disabilities."

Once again, the gospel lay at the heart of Rogers' approach. Baggett explained, "Fred kept in view that the children with whom he interacted were themselves made in the image of God, and his ministry was indelibly shaped by that principle."

Whoever welcomes one such child in My name welcomes Me. (Mark 9:37)

May we recognize Your image in all children, Lord.

Only a Drop in the Ocean

Mother Teresa of Calcutta was once asked about the difference being made by the work of her religious community for the dying poor of India. "What we are doing is just a drop in the ocean," she admitted. "But if the drop was not in the ocean, I think the ocean would be less because of the missing drop."

Others have expressed similar sentiments. The great Protestant clergyman, physician, philosopher, and humanitarian Albert Schweitzer observed, "Each of us can do a little to bring some portion of misery to an end."

Another person noted, "One of the most serious thoughts that life provokes is the reflection that we can never tell, at the time, whether a word, a look, an occurrence of any kind is trivial or important."

When you think that your efforts seem insignificant, keep in mind the words of St. Madeleine Sophie Barat: "Nothing that can please the heart of our Lord is small."

The kingdom of heaven is like a mustard seed...it is the smallest of all the seeds, but when it has grown it is the greatest of shrubs and becomes a tree. (Matthew 13:31-32)

Jesus, remind me that small deeds can have a great impact.

A Mile a Day Keeps the Doctor Away

World War II veteran John Hamilton, age 105, has led a remarkable life. A retired British Army major who served his country for 25 years, Hamilton helped defend and evacuate thousands of Allied soldiers in the 1940 Battle of Dunkirk.

According to Britain's *SWNS*, John met his wife, Elsa, that same year, when they took cover under a tree in Hyde Park during a terrible rainstorm. They wed three years later, and were married for 67 years, until her death from dementia in 2006.

Hamilton currently lives in a bungalow on the grounds of a care facility in Warminster and enjoys good mental and physical health. Always a strong athlete, playing everything from rugby to polo in his youth, John still walks one mile every day. Ten years ago, he even broke "the world record for the 100 mm time trial" in a rowing competition, in the 94 to 99 age division.

"The key to a long life is exercising," Hamilton pointed out. "It makes you physically well, but is mentally stimulating, too." The grandfather of eight and great-grandfather of 10 added, "My big family helps to keep me going."

There is no wealth better than health. (Sirach 30:16)

God, may we always value our physical and mental health.

The Ministry of Listening

After growing up in Mexico, Father Hugo Medellin, C.M., moved to North Carolina and joined the Vincentian order of the priesthood because of their "service to the poor." One day, his pastor assigned him to take a Spanish man with obsessive-compulsive disorder to the hospital. The wait lasted hours, but Father Medellin kept the man calm and translated for him.

Several months later, this same man called Father Medellin because he was feeling suicidal. With no training in this kind of situation, the priest kept him on the phone and tried to give him hope. It worked. The man said he would not harm himself because he knew he was loved.

Whenever people with troubles come to Father Medellin now in his role as chaplain at St. John's University in Queens, New York, he offers them spiritual guidance, but also refers them to professional help if needed. He told *St. John's Magazine* that some people simply need to feel heard: "I listen to their suffering, and they feel understood. Often, people come to the solution on their own. You have to be a calming presence... This is what I do."

I love the Lord, because He has heard my voice. (Psalm 116:1)

Improve my listening skills, Divine Healer.

A Chef's Prison Ministry, Part 1

Chef Bruno Abate, a native of Naples, Italy, is teaching his students in Chicago how to make some of the city's best pizza. But these pupils are not enrolled in a traditional school. Rather, they are prisoners in Cook County Jail.

Many years ago, when Abate first immigrated to the U.S., he watched a TV program on the prison system and felt called by God to assist the rehabilitation process for inmates. He created the program "Recipe for Change," and was welcomed into the jail to give it a go.

As reported by Mack Liederman for *Block Club Chicago,* Abate runs his program from the jail's basement, which includes a brick pizza oven and ingredients he imports from Italy. Classes include 48 inmates, whose pizza is so tasty that even the jail's bosses ask for it.

Since 2014, "Recipe for Change" has had 4,000 inmates graduate. A participant named Ethan looks forward to making his grandmother steak tortas when he is eventually released. He said, "When I come home, I want to be able to contribute something."

**I was in prison, and you visited me.
(Matthew 25:36)**

Father, send messengers to people in prison to guide them towards means of rehabilitation.

A Chef's Prison Ministry, Part 2

Chef Bruno Abate's "Recipe for Change" program in Chicago's Cook County Jail has become so successful that they are expanding. Twelve recently released inmates will take their pizza making skills onto a food truck to be stationed outside the criminal courthouse. Chef Abate hopes the food truck teaches the public that those who were in jail can turn over a new leaf.

He told Mack Liederman of *Block Club Chicago,* "Try this pizza, and you'll find there's more humanity to be given to people, more education, compassion, self-esteem, more hope. We're capable of being more creative to make the world a better place."

In an interview with *America,* Chef Abate added, "When I wake up in the morning, I ask God to give me the energy to carry on helping other persons. In the future, I want to try and enter other prisons...The solution is not just getting them work; it's to restore what's broken inside of these people, giving them back their dignity, their self-esteem, their self-confidence, and hope."

I have called you...to bring out...from the prison those who sit in darkness. (Isaiah 42:6-7)

May people in prison choose light over darkness, Jesus.

Listening Heart-to-Heart

This story was told more than 700 years ago by the Persian mystic poet Attar. A man was weeping bitterly. Someone went up to him and asked, "Why are you crying?"

The man answered, "I am crying to attract the pity of God's heart." The questioner said, "You're talking nonsense, for God doesn't have a physical heart."

The man replied, "It's you who are wrong. He is the owner of all the hearts that exist. It is through the heart that you can make your connection with God."

The message of this story still speaks to people of all faiths today. When our hearts are open to the needs of others, we can become the instrument of God's help to them.

We must also remember that cries for help take many forms. We often have to listen for the feeling behind a person's words or behavior. For instance, an angry relative may lash out because of a difficulty they are facing—and a misbehaving child may feel neglected and simply need more attention. When we listen with our hearts, we can become a channel of God's love.

My Lord, I cried to You for help, and You have healed me. (Psalm 30:2)

Lord, allow me to be Your heart to someone in distress.

From 9/11 to the Priesthood

On September 11, 2001, Firefighter Tom Colucci was at the World Trade Center when he witnessed the collapse of the North Tower. In the following days and weeks, he dealt with the trauma of the unimaginable loss of life that day brought, along with continuing to perform his duties on the job.

Coluccci was impressed by the presence of priests at Ground Zero, who always showed up to bless human remains and offer physical and spiritual support to whoever needed it. He was already known for being a religious person, to the point that his co-workers dubbed him "Father Tom."

Colucci had thought about joining the priesthood once he retired, and 9/11 "sealed the decision," he told *Aleteia's* John Burger. In 2016, Father Tom Colucci became the first retired firefighter to be ordained a New York City priest.

He observed, "We're body and soul, the human person, and when we rise again at the Last Judgment, we're gonna rise body and soul. So, they're both important: saving lives and to save souls."

Let yourselves be built into a spiritual house, to be a holy priesthood. (1 Peter 2:5)

Help us bring goodness out of the ashes of 9/11, Lord.

For Love of the Broken Body, Part 1

Shortly after entering the novitiate for the Franciscan Sisters of Perpetual Adoration at age 25, Sister Julia Walsh learned that her parents were selling the farm in Iowa where she and her siblings had grown up. The prospect of that loss made her want to return to her old home one last time to "pray my goodbyes" and come to terms with her new direction in life.

While she was there, she decided to climb down a cliff to go swimming in the creek below. It was something she had done many times as a child, without incident. But not this time.

During a *Christopher Closeup* interview about her memoir *For Love of the Broken Body,* Sister Julia recalled, "As I climbed down, one of the rocks I stepped on crumbled, and I fell face first, maybe 15, 20 feet. My hand went up to my forehead. It protected my skull, so my knuckle and my wrist were broken.

"I felt teeth break and fall out of my face immediately, and I felt my jaw crack into two. I was all alone in the woods. Nobody was home on the farm, and I had to make my way back to the farmhouse. It was a major 'choose life' moment for me."

God is our refuge and strength, a very present help in trouble. (Psalm 46:1)

Sustain me during times of trial, Savior.

For Love of the Broken Body, Part 2

As the ambulance raced her to the hospital, Sister Julia Walsh felt ashamed that she had done something so risky as climb down a cliff because her actions were now inconveniencing many friends and family. At the same time, she experienced a profound sense of gratitude and even began singing songs of praise in the emergency room.

"Only after I made my final vows and I dove deeper into the memories," Sister Julia explained on *Christopher Closeup*, "did I start to recognize that I was living the charism of my congregation."

"The Franciscan Sisters of Perpetual Adoration are a Eucharistic community. We're adoring the Eucharist, the Blessed Sacrament, in our chapel in La Crosse, Wisconsin, all the time... Eucharist means 'thank you' or 'thanksgiving.' Besides the shame and the pain, [I was feeling] joy and gratitude...that God had saved my life, that I was being well taken care of by a phenomenal medical team, that even...my friends drove hours to visit me...in the ICU."

Give thanks in all circumstances.
(1 Thessalonians 5:18)

God, even in times of darkness, show me reasons to be grateful.

For Love of the Broken Body, Part 3

The injuries and lengthy recovery that Sister Julia Walsh endured made her better appreciate the incarnational nature of Christianity and how it forges a common bond with all people.

During an interview about her memoir *For Love of the Broken Body,* she said, "I came to recognize that everyone has an experience of brokenness. Everyone can unite with Christ in their own woundedness, and that is one of the ways that we can know intimacy with Christ."

"At the same time, we live in a society and a culture where we're taught to hide our brokenness. If our sense of brokenness is preventing us from...being a loving presence to others, then, in a way, we're saying no to an opportunity for union with Christ."

"My hope is that readers [of my book] will come to recognize the sacredness of their authenticity. There is actually something holy in being raw and real for one another because...we're showing up in our woundedness for one another. And we're able to lean on each other. I believe that increases our compassion."

Since God loved us so much, we also ought to love one another. (1 John 4:11)

Allow my woundedness to bring healing to others, Jesus.

For Love of the Broken Body, Part 4

Though she has experienced much hardship, Sister Julia Walsh is no doom-and-gloom Christian. In fact, she remains a person with a joyful spirit and easy laugh. Following her accident, however, she began living with an intensity as if every day could be her last. She got a little too intense, leading her fellow Sisters to gently tell her to chill out.

During a *Christopher Closeup* interview, Sister Julia explained, "That was a gift that they gave me, and they helped me to increase the levity, to increase the joy, and find greater freedom in the recognition that every day could be my last day.

"That's nothing to be afraid of because, well, maybe I'm a rare bird, but I'm not afraid to die. Our mortality is a very important part of our faith, and to be conscious of that and to be preparing for our death is a holy and good act.

"So, as cliché as it may sound, I do want to be living every day like it's my last. I'm trying to bring joy and light into the world, and I think it helps to have a light heart and to see the beauty in all things and all people the best we can."

May the God of hope fill you with all joy and peace in believing. (Romans 15:13)

Holy Spirit, help me bring joy and light to the world.

For Love of the Broken Body, Part 5

Though she is generally a happy person, Sister Julia Walsh does experience the occasional dark night of the soul. But as she reveals in her memoir *For Love of the Broken Body,* she knows there will be joy and light on the other end.

Sister Julia concluded, "There [are] definitely times where I feel like I'm in a 'Good Friday' phase, and the darkness is intense. Grief can wake me up in the middle of the night, and sadness can haunt me. This is not a Pollyanna joy [that I have]. This is the type of joy that St. Francis of Assisi talks about when he talks about perfect joy.

"In the midst of suffering, rejection, sorrow...I am somehow graced with this contentment that I have encountered in Christ, deep in my heart...All that is grace, all that is transformative. I do think, when you know an intimacy with Christ—which is a grace and doesn't come easily to all—but when it starts to come, we can do a dance with God together, and God can transform the heartache if we hold it out to Him."

He will transform the body of our humiliation that it may be conformed to the body of His glory. (Philippians 3:21)

Transform my heartaches into joys, Savior.

Young Painter Helps Hurting People

For his eighth birthday, Arsh Pal received acrylic painting supplies from his family. No one had any idea how that simple gift would shape the course of his young life.

Arsh quickly developed a passion for painting, inspired by nature and the world around him. His mom, Divya, started taking him along to her job as an occupational therapist at a nursing home. Arsh enjoyed interacting with the residents and started giving them painting lessons. They loved it, and so did he.

As reported by Betsy Taylor in *St. Jude Inspire* magazine, Arsh realized that "the residents, though decades older, had the same desire for connection and fun that he did. But he also saw that sometimes they were hurting and lonely."

Arsh decided to use his talents to help people who were hurting. Not only did he continue volunteering with the seniors, he began selling paintings to raise money for St. Jude Children's Research Hospital, because he wanted his work to benefit kids with cancer. For the past five years, Arsh has raised $1,000 a year for the hospital.

Let no one despise your youth, but set the believers an example in...conduct, in love. (1 Timothy 4:12)

Give our youth charitable hearts, Creator.

Off-Duty Nurses Make a Difference

When Doreen Thrash attended a basketball game in East Bay, San Francisco, she thought she would be getting a break from her work as a nurse at Kaiser Permanente Medical Center. But when a player collapsed and stopped breathing, Thrash sprang into action.

When she got to the court, she was joined by John Muir, another off-duty nurse. As reported by Jodi Hernandez of *NBC Bay Area,* the two nurses began CPR because the patient had no pulse. They then got the gym's portable defibrillator and were able to shock the man's heart back to life.

Their heroics were captured on video by Nolie Caldetera, who was there recording the game. He shared the video online, saying, "I wanted to give these people recognition and show that there is still humanity out there and people still care."

The patient was taken to the hospital and expected to recover. Nurse Thrash said, "I felt elated...What a blessing. What a blessing. There's no words for it. I pray that he continues to heal, and I pray nothing like that ever happens to him again."

I pray that all may go well with you and that you may be in good health. (3 John 1:2)

Thank You for people who care, Paraclete.

A Miraculous Union

It was truly a love story for the ages, straight out of the pages of a fairy tale. Just shy of 31 years ago, Jack Richardson and Bronwyn Tacey were both born prematurely, at 30 and 26 weeks respectively, at Queens Medical Center in Nottingham, England. Both of their families, their mothers especially, bonded closely over the shared difficulties of their children's labors.

"I had growth hormone injections until I was 16 to ensure I was not really short," Bronwyn recalled to *South West News Service*. "Jack was in intensive care…It was touch and go whether we would both make it. It's a complete miracle…we are…here."

It is even more miraculous that, despite growing apart over the years, Jack and Bronwyn reconnected on Facebook in 2021 and started dating. Within two years, the pair was engaged and in 2024, they had a daughter of their own, Sienna, at the same medical center where they entered the world together. "I don't know anyone else or any other relationships that are like this," Tacey concluded. "It's a great partnership…We're like best friends…Just feels really natural to be together."

What God has joined…let no one separate. (Mark 10:9)

Father, may we trust in Your guiding hand in life and love.

Senior Couples Teach True Love

Though many physicians write off a dying patient's visions or dreams of deceased loved ones as delirium, Dr. Christopher Kerr does not. He has studied these common phenomena and found them to be life-affirming.

In addition, he has gained much wisdom on both living and dying that would be of value to anyone. Paul Lauritzen profiled Dr. Kerr in *Commonweal Magazine,* and shared this lesson he learned from elderly husbands and wives.

"Old couples have much to teach us about true love," Dr. Kerr said. "Their bond requires no big declarations, loyalty tests, or dramatic endings...They continue to feel and believe in it even when the person through whom that love originated leaves them."

"Jobs, ambitions, hobbies, mortgages, and plans have come and gone. What is left and what matters is the relationships they have maintained, cherished, and tended to through a lifetime of small gestures and greetings, loving glances and humorous words, shared stories, and forgiven faults."

With old age is wisdom, and with length of days understanding. (Job 12:12)

Lord, may we treasure the love and wisdom of our elders.

Music and Memories

Alzheimer's patients undergo a long, slow change in their brains that leads to memory loss and an inability to reason and function. One bright spot is that music from their past can often spark an improvement, even if it's short-lived. Neuroscientist Michael Thaut set out to investigate this mystery.

In one study, patients in an fMRI scanner listened to music they had enjoyed for more than 25 years. As reported in *AARP: The Magazine,* that "beloved, familiar music" lit up parts of the brain "where higher order reasoning and memory are processed."

In another study, Alzheimer's patients listened to their favorite music every day for four weeks, while also engaging in conversation about past memories for one hour a day with a spouse or caregiver.

This led to "significant improvement on memory tests" and, in some cases, an increase in density in the brain's white matter. While dead neurons cannot be resurrected, "music appears to bolster connections between preserved neurons."

An intelligent mind acquires knowledge. (Proverbs 18:15)

Creator, guide researchers toward help for dementia patients.

A Selfless, Sainted Sister, Part 1

In 2016, Pope Francis canonized Maria Elisabeth Hesselblad, who was born Lutheran in Sweden, converted to Catholicism, and restored the Bridgettine order of nuns. Following her canonization, Paulist Father Don Campbell recalled some details from her biography.

Around 1890, before she became Catholic, Maria worked as a nurse in New York's Roosevelt Hospital. Her personal devotion to God led her to always be conscientious about getting a priest for any Catholic patient who asked for one. The Paulists lived across the street from the hospital, so she often went to request their presence, even in the worst weather.

"One night," the story goes, "when she had run out in a frightful storm to call a priest for a dying man who had really wandered from the 'narrow path,' the old Father said to her, as he went back to his church: 'God bless you, dear little sister. God reward you for your thoughtfulness, your warmth. You cannot yet understand…what a wonderful service you are doing for so many…Someday, you will understand…You will find the way.'"

This is my comfort in my distress, that Your promise gives me life. (Psalm 119:50)

May the dying experience divine comfort and love, Jesus.

A Selfless, Sainted Sister, Part 2

After converting to Catholicism, St. Maria Elisabeth Hesselblad went on to live in Rome and become a nun. Having always felt a devotion to St. Brigid of Ireland, despite being Swedish herself, St. Maria revived the Bridgettine order.

As Mother Superior at their monastery in Rome during World War II, St. Maria offered refuge to 12 members of the Jewish Piperno-Sed families, who feared Nazi persecution. As reported on the *Yad Vashem* website, she "revealed herself as a charismatic personality who took great risks in saving them and helping other persons in need."

"The children of the Piperno-Sed families were then 18, 16, and eight years old, and were impressed by the openness of Mother Maria who never tried to convince them to convert, on the contrary, insisting that they say their Hebrew prayers and fulfill other obligations of their religion. After the war, the rescued Jews retained a vivid memory of their benefactor, regarding themselves very fortunate to have met such an outstanding person."

You shall love your neighbor as yourself. (Mark 12:31)

Lord, may we remember one of the best gifts we can impart to others is that of acceptance and understanding.

Creativity at Work

When Jim Henson died unexpectedly in 1990, New York's Cathedral of St. John the Divine was jammed not only with family, friends and associates, but with admirers young and old. They were there to celebrate his unique legacy: a family of Muppet characters created by Henson's ingenuity.

He made his unusual puppetry seem effortless and simple. But he realized that "the only way the magic works is by hard work. But hard work can be fun."

Jim Henson's fascination with his art began as an adolescent and developed through college. He made local TV appearances accompanied by a frog named Kermit, made from a piece of cloth from an old green coat of his mother's. Now, young and old alike have come to know and love his creations through *The Muppet Show* and *Sesame Street*.

Jim Henson left behind him great wealth: joy, humor, and childlike fun. One person can enrich so many.

We intend to do what is right not only in the Lord's sight but also in the sight of others. (2 Corinthians 8:21)

May human creativity channel more of Your joy and light into the world, Jesus.

Faith Inspires Wheelchair Ministry

Because of Duchenne muscular dystrophy, a progressive genetic condition which affects the muscles, 24-year-old Louis Bouffard lost the use of his arms and legs. However, this young man is not letting his disease stop him from doing God's work.

"We have to make ourselves available to God's grace: a little like a stained-glass window, we are called to let His light shine through," Bouffard told *Aleteia*.

Bouffard believes God is calling him to be a missionary in a wheelchair. He also believes that God shares in his suffering and is there by his side helping him to live a meaningful life.

Bouffard explained, "In our lives, we all suffer at some point: we just have to give another dimension to that suffering. Faith is what makes that possible...I firmly believe that Christ came to share my suffering. He doesn't shrink from it; He comes close to it. This helps us understand that God doesn't want suffering; He fights it. And more than that, He comes to join us in it."

The king himself and those with him were astonished at the young man's spirit, for he regarded his sufferings as nothing.
(2 Maccabees 7:12)

Jesus, may I see Your light shine through my sufferings.

A Bright Future

Mercy Center in the Bronx, New York, has been serving men, women, and children struggling with poverty for more than three decades. Some of the young people who were once helped by the Center are now helping others there.

For instance, there is Jose Galindo, who began attending Mercy's After School program when he was in the second grade. Currently a senior in high school, he has been volunteering with younger kids for four years, acting as a "big brother" by tutoring them in subjects like math, talking to them about their personal lives, and offering good advice to them when they need it.

Jose credits his motivation to be successful to his father's repeated mantra, "If you work hard, you will have a bright future." With a 3.7 grade point average and a Charles Hayden Foundation Scholarship to take several college courses early over the summer, he is well on his way to reaching his full potential.

As reported in Mercy Center's newsletter, Jose said, "I believe this is the opportunity of a lifetime...Anything good in life must be obtained through hard work and dedication."

I know the plans I have for you, says the Lord... to give you a future with hope. (Jeremiah 29:11)

Inspire young people to work hard and be kind, Creator.

The Spirit of St. Vincent de Paul

The St. John's University Vincentian Mission Certificate (VMC) cohort had a spiritual experience traveling to the Germantown neighborhood of Philadelphia, Pennsylvania, to witness the "beating heart of the Vincentian community on the East Coast," reported the campus website *StJohns.edu*.

The VMC participated in a 16-month program to learn about the life and ministry of St. Vincent de Paul. During their trip to Germantown, the cohort toured several holy sites and social service agencies that continue to advocate and serve others, as per the Vincentian mission.

MaryAnna Schaefer, the Office of Advancement's Director of Annual Giving, said, "While we witnessed the many struggles of a community, we also witnessed a great love within the community for one another as they help the most vulnerable move forward with great dignity and respect. There are so many really deeply good people in our world who are present 24/7, doing a myriad of small things together with care and love. It was uplifting."

Since it is by God's mercy that we are engaged in this ministry, we do not lose heart.
(2 Corinthians 4:1)

Father, may we follow in St. Vincent de Paul's footsteps.

Baking Changes a Life

Though she had a good upbringing and loving parents, Janie Deegan endured crippling anxiety, which led her down a path of drug and alcohol addiction, as well as homelessness. At age 25, she finally found the motivation to get sober. But she still felt a lack of purpose in her life.

That's when Janie started baking in her tiny New York City apartment, reported *Guideposts* magazine. She had enjoyed it as a child and found it meditative, so she decided to bake brownies and cupcakes for her friends' birthday parties. When a guest asked Janie if she could buy one of her cakes, the idea of turning her hobby into a business began to blossom.

In the years that followed, she opened Janie's Life-Changing Baked Goods, and even created the first "pie crust cookie." The business has become a success and allowed Janie to hire employees who are looking to change their lives for the better following periods of homelessness, prison, or addiction.

Janie said, "It's a miracle I'm still here. For so many people, they don't have that moment of grace...I succeeded because people believed in me, so I want to do that for others."

God...gives grace to the humble. (James 4:6)

Holy Spirit, guide me through struggles towards victories.

Heart Attack Leads to a Job

Drew Andrews had spent most of his life as a healer. For 23 years, he served in the Air Force as a medic in the Middle East's war zones and as a nurse in CVICUs (Cardiovascular Intensive Care Units). He was so good at his job that he was dubbed a "one person hospital."

Upon retiring from military service, Andrews wasn't sure what his next season of life would bring, though he knew he wanted to "make people feel better," reported *Good News Movement* on Instagram.

While walking his dogs in his Tampa, Florida hometown one day, Andrews felt severe pain in his chest. He knew he was having a heart attack. After arriving at AdventHealth Tampa, doctors and nurses saved his life. They also discovered his medical background and offered him a job.

After being discharged and recovering, Andrews accepted the hospital's offer and is now working in the CVICU. He also makes it a point to engage in outreach to veterans who need care. "I'm blessed," Andrews concluded.

Their gift of healing comes from the Most High. (Sirach 38:2)

Help me be a healer in my own unique way, Lord.

Friars Offer Hope to Addicts

For many years, Larry was a slave to his drug addiction. Not even rehab centers were able to help him. Then, Larry and his mother, Tracy, discovered St. Christopher's Inn, run by the Franciscan Friars of the Atonement in Garrison, New York.

The staff at St. Christopher's Inn guided Larry down the path of facing his demons and building his sense of self in the company of others who were struggling with similar issues. In addition, he received spiritual support that helped grow his faith and gave him the strength to forgive himself.

Tracy told the publication *In At-One-Ment,* "I will never forget the day I saw the light in my son's eyes return with a flicker of determination as he embraced his healing journey offered by the Friars. With their compassionate care, he embarked on a path of recovery, one step at a time."

Tracy concluded, "The Friars of the Atonement not only restored my son to me; they have restored our family to wholeness. The Friars never gave up on Larry, and they illuminated his path with hope."

Call on Me in the day of trouble. (Psalm 50:15)

Divine Healer, guide those struggling with addiction towards healing and recovery.

Why God Loves Us

St. Therese of Lisieux was known for living her "little way" of trusting God and realizing that the smallest acts of love will make God happy. Yet this view clashed with the Jansenist philosophy which was pervading her culture at the time.

In the Society of the Little Flower's newsletter *Between Friends,* Father Bob Colaresi, O. Carm. explained that Jansenism promoted "an angry God who was vengeful and vindictive...a God ready to pounce in judgment...Jansenism proclaims that God loves us *if* we are good—instead of the good news that God loves us *because* God is good."

Father Bob takes comfort in St. Therese's simpler, more grace-filled way of thinking. He noted, "Her inner graced experience was that God loved her because she was imperfect (not in spite of being imperfect). That is where the Divine could most affect her...In our broken imperfection, God works well as light. St. Therese learned this lesson early...God could be close and intimate and make her whole and complete."

I have loved you with an everlasting love. (Jeremiah 31:3)

Creator, meet me in my imperfections, and fill me with Your grace and light.

Music for Healing

Ordinarily, a new choir director would be discouraged when the first question asked by a member is, "What's a note?" But Deborah Staiman was not leading an ordinary choir.

The members were drug addicts undergoing treatment at Phoenix House in New York City. Most had no background in music.

This all happened decades ago, but the story remains a shining example of sharing God's love with others.

Staiman is a cantor, the leader of liturgical songs in a synagogue. During Yom Kippur, the Day of Atonement, she realized she wanted to do more for others. She soon found an unusual opportunity to lead the singing of Christmas carols at a drug treatment center.

Her beautiful music and encouragement provided valuable support to people on the difficult road back from addiction.

I will sing to the Lord, for He has triumphed gloriously. (Exodus 15:1)

Father, make it possible for me to enjoy beautiful music and, through it, to be led to You.

Barbershop Books

In 2008, while getting a haircut at a local barber shop in Harlem, New York, first-grade teacher Alvin Irby noticed one of his students there "looking bored." Ever the teacher, Irby thought it was a shame that he didn't have a book with him to lend to his pupil. Thus, the idea for Barbershop Books was born.

It wasn't until five years later, however, that Irby was able to create this nonprofit organization. For more than 10 years, Barbershop Books "has brought more than 50,000 free children's books to more than 200 barbershops in predominantly Black neighborhoods across the country."

"Our goal is not to turn barbers into tutors," Alvin pointed out to *CNN*. "This is an opportunity to provide boys with male role models...Less than two percent of teachers are Black males, and many Black boys are raised by single moms."

"We want [barbers] to encourage kids to use the reading spaces," Irby concluded. "So many kids associate reading with something you do in or for school...Our program is about getting kids to say three words: 'I'm a reader.'"

**Reading...will enable you to perceive.
(Ephesians 3:4)**

Abba, help us instill a love of reading in our children.

The Humility of St. Francis

St. Francis of Assisi remains one of our most beloved saints, having renounced all his worldly possessions to lovingly serve God and the poor. Theologian Bruce Epperly reflected on the saint's life in his book *Walking with Francis of Assisi:*

"Francis patterned his life…after the gospel simplicity and humility of Jesus, whose self-emptying and letting go of power and prestige was at the heart of His divinity…Francis discovered that the glory of God is found in identification with the salt of the earth, the most vulnerable people, the poor, disabled, and leprous. The incarnation of Christ means that Christ is one of us, not lording it over like presidents and prelates, but living among the poor and dispossessed."

"Francis, Clare [of Assisi], and their followers sought the way of holy poverty or spiritual simplicity that breaks down walls and builds bridges with all God's creatures. Better than none, equal to all in need of God's grace, and depending on God's gifts for life itself, Francis and Clare found God in the least of these."

Just as you did it to one of the least of these… you did it to Me. (Matthew 25:40)

Help me emulate Your holy humility, Jesus.

Safe Haven Baby Boxes

Monica Kelsey was abandoned shortly after her birth, but was adopted quickly by a loving family. When grown, she heard that babies were dying in the USA after being left outside safe haven locations, where mothers who could not raise their children could drop them off, no questions asked. Kelsey yearned to protect the wellbeing and safety of these babies.

That's when she created Safe Haven Baby Boxes. If a parent wishes to surrender their baby anonymously, they can leave their newborn in this temperature-regulated baby box, typically located at a firehouse. The box alerts 911 on its own, and the fire department responds, typically within two minutes. After a hospital visit, the baby is transferred either to an adoption agency or to the Department of Child Services.

The baby box program has saved 180 babies and counting, and is now offered in 15 states. Kelsey told *Good Morning America*, "How blessed am I that I was abandoned as an infant and now I'm saving abandoned children."

Protect me, O God, for in You I take refuge. (Psalm 16:1)

Jesus, protect abandoned children and find them loving homes.

The $10,000 Tip

For friends Steven Harward and Nikisha Timms, it has become a mission of theirs to dole out extra generous tips at their favorite restaurants. Typically, that amounts to $1,000 per meal. But for one special eatery—the Mexican restaurant Monarca in Salt Lake City, Utah—they gathered 20 of their friends to give the entire staff a whopping $10,000!

Immigrants Alfonso Brito and his wife opened Monarca just four years ago. "When we moved to America, we had nothing to our names," Brito told *KSL TV News*. "We had $20 in our pocket, and we started working as dishwashers."

Never in Alfonso's wildest dreams did he think he and his workers would be presented with "$10,000...in 100s." It was a moving experience, as seen in cell phone footage of this benevolent act. Harward and Timms asked that $2,000 be given to their waiter, but the rest was Brito's to distribute as he chose.

"The impact of the generosity extends not only to our staff, but also to their families and our entire community," Brito wrote on Facebook. "An act of kindness goes far beyond what words can express...Gracias from the bottom of our hearts."

**A generous person will be enriched.
(Proverbs 11:25)**

Abba, inspire us to selfless acts of generosity.

A Baseball Game with Mom

When the *Philadelphia Inquirer's* Kristen A. Graham was given the assignment to cover Game Two of Major League Baseball's 2023 National League Championship Series, which pitted the Phillies against the Arizona Diamondbacks, she was thrilled. Even more excited was her 10-year-old son, Kieran, who accompanied her to the game.

Since it was a school night, Graham wrote a note to Kieran's teacher, asking her to accept his math and spelling homework a little late this one time. (The teacher happily obliged.) After all, no mother could pass up the opportunity to bond with her son, a die-hard Phillies fan, in this special way.

Once they arrived at the stadium, they roamed around hand-in-hand, ate ice cream, talked baseball with other fans at the game, and enjoyed the lopsided 10-0 Phillies win.

Mother and son didn't arrive home until 1:00 a.m., the latest Kieran had ever stayed up. Graham asked Kieran what his favorite part of the evening was. His answer: "The win…but also I just like talking baseball with you."

His mother treasured all these things in her heart. (Luke 2:51)

Strengthen the bonds between parents and children, Jesus.

Life with Lidia, Part 1

If you've tuned in to any of Lidia Bastianich's cooking series on *PBS* over the last 26 years, you'll know they are multi-generational affairs. Her grandchildren were always a presence, and still remain so today.

In addition, her mother Erminia, who passed away at age 100 in 2021, also frequently joined Lidia in the kitchen. And though she is not physically present on the program anymore, audio of Erminia and Lidia singing together continues to be a staple of each episode.

Keeping her mom involved with the show in her senior years was important to Lidia. During a *Christopher Closeup* interview, she said, "I think that in today's world, the grandma generation is kind of left behind, and it's such a loss for the children because grandparents have unconditional love. They don't question. They just give and have life experience to share."

"For a while there, we were four generations...So, I feel very strongly about being together. It brings strength to everybody in the family."

Grandchildren are the crown of the aged, and the glory of children is their parents. (Proverbs 17:6)

May children appreciate their grandparents, Abba.

Life with Lidia, Part 2

The bonds of family were forged early in Lidia Bastianich's life. The section of Italy in which she was born was given to communist Yugoslavia after World War II. As a result, both the practice of the Catholic faith and private enterprise were both outlawed. Still, Lidia spent her formative years—from birth to age 10—around her grandmother, Nonna Rosa.

Lidia recalled, "We lived in a big city, but [my mother] put my brother and I with grandma out in the country...We fed the animals, we milked the goats...We had olive trees. In November, we'd harvest the olives, make the olive oil. Grandpa would make the wine...And the love was unconditional."

"I had to help [Grandma]...I would run around with the hose to wet the garden, to collect the potatoes. But...it was such a great period of learning, of forming who I am as a person, in appreciation of the gifts of nature, in appreciation of God. Because under communism, we couldn't go to church. But grandma would say prayers at night with me, so I felt connected, to some extent, to my faith, even though it was forbidden."

O Lord, how manifold are Your works! In wisdom You have made them all. (Psalm 104:24)

Teach us to appreciate the beauty of nature, Creator.

Life with Lidia, Part 3

During her childhood in communist Yugoslavia, Lidia Bastianich witnessed the selflessness of her mother, Erminia, who worked as a teacher and went out of her way to help students with special needs and those who had to work in the fields. She taught Lidia the importance of helping those in need. Soon, however, it would be Lidia's family who were in need.

Because Lidia's father owned a truck and ran something of a private business, he was arrested and held for weeks by communist authorities. When he was finally released, the family knew it was time to escape from their native region.

Lidia, her brother, and mother made it to Italy under the pretense of visiting a relative, while her father had to escape through the woods in an attempt to cross the border. In his pocket, he carried a picture of the Sacred Heart of Jesus that his mother had given him before she died. He had a harrowing journey, but eventually arrived safely. Lidia's family soon joined the many other refugees in Italy, looking to build a new life somewhere else.

We have escaped like a bird from the snare of the fowlers. (Psalm 124:7)

Protect and guide those fleeing persecution, Holy Spirit.

Life with Lidia, Part 4

Life in the Italian refugee camp was difficult for Lidia Bastianich's family, but they made the best of it. Lidia was even able to attend a school run by the Canossian Sisters. During a *Christopher Closeup* interview, she recalled, "That was my reentry into Catholicism...They took me in, taught me, but I also got a chance to work with them. They put me in the kitchen with the other nuns...In those two years, I got back into understanding the Catholic religion and the whole gospel."

Catholic Relief Services helped Lidia's family in the camp, while Catholic Charities and the Red Cross brought them to the U.S. Lidia said, "Learning the new language was the most important thing for us, and so we did."

"Catholic Charities set us up in an apartment. The people of Italian descent, part of the Catholic community, they would bring food [and] everything that a new family would need. We were amazed that after being forbidden to do many human things...[we were able] to be free, to be open, to go to church, to speak Italian, and to become part of this wonderful America."

Let us work for the good of all, and especially for those of the family of faith. (Galatians 6:10)

May a spirit of giving guide me, Paraclete.

Life with Lidia, Part 5

Lidia Bastianich took full advantage of the opportunities offered in the U.S. She turned her talent for cooking into several successful restaurants and numerous cooking series on *PBS*. In more recent years, her gratitude for the U.S. led to a series of specials titled *Lidia Celebrates America*. One of its episodes, *Overcoming the Odds*, earned a 2022 Christopher Award.

Lidia explained that she wanted to highlight an immigrant's point of view, how she was given the opportunity to start a new life, get an education, and pursue her dreams of becoming a chef and restaurateur.

"The last one that I did," Lidia said, "was about different refugees, like me, from Nepal, from Vietnam, from Palestine. How these people, as refugees, made their life in America. I wanted to show how these people really appreciate America, the opportunity, and how they've made a full life, a family. They're workers, they're contributors to America, and they are successes in their own right."

I do not cease to give thanks for you as I remember you in my prayers. (Ephesians 1:16)

Lord, I thank You for all the opportunities you have put in my path.

Life with Lidia, Part 6

Two career highlights for chef and *PBS* host Lidia Bastianich's career are cooking for Pope Benedict XVI and Pope Francis during their respective stays in New York. Pope Francis even surprised Lidia and her team one day.

During a *Christopher Closeup* interview, she recalled, "After lunch, the staff was sitting around the table downstairs in the kitchen having coffee... and [we saw] this white thing floating down the hallway. And here [Pope Francis] was. We jumped up, and he said [in Italian], 'May I have a coffee with you?' Of course, we made coffee, and he stayed for 15 minutes.

"He talked to us, blessed everybody. Then, he went into his pocket, gave a blessed rosary to each one of us, and he left by asking us to pray for him as well...I think that's the grandeur of Pope Francis and people of that stature. One would think, even for me cooking, you would think that these people are on another sort of strata than you are. But at the end, you find out that they're human beings, just like us. They just have a special mission in life."

When pride comes, then comes disgrace; but wisdom is with the humble. (Proverbs 11:2)

No matter my successes, keep me humble, Jesus.

Life with Lidia, Part 7

Acclaimed chef and Christopher Award-winning *PBS* host Lidia Bastianich continues with her mission of showing people that cooking can be easy, fun, and provide bonding moments for the family. She also remains committed to giving back through various charities, including Catholic Charities, for the help they gave her family when they immigrated to the U.S.

Lidia has always relied on her faith to get her through life's highs and lows, and in her senior years, that has not changed. During a *Christopher Closeup* interview, she concluded, "I [say] my prayers, whether it's at night or the rosary, but I talk to God.

"So, whenever I'm in a situation [that's] beautiful...I thank God for giving me this opportunity, for whatever I see, whatever music I hear, whatever food. I just talk to Him and thank Him like I would talk to you. And when in difficulties, I talk to Him: please get me through... and get me where You want me to be...So, I do a lot of talking to God."

Pray in the Spirit at all times in every prayer and supplication. (Ephesians 6:18)

Thank You, Lord, for all You have given me. Also, help and guide me to where You want me to be.

No Longer Suffering in Silence

Katie Grogan and Shaunda Penny are spearheading new ministries at various churches in the Diocese of Albany, New York, inspired by their own experiences with miscarriage. It's a topic that has rarely been discussed in the Church, even though it is estimated that between 10 to 28 percent of pregnancies end in pregnancy loss.

Enduring the loss of an unborn child can result in physical problems and psychological repercussions, such as "grief, anxiety, and depression," writes Emily Benson in *The Evangelist*. "Some women said they weren't aware a funeral or memorial Mass could be offered for their baby."

Having a community of faith support a woman through this tragic event can make a positive difference. Grogan explained, "I had three miscarriages but...I had a funeral Mass and burial for each one, and I can tell you that really helped me with closure, that I know where my babies are buried."

Penny added, "I don't want anyone to suffer alone."

Blessed are those who mourn for they will be comforted. (Matthew 5:4)

Bring comfort and healing to parents who endure pregnancy loss, Jesus.

EJ's PJs

In 2024 in Louisville, Kentucky, Jefferson County Public Schools' bus driver Larry Farrish, Jr., went viral for his act of kindness towards Engelhard Elementary School first grader, Levi Carrier.

Driving Carrier on the bus that morning, Farrish noticed the boy was not his usual cheerful self. When Larry learned that Levi did not have any sleepwear to wear to his school's Pajama Day, he went out and brought back two pairs of pajamas for the youngster. Pictures of this heartwarming exchange were soon posted all over social media, receiving an overwhelmingly positive response from around the world.

The most generous reaction came from Patricia Poggi, the founder of EJ's PJs, based in Long Island, New York. Poggi partnered with Toys for Tots and traveled 800 miles to gift all 300 students at the school with a free pair of pajamas.

"Pay attention to the kids," Farrish told *WDRB News.* "Every kid deserves something. They're oblivious to what we go through as adults, so just let them be kids and guide them."

The good leave an inheritance to their children's children. (Proverbs 13:22)

Abba, may we work to protect the innocence of our youth.

Family Considerations

Lucy was 12 years old, and she had all the wisdom that comes at that age. She knew that her parents were going to argue on occasion, that people simply don't agree about everything all the time.

Still, it depressed her when her parents argued in front of her. She didn't think they ought to do that.

"It would be good," she said, "if they'd apologize to me when they did that. It would show that they are taking you into consideration, that they are thinking of your feelings, too."

An interesting point. Try not to involve your children in your disputes. But if you do, remember Lucy's suggestion, and be ready to apologize. Every member of the family, especially your children, has feelings that should be considered.

Let the little children come to Me...for it is to such as these that the kingdom of God belongs. (Mark 10:14)

I know adults are supposed to teach children, Lord, but help me remember that sometimes children possess wisdom that is helpful for adults.

Centenarian Priest's Full-Time Job

Father John McMillan, a Passionist priest who celebrated his 100th birthday in October 2023, may be officially retired, but he still considers his active prayer life to be his most important daily work. Born in Linden, New Jersey, to a Presbyterian father and Catholic mother, McMillan discovered his faith when he became a draftsman for the Bell Telephone company in 1941.

On his lengthy work commute to Lower Manhattan, McMillan picked up a spiritual book that touched his soul, particularly the chapter highlighting the "Passion of Christ." This religious yearning remained in him, even after he finished serving in the U.S. Army Air Corps during World War II.

Ordained into the Passionist priesthood in 1956, Father John has been employed in many rewarding vocations, including being a chaplain to residents at an alcohol and drug treatment center. However, the activity he values most is praying for others, especially crime victims and perpetrators he reads about in the news.

"I pray for the salvation of those who are guilty," Father John told *The Tablet's* Bill Miller, "and pray for some peace for those who have been hurt. It's a full-time job."

The prayer of the righteous is powerful. (James 5:16)

Lord, may we value the power of prayer.

Courage to Contribute

The late senator from New York, Jacob Javits, once held a memorable speech at a conference of doctors.

At the time, Javits was suffering from Lou Gehrig's disease. His condition had been diagnosed as terminal. He was in a wheelchair and had lost control of his muscles. He could speak only with the aid of a portable respirator. Yet he spoke to the doctors for an hour. This is what he told them:

"We are all terminal. We all die some time. So why should terminal illness be different from terminal life? There is no difference. As long as your brain can function, you can contribute."

To be able to contribute in difficult circumstances is a formidable challenge. But courage is one of the qualities that makes life worthwhile. If you find yourself in this type of situation, pray for the strength and guidance to deal with it as best you can.

I was hard pressed and falling, but the Lord helped me. My strength and my courage is the Lord. (Psalm 118:13-14)

Redeemer, enable me to find strength in difficult times.

Native Women Running

The first time that Verna NezBegay Volker went for a run, she just hoped to work off some of the stress she was dealing with in her life. When she realized how running improved her mood, she made it a regular practice. "I began to feel better and stronger," Volker wrote in *AARP: The Magazine*.

As a member of the Navajo Nation living in Minneapolis, Volker came to notice there were no other Native American women participating in races, despite the fact that Indigenous people had always found running to be "a form of meditation and a connection to the land."

Volker created an Instagram page called Native Women Running, intending to build a community that would get more women involved in the sport, while also raising money for charity. It has since become a success.

Volker said, "The majority of Native women I interact with tell me they run for spiritual reasons. They'll say running is healing, running is prayer, running is our medicine."

Those who wait for the Lord shall renew their strength...they shall run and not be weary. (Isaiah 40:31)

Guide me towards healing, prayerful activities, Lord.

Nurture Friendships for Brain Health

The nonprofit Mind What Matters financially supports caregivers for Alzheimer's and dementia patients, and also offers advice on improving brain health to younger people to help them avoid getting these conditions. One of their tips involves social interaction. The Mind What Matters Instagram page stated:

"Humans are social beings, and our brains and hearts need the interaction of others. Who is on your team? Who do you support and care for? If you don't know, you need to work on building one. It is important to nurture and cultivate real friendships, not just acquaintances. Focusing on a few that truly matter is so important. Not everything is better in quantity.

"If you're having trouble, joining a community center or religious organization can be a great way to start. Another easy way to meet people as adults is by volunteering!...If you're a caregiver currently and it's hard to go out, join an online support group...Remember, your friends and family are who nurture you through tough life events. Make sure you nurture those relationships."

It is not good that...man should be alone. (Genesis 2:18)

Help me find loving and caring friends, Savior, and allow me to be a loving and caring friend to others.

Polish Painter Praises God's Guiding Hand

For 70-year-old Polish Catholic artist Christopher Zacharow, God has always been in the details—especially when it comes to designing his creations. Inspired by the "Italian Renaissance architecture" of his home city of Zamosc, located in eastern Poland, Zacharow started both painting and carving at a young age. "My mother would give me potatoes," he recalled in *The Tablet,* "and I would carve things with them."

Zacharow's educational background includes a degree from Krakow's Academy of Fine Arts. In 1981, he moved to New York, where a chance meeting with a Madison Avenue art gallery owner led him to his first job. His reputation as a talented artist only grew from there.

Zacharow's paintings have been displayed in galleries all over the world, and he currently teaches and lectures at several renowned art schools in the tri-state area. He finds special fulfillment, however, as a painting instructor at the Pete McGuiness Older Adult Center in Greenpoint, a program run by Catholic Charities. No matter where his artistic journey has taken him, Zacharow credits God as his constant guide.

We are all the work of Your hand. (Isaiah 64:8)

Lord, may we see Your guiding hand in all we do.

You Can Keep Moving On

Many years ago, Michael King had something he wanted to say to other people with disabilities. So, he decided to travel from Fairbanks, Alaska, to Washington, D.C., in a wheelchair.

You see, Michael King is a paraplegic who lost the use of both of his legs in a motorcycle accident. He made the 5,600-mile journey in four months, and along the way repeated this message: "You can still make something of your life in spite of difficulties and circumstances."

King said his goal was to reach out to others and encourage them to live to the fullest extent possible. For King himself, that meant beginning graduate studies in social work as soon as the trip was over. Years later, he created Powered to Move, which puts "Christ's love into action by providing people with intellectual and physical disabilities opportunities for physical fitness."

King is an inspiration to everyone because life is a series of challenges. To meet them, it's wise to rely on all the resources God has given you. And while you're at it, remember to pray.

Continue steadfastly in prayer, being watchful in it with thanksgiving. (Colossians 4:2)

God, guide me through challenges and hard times.

Loving Those Who Are Addicted

Even when she was a child growing up in Italy, Blessed Sandra Sabattini felt called to love and care for the less fortunate and people shunned by society. By age 20, she was a medical student determined to help those living with addictions.

This was the early 1980s so, as Meg Hunter-Kilmer wrote in *Our Sunday Visitor,* "There was little understanding of the trauma that often leads to substance abuse issues or the ways that addiction impairs our freedom, making many who are dependent on drugs all but incapable of stopping without help. Still, Sandra saw the dignity of those she served."

Sandra came to see all the patients in the rehab center where she worked as beloved children of God and reflected the love of Jesus to them, even when they rejected her or raged at her. "It was her smile and her eagerness to listen that helped the patients to open up," Hunter-Kilmer observed. "One man later wrote of her contagious joy, which enabled him to work toward recovery; he has now been sober for 40 years."

Tragically, Sandra died in a car accident at age 22. Her example of love and mercy, however, can guide us all.

Clothe yourselves with love. (Colossians 3:14)

Guide those with addictions toward recovery, Savior.

Donor Heart Saves a Life

Carlos Toro spent 30 years working more than 70 hours a week as a supermarket manager in Brooklyn, New York. Then, the hectic pace of his life caught up with him. As reported by Barry Paddock in the *Daily News,* Toro suffered a major heart attack after developing "lethally high blood pressure." The only thing that could save him would be a heart transplant.

The wait for a donor heart can be long and difficult in general, but because the 57-year-old Toro has "O negative" blood, his body could only accept the organ from someone with the same blood type. After two instances in which Toro was prepped for surgery, but had it cancelled at the last minute, he finally received a heart at Mount Sinai Hospital in 2023.

With his ever-improving health, Toro felt grateful to spend Christmas with his granddaughter that year. However, he knows that his good fortune is grounded in someone else's loss of life. He said, "I believe in God, and I believe in fate. The day I got out of the hospital, I decided to light a candle for my donor for the next six months, and not a day goes by when I don't do it."

I will give thanks to the Lord with my whole heart. (Psalm 9:1)

Remind me to be grateful for the gift of life, Jesus.

Jeff Foxworthy's Bible Study Mission

Though comedian Jeff Foxworthy has achieved great success over the course of his decades-long career, he has managed to remain grounded in both his personal and spiritual life. For instance, once he had children, he decided to move from Los Angeles back to his home state of Georgia because he wanted his kids to grow up around family.

During an interview on the podcast *Mayim Bialik's Breakdown*, Foxworthy shared this story: "For 12 years, I would get up every Tuesday at 5:00 in the morning and go teach a small group Bible study at the homeless mission downtown. After a dozen years of doing it, people would find out about it, and they would go, 'How come I don't know that you do this?' And I would [say], 'I'm not doing it for [the attention].'

"I met somebody who was homeless and learned their story, and I realized this was something I needed in my life. I needed to be able to have these conversations with other human beings that were just as important as me…I'm so grateful for that in my life."

Whenever you give alms, do not sound a trumpet before you, as the hypocrites do. (Matthew 6:2)

Guide me in quietly performing good deeds, Savior.

Just Hard Work

In 1985, there was a lot of excitement surrounding the discovery of the treasure trove that sank with the Spanish ship, Nuestra Señora de Atocha, in 1622.

The ship carried gold, silver, and jewelry valued at $400 million. And everyone thought how lucky the finders were.

Except, it wasn't luck that led them to the Atocha. The man who directed the search had been looking for the vessel for 15 years.

He hired expert drivers and searched everywhere. Spanish specialists were consulted. There were numerous disappointments, false starts, and lawsuits before success was achieved.

Success is like that—one part luck, perhaps, but nine parts hard work. Don't be caught short. Expect to work hard, regardless of what goals you pursue.

Commit your work to the Lord, and your plans will be established. (Proverbs 16:3)

Direct my plans, Jesus.

Jeopardy! Champ's Unexpected Friendship

Doris Rabideau, age 89 and the mother of 12, always enjoyed having a few friends over to watch *Jeopardy!* So, when her fellow Green Bay, Wisconsin resident Ben Chan won nine games on the show, she sent a congratulatory postcard to him where he worked, St. Norbert College. Rabideau told the *Green Bay Press Gazette*, "I said I'm so proud of him, and he's giving Green Bay and Wisconsin a good name. We're not just football."

After receiving her note, Chan responded, saying he would love to attend one of her watch parties. Rabideau was thrilled to welcome him into the fold—and he has since attended more than one of her gatherings. She noted that he is soft-spoken and doesn't shout out answers like she and her friends do.

While Chan was taking part in *Jeopardy's* annual Tournament of Champions, he told host Ken Jennings that one of the best things about gaining a level of fame from the show was getting to befriend Doris. Rabideau was happy to hear how much their connection meant to Chan. She concluded, "We're going to be friends, because he's such a sweetie."

You shall rise before the aged, and defer to the old. (Leviticus 19:32)

Abba, foster the bonds of friendships between generations.

Childhood Cancer Leads to Foundation

In 2019, *WGHP News* anchor Chad Tucker and his wife, Meredith, received news no parents want to hear: their three-year-old daughter Pearl Monroe—nicknamed Roe Roe—was diagnosed with leukemia. For the next two plus years, she received chemo at Brenner Children's in Winston-Salem, North Carolina, that has left her cancer free so far.

Because of all the love and support they received during this difficult time, the Tuckers chose to create the Roe Roe's Heroes Childhood Cancer Foundation. This organization assists families in similar situations and lobbies the government for more financial resources for childhood cancer research.

An initiative close to Roe Roe's heart is The Hero Library, which gives away books to kids going through cancer treatments. The idea was inspired by Roe Roe's love for Dolly Parton's music and her mission of giving away books through The Imagination Library. In 2024, Roe Roe got to meet Dolly and tell her how much her work meant to her. Dolly was thrilled for the little girl, who had endured so much at such a young age.

Their children become a blessing. (Psalm 37:26)

Bring strength and healing to children and families dealing with cancer, Divine Physician.

Palace for the Poor, Part 1

In the 19th century, Rome's Palazzo Migliori served as the home of the wealthy Migliori family. The four-story palace boasted 16 bedrooms and 13 bathrooms, among other facilities and amenities. In the 1930s, the building came to house the Calasanziane religious order, which used it to support young mothers who had nowhere else to turn.

When the Calasanzianes moved to a different location, there was a question of what to do with the Palazzo. Some suggested converting it into a luxury hotel. But since the building belongs to the Vatican, Pope Francis had another idea. He had it turned into a shelter for the homeless.

This "palace for the poor" opened in 2019 and can house up to 50 people. Each day, volunteers arrive to cook delicious meals. Before dinner, the residents meet in the chapel to pray. Afterwards, volunteers and residents sit together, eat, and engage in friendly conversation.

Some complain that the palazzo's accommodations are too fancy for the homeless. But as the shelter's director, Carlo Santoro, told *As It Happens* host Carol Off, "Beauty heals."

Happy are those who consider the poor. (Psalm 41:1)

Remind us that the poor are our brothers and sisters, Lord.

Palace for the Poor, Part 2

Plough.com's Sharon Rose Christner visited Rome's "palace for the poor" and noted that all the homeless residents, as well as the volunteers who cook and clean, know each other's names and life stories. Genuine human bonds are formed, as they should be since we all need to experience kindness and compassion in order to find our best selves.

Anna, one of the residents, told Christner that her life took a dark turn during her youth, and she often found herself in regular homeless shelters that could be dangerous. While living on the streets, Anna observed people avoiding her "because everybody...is afraid of poorness."

"And then?" Anna continued. "God is good. He, the big Father, saw this little thing falling down, and He picked me out and put me here...Without any important reason either. Because I didn't do anything so *great* to stay in a palace next door to the pope! Like a *princess,* oh my. So, if anyone doesn't believe that miracles can happen...Now, I am in the place of a princess."

When you give a banquet, invite the poor...You will be blessed, because they cannot repay you. (Luke 14:13-14)

Jesus, open our eyes to the inherent beauty in others.

**The unfolding
of Your words
gives light.**

(Psalm 119:130)

St. Francis and the Leper

St. Francis of Assisi gave up riches in order to embrace poverty and follow Jesus, but he still faced some obstacles along the way. One of them was his fear of lepers.

Leprosy (now known as Hansen's Disease) causes nerve damage and severe skin sores all over a person's body. In the 13th century, when St. Francis lived, there was no treatment or cure. The sight of lepers revolted St. Francis, noted Murray Bodo, O.F.M., at *Franciscan Media*.

One day, while riding his horse, St. Francis was approached by a leper. Despite his misgivings, the saint embraced the man and gave him money. After getting back on his horse, St. Francis couldn't see the leper anywhere. He came to believe the leper was Jesus in disguise.

From that moment on, St. Francis found "spiritual and physical consolation" in the company of lepers. In his work *My Testament*, he instructed his friars to "be glad to live among social outcasts, among the poor and helpless, the sick and the lepers, and those who beg by the wayside."

I will bind up the injured, and I will strengthen the weak. (Ezekiel 34:16)

Give me compassion for those rejected by society, Jesus.

The Sign of Our Love for God

Born in Italy in 1894, Mother Thecla Merlo went on to cofound the Daughters of St. Paul with Father James Alberione. Their goal was to use media to evangelize, a mission which expanded as print, radio, film, and television evolved.

Though Mother Thecla experienced some health problems, she never let them affect her work. Father Alberione said of her, "In various everyday instances, whether pleasant or not, her outlook and manner of speaking flowed from her love for God, to whom she abandoned herself completely and absolutely."

In fact, love for all souls remained her chief motivation. These words from Mother Thecla can serve as a good reminder to us all: "The sign of our love for God is the love of our neighbor. It's easy to love those who are far away. We must love all the people in the world, pray that all may be saved. But then we must love and treat well those closer to us. This is what's more difficult."

Let us love one another, because love is from God. (1 John 4:7)

Father, teach me to offer Your life-affirming love to all those around me.

Heroic Sergeant Becomes an Uncle

Sergeant David Musgrove from Florida's Charlotte County Sheriff's Office was on patrol one night when a motorcycle zoomed past his car. Soon after, he heard a loud crash and rushed to the scene.

As reported by Katie Kindelan for *Good Morning America,* the motorcyclist, traveling at 90 mph, had crashed into a car which held single mom Kayleigh Foley, her three-year-old daughter Ariel, and six-month-old infant Lola. The driver of the motorcycle died immediately, but Kayleigh screamed for help for her family.

Though Kayleigh and Ariel suffered only minor injuries, Sgt. Musgrove couldn't find a pulse on Lola, so he started CPR on the side of the road. Just as paramedics arrived, Lola gasped and took a breath. Sgt. Musgrove had saved her life.

Though Lola still faces a long road of recovery, her family is grateful she is alive. "He's our angel, that's for sure," Lola's grandmother, Lisa, said. And the Foleys have now unofficially adopted Sgt. Musgrove as an "uncle."

Rescue the weak and the needy. (Psalm 82:4)

Guide and protect police officers who do their best to save lives, Jesus.

Café Brings Worshipers Together

As rector of Baltimore's Basilica of the National Shrine of the Assumption of the Blessed Virgin Mary, Father Brendan Fitzgerald often sees homeless people come into the church for shelter from the heat or cold. Sadly, they leave after a few hours, without anyone engaging them in conversation about their lives or faith. With the opening of Sexton's Lodge Café, however, Father Fitzgerald hopes this will change.

As reported by George P. Matysek Jr. in the *Catholic Review*, "The new café, erected inside a structure built north of the cathedral in 1840, is meant to be a place where basilica parishioners can develop relationships with people who live on the streets." It offers free refreshments after two weekly Masses.

Father Fitzgerald observed, "It's good for families to see the poor and to encounter the poor and to love the poor before they head back to the suburbs. I think it's a beautiful witness to see some of the poor genuinely worship with us on Sundays. We have some who have been baptized, and they participate in the liturgy."

The righteous know...the poor. (Proverbs 29:7)

Lord, may we seek to know and uplift the poor.

An Antidote to Loneliness

Loneliness and isolation have become an epidemic in the United States. The solution, however, could lie right in your own neighborhood: volunteering.

Writing for *America* magazine, Catholic Charities USA President and CEO Kerry Alys Robinson observed, "Volunteering nourishes the soul. As we grapple with fragmentation, political polarization, and rising distrust in institutions, a national embrace of volunteerism could go a long way toward healing what ails us as a society."

Robinson knows whereof she speaks. Catholic Charities relies on 45,000 staff members and 215,000 volunteers to accomplish all they do. She said, "Generosity is humankind's birthright, and volunteer work allows us to be generous with our most valuable assets: our time and attention.

"Central to Christianity is a disposition of other-centeredness...All the volunteers I encounter say to me that, paradoxically, they are the true beneficiaries of their encounters with others in merciful service."

Serve one another with whatever gift each of you has received. (1 Peter 4:10)

Increase my desire to be of service to others, Lord.

Motel to Home

Though she had a job, Tracy Neal didn't earn enough money to afford an apartment for herself and her two children. So, like thousands of other Georgia residents, she opted to live in an extended-stay motel.

After two years, Neal found new hope through her local St. Vincent de Paul Society's Motel to Home initiative, which provides "support and resources to help families transition into secure, long-term housing," reported the *Georgia Bulletin*. The assistance allowed Neal to move into a townhome.

To qualify for Motel to Home, "applicants must have a steady income and children." Once accepted, they receive financial assistance, but must also cooperate with caseworkers on budgeting, credit score improvement, and goal setting.

Neal credited these budgeting lessons with teaching her to become more financially responsible. Now serving as a mentor to other participants, she concluded, "Motel to Home isn't just an organization that throws money at people. They're really saving lives because they literally saved mine."

The plans of the diligent lead surely to abundance. (Proverbs 21:5)

God, show us the means to better our lives.

Teaching Children to Be Generous

Who helps a child learn how to give, how to sidestep selfish behavior? According to Victor Parachin in *Catholic Digest*, "parents still have the greatest opportunity to provide moral formation." How do children develop caring and sharing attitudes? He suggests the following:

- Start early. Even a one-year-old has generous instincts.

- Love and nurture your children, and shower them with respect.

- Be a role model. Practice what you preach about generosity and giving.

- Make holidays a time to give and receive, especially to those in need.

- Create opportunities for sharing and caring. Actively give help, consolation, or support to others. Write a letter, give flowers, or donate supplies when such gestures are called for—and encourage your children to do the same.

- Commend your children for acts of caring and kindness.

- Promote tolerance and acceptance. Let your children know that differences are acceptable.

**Let us conduct ourselves becomingly.
(Romans 13:13)**

Jesus, help us set good examples for children.

When You Love People

Dorothy Day founded the Catholic Worker movement and embraced poverty herself while living among, and serving those, who were poor and hungry. She also shared much wisdom in her books. John Touhey, writing at *Aleteia,* shared some of her memorable quotes.

In her 1948 book *On Pilgrimage,* Day noted, "Whenever I groan within myself and think how hard it is to keep writing about love in these times of tension and strife which may at any moment become for us all a time of terror, I think to myself, 'What else is the world interested in?' What else do we all want, each one of us, except to love and be loved, in our families, in our work, in all our relationships. God is Love. Love casts out fear."

Continuing with the theme of love, Day added, "When you love people, you see all the good in them, all the Christ in them. God sees Christ, His Son, in us and loves us. And so we should see Christ in others, and nothing else, and love them. There can never be enough of it."

If we love one another, God remains in us, and His love is brought to perfection in us. (1 John 4:12)

Jesus, help me see Your loving presence in all I meet.

The Baking Benedictines

It's not surprising that the Benedictine nuns at Transfiguration Hermitage in Windsor, Maine, are devoted to prayer. What is unusual is how committed they also are to baking fruit and rum cakes, and selling them during the Thanksgiving, Advent, and Christmas seasons to support themselves.

As reported by Dan McQuillan in *The Rhode Island Catholic,* Sister Elizabeth, Sister Bernadette, and Sister Anastasia try to incorporate prayer and an awareness of God's presence into everything they do, including their hours spent in the kitchen. They focus on fruit and rum cakes, Sister Elizabeth explained, because "they ship and keep well. We start making them in January and finish our production sometime in May."

The Sisters also welcome the occasional visitors to their small retreat house. Sister Elizabeth noted, "A few people join us for communal prayers. Most, though, just need quiet and nothing to do." Regarding prayer in general, she added, "Don't worry about how you're praying. Just quiet down. See what surfaces and talk to God about that. That's all people need, really."

Whatever you do, in word or deed, do everything in the name of the Lord Jesus. (Colossians 3:17)

Teach me to see Your presence in all I do, Creator.

War Horses for Veterans

Eight years after Iraq War veteran Patrick Benson retired from the military, he found himself experiencing symptoms of post-traumatic stress. His chosen career of training horses became a healing lifeline for him—and he realized that it could play the same role for other veterans who were struggling.

Benson co-founded the program War Horses for Veterans (WHFV) on a 30-acre horse ranch in Stilwell, Kansas. Donations from individuals and corporations cover workshops and multi-day sessions with horses for veterans and first responders, allowing them to reconnect with their talents, families, workplaces, and communities in new ways, reported *Costco Connection* magazine. One Iraq War veteran credited the program with saving his life.

"Horses are great teachers," Benson explained. "You can't fool them. They will humble you, if that's what you need, but they can build you up, too. We see amazing transformations here."

Ask the animals and they will teach you. (Job 12:7)

Guide those experiencing trauma towards healing, Divine Physician.

Army Veteran Saves a Life

When Army veteran Juan Serrano left a church community event in Petersburg, Virginia, little did he expect to do God's will by saving a person's life.

Serrano and his wife were driving home when they spotted a young man walking along the edge of a bridge that crossed the Appomattox River. Serrano felt something was wrong, so he stepped out of the car and called out to the young man to see if he needed help. Then, the unimaginable happened—the young man jumped off the bridge!

Picturing the troubled man as one of his kids, Serrano told *WTVR* that he was determined to rescue him. His training came back in full force, and Serrano jumped into the cold water, grabbed the man, and they travelled about a mile down the river, ultimately landing at the gates of a water treatment plant when help arrived.

Serrano is sharing his story to help spread the need for more mental health resources in all communities. "Hero is a big word," he said. "I was just a guy with my wife, passing by, and God put us there for a reason."

He might rescue him out of their hand and restore him to his father. (Genesis 37:22)

Merciful Jesus, bless all kind and caring veterans.

The Hero of the Video

Last year, 28-year-old Tik Tok influencer Jimmy Darts released a video that conveyed just how much one kind gesture can impact the lives of many. The film starts with the California native approaching 75-year-old Linda Witt-King in a Costa Mesa library. When Darts asks her for something to eat, Witt-King gives him most of the food she has.

The footage then goes on to witness Linda's shocked and tearful reaction when Jimmy gifts her with $1,000, telling her he was just "helping out the first person who helped" him. When Witt-King told Darts that because of his generosity, she would be able to stay in a motel that night, the young man was amazed to learn that his benefactor was homeless herself, having given up everything she had to help those in need.

According to *Newsweek*, Witt-King's inspiring story got over "7.2 million views." The next day, Jimmy was thrilled to be able to tell his new friend, whom he declared the "hero of the video," that $32,000 had been raised for her through a GoFundMe page. "I have been blessed, this time in a major way," Linda told *ABC 7*. "My life has completely changed."

Do good...share what you have. (Hebrews 13:16)

Jesus, infuse us with generous and loving spirits.

Sister's Road to Bread and Life, Part 1

Sister Caroline Tweedy, RSM, grew up thinking that coaching sports would be her dream job. Life didn't exactly turn out that way for the Sister of Mercy, who now serves as Executive Director of the St. John's Bread and Life food pantry program in Brooklyn, New York.

When Sister Caroline was a child, she helped out in the restaurant/bakery that her grandmother owned. "At the end of the day, my grandmother would give whatever was left to whoever was there, whoever needed it," she recalled during a *Christopher Closeup* interview. "She never turned anybody away."

The Catholic faith that Sister Caroline saw modeled by her family also left a lasting impression. She noted, "We were always taught that God is loving and compassionate, and God forgives, and that as a Christian, your mission in life is to do good. Whatever road that takes you down, everybody has something to offer. Everyone. That stuck in my mind the most. You're part of a group, but you're also your own person, and you have to give back."

The one who sows bountifully will also reap bountifully. (2 Corinthians 9:6)

Teach me to share what I have with others in need, Savior.

Sister's Road to Bread and Life, Part 2

Young Caroline Tweedy went on to attend a Mercy High School, run by the Sisters of Mercy, who impressed her with the joy with which they served. But the thought of joining them herself was still far in the future. Instead, she excelled in athletics, which resulted in her getting college scholarships that allowed her to earn a degree in comparative literature in history.

After graduating, however, Tweedy was offered a job teaching physical education at her old high school. The work involved coaching, so she felt drawn to it: "I saw people who gave back and how happy they were and the fruits of that: to train the next generation to be good sports, and to understand what their faith is and how to share their faith with one another. That was really important to me."

When someone asked Tweedy if she considered joining the Sisters of Mercy, she replied, "Oh, no, I've got other fish to fry." Eventually, the other fish got fried, and Tweedy found herself attracted to the Sisters of Mercy's mission and work—and the idea of living in community.

Serve one another with whatever gift each of you has received. (1 Peter 4:10)

Reveal Your divine purpose within me, Holy Spirit.

Sister's Road to Bread and Life, Part 3

After joining the Sisters of Mercy, Sister Caroline Tweedy went on to hold various jobs at Mercy Home for Children, which cares for developmentally disabled children and adults, both in residential programs and in respite care programs. It was a life-changing experience that allowed her to see the world through God's eyes.

During a *Christopher Closeup* interview, Sister Caroline said, "You see the face of God in those that are most fragile, those who don't have a voice. You become their voice. You take a stand for them...There are people whose voices are not heard, people who are undercounted or undervalued, and that shouldn't be. We're all equal, and we all have something to contribute. Because someone has a disability doesn't mean they can't do the job. It just might take them a little longer."

That experience proved to be the perfect foundation for Sister Caroline's current work at the St. John's Bread and Life food pantry program.

Speak out for those who cannot speak...defend the rights of the poor and needy. (Proverbs 31:8-9)

Make our society more welcoming to those who live with disabilities, Father.

Sister's Road to Bread and Life, Part 4

St. John's Bread and Life in Brooklyn, New York, provides four and a half million meals to food insecure people each year through its soup kitchen and food pantry programs. As Executive Director, Sister Caroline Tweedy, RSM, oversees every detail.

When we refer to "the poor" or "the homeless," we can depersonalize these groups of people. But Sister Caroline and her team are meeting them face-to-face as children of God. She explained, "You are putting a face on someone who is in need of a service, who might be in crisis. And when you look at that person, you see the face of God...That's really what we're doing.

"You can learn about...religious life and service in the Church by reading it or watching somebody else. But until you actually have that interaction with folks, and you see progress, that's when you've made a significant difference. For all of us, it's very important to have that one-to-one relationship. We could walk through the neighborhood, and everybody knows who [we] are."

I was hungry and you gave Me food...I was a stranger and you welcomed Me. (Matthew 25:35)

Help me to see Your face in other people, Jesus.

Sister's Road to Bread and Life, Part 5

Out of St. John's Bread and Life's 35 staff members, 10 are former clients who were able to get back on their feet with the assistance of the program, which also includes counseling on government benefits that can help those struggling through a hard time. And food for the soul is always available to the guests through compassionate interactions with the staff.

During a *Christopher Closeup* interview, Sister Caroline Tweedy concluded, "For me personally, the greatest gift is to know that you've helped someone…That person may come one time or that person may come multiple times, and you see their success. You'll get a letter from the city or the state or an agency that we've worked with that says, 'So-and-so is now housed,' or, 'So-and-so no longer needs SNAP benefits. They have a job.'

"Those are the things that are exciting for us. Sometimes we see the fruits of our labor, and sometimes we just have to hope for the best. You can get a little jaded sometimes, but certainly the joy outweighs the jadedness multiple times."

There will never cease to be some in need…I therefore command you, "Open your hand to the poor and needy neighbor in your land." (Deuteronomy 15:11)

Allow me the blessing of helping someone, Messiah.

St. Lucy's Gift Giveaway

For 22 years, St. Lucy's Church, located in Syracuse, New York, has orchestrated an annual "gift giveaway" for Christmas. The inventory for this drive has grown so much that a warehouse is needed to store all the presents.

In 2023, all the donated gifts, worth approximately $15,000, were stolen. The community's reaction was nothing short of inspirational. There were no "negative" responses, recalled co-coordinator of this event, Kay Scharoun, in *The Catholic Sun,* only "a cast of 1000s," ready and willing to help!

By the beginning of December, 2,000 replacement items had been bought and dropped off at the church's gym, ready to be organized and delivered to 230 local families in need. When asked what message Kay would share with the robbers, she had these uplifting words to say:

"If you have needs that are so great that you're tempted to steal, come to us; we have a clothing room…a food pantry…Let me help you. Let me help you out of the situation that you feel is so desperate that you have to steal."

Let us consider how to provoke one another to love and good deeds. (Hebrews 10:24)

Jesus, help us to be messengers of peace and goodwill.

The Best Medicine

Though hospice physician Dr. Christopher Kerr is not a religious man, he respects the faith of his patients and does whatever he can to accommodate their wishes. As Paul Lauritzen notes in a profile of Dr. Kerr in *Commonweal,* he once had a 56-year-old Catholic patient, Ann Gadanyi. She entered hospice around Thanksgiving because she was dying of breast cancer.

With Christmas approaching, she told Dr. Kerr that her one wish was to "attend Christmas Eve Mass to hear her daughter sing, and wake on Christmas morning at home."

"Kerr explained that this plan would be difficult," Lauritzen wrote, "because Ann was receiving medication through IV lines…Without the IVs, pain and bleeding could be serious problems. However, he told her, if she had her heart set on this plan, they could probably make it happen."

And make it happen he did! In gratitude, Ann called the local newspaper, asking them to do a story on Dr. Kerr. When a reporter asked him why he went out of his way to help Ann, Dr. Kerr responded, "Sometimes the best medicine is not medicine."

Honor physicians for their services, for the Lord created them. (Sirach 38:1)

God, may we remember there is more than one way to heal.

'Postboxes to Heaven' Installed Across UK

Ten-year-old Matilda Handy from the United Kingdom wished to send her deceased grandparents a Christmas card and say how much she still loved them. It was then that she had the idea for a postbox to heaven, and to have it available to people to help them with the grieving process around the holidays.

Matilda, along with her mother, Leanne, approached Gedling Crematorium in Nottingham in 2022 with the postbox idea. The crematorium agreed and erected an old postbox, painting it white and gold just in time for Christmas. The response was overwhelming, with more than 100 letters dropped.

The "Letters to Heaven" box was rolled out across 40 sites in England, Scotland, and Wales. It became a way of helping relatives who were grieving their lost loved ones on anniversaries and holidays. Leanne told *Good News Network*:

"A lot of people miss sending cards at Christmas time, and they find real comfort in sending something, whether it's a child drawing a picture or an older person sending something to their loved ones…It helps with the process."

This is my comfort in my distress, that Your promise gives me life. (Psalm 119:50)

Loving Lord, comfort me in my time of grief.

Finding God in Mongolia, Part 1

When Father Peter Turrone of the Archdiocese of Toronto, Canada, became a priest, he embarked on a unique missionary experience. He traveled to Mongolia in central Asia and set up a church in a tentlike structure called a "ger" or "yurt." This church was named Mother of Mercy, and it remains there today.

Outside of the city, Father Turrone was surrounded by grasslands and desert, leaving him in awe of the country's beauty. In an *Aleteia* profile, John Burger wrote, "A hermit priest [that Father Turrone] met there told him not to be surprised if he someday realizes that God led him to Mongolia so that 'He could first evangelize *you*.'"

With only 1,500 Catholics in the entire country, Father Turrone's ministry started out small. But people soon came to pitch their own yurts, to be used as their homes, around the church in order to be close to it. The priest discovered that despite their poverty, the people of Mongolia possess a "spiritual richness" the Western world could learn from.

More tomorrow…

Go into all the world and proclaim the good news. (Mark 16:15)

Guide me in developing a "spiritual richness," Paraclete.

Finding God in Mongolia, Part 2

In light of his missionary work in Mongolia, Father Peter Turrone couldn't help but think of the line from John's gospel, "The Word became flesh and made His dwelling among us." The proper translation of that line from Greek, the priest had learned, stated "pitched His tent among us." This connected perfectly to a church in a tent surrounded by people's tented residences.

During a Christmas Eve service, Father Turrone preached, "God has pitched His tent among us. What is also incredible is the way in which He chose to do so. Jesus could have chosen to be born in a grand palace with a bed made out of the finest linens and precious metals...But He didn't. He chose to lie in the same place where animals came to eat."

In an *Aleteia* profile, Father Turrone recalled that several shepherds he had never seen before came into Mass that night to get out of the cold. They seemed "curious" and examined the Nativity scene. Father Turrone found it spiritually profound to be around shepherds, like those in Bethlehem, at this special service. He called it "one of the most moving experiences of my life as a priest."

Shepherds, hear the word of the Lord. (Ezekiel 34:7)

Thank You for "pitching Your tent" among us, Jesus.

The Dog that Saved Christmas

It was the week before Christmas 2023, and Philadelphia resident Chanell Bell could not believe what her husky, Kobe, had dug up in her front yard: a gas leak.

Since Bell had experienced a recent gas leak in her home, she got a gas level reader to further investigate. The reader didn't indicate anything harmful, but when Kobe persisted in digging in that same area a few days later, Chanell pulled out her reader again. This time, "it detected the presence of gas."

As she was told by the repairmen, who worked three days to fix the leak, if left unchecked for much longer, Chanell's home could have blown up and endangered the rest of her block as well. "[It] was really, really mind-blowing," Chanell exclaimed, as quoted in *The Guardian*. "I'm so thankful for God, thankful for...[Kobe]."

At the suggestion of an inspired viewer of her shared video on digital media, Bell chronicled the story of Kobe's life-saving sense of smell in her 2024 independently published children's book, *The Dog that Saved the Block Before Christmas*. What a fitting tribute to an extremely good boy!

Who teaches us more than the animals?
(Job 35:11)

Abba, bless our pets, healers and guardians of us all.

One Volunteer's Courageous Choice

Grazyna Slawinska of Krakow, Poland, already had a heart for the disabled. The 33-year-old's job consisted of teaching university students how to work with people who have disabilities. She never expected, however, to become a person with a disability herself.

After Russia invaded Ukraine in 2022, Slawinksa knew that she had a personal calling to help Ukrainians with disabilities. "War is challenging for a healthy person, it is a nightmare for a disabled one," she told *OSV News*. Ukraine lacks accessible infrastructure for the disabled, and many cannot physically descend to bomb shelters for safety.

That Christmas, Slawinksa was volunteering in the Ukrainian city of Bakhmut to bring the disabled food and a sense of normalcy. It was there that tragedy struck. She had to have her right leg amputated after it was hit by a Russian mortar shell.

Following months of recuperation, Slawinska bravely returned to Ukraine for Christmas 2023, saying, "I went to Ukraine because my heart told me I must go."

It is more blessed to give than to receive. (Acts 20:35)

Jesus, bless all the volunteers who are working to help those most vulnerable during times of war.

A Happy Accident for Thanksgiving

In 2016, Wanda Dench of Mesa, Arizona, thought she was texting her grandson and inviting him to Thanksgiving dinner. But her grandson had changed his number, so the text instead went to 17-year-old stranger, Jamal Hinton.

He explained the error to Dench, but also asked if he could come over anyway. Dench told Hinton, "Of course you can. That's what grandmas do...feed everyone."

That began a new tradition, with Hinton joining Dench for Thanksgiving for eight years and counting. The bond between the two became even more important after Dench's husband died and she needed the support of family and friends.

The experience inspired Dench to open her home to more strangers who longed for a homemade Thanksgiving meal and a friendly environment. Both Dench and Hinton feel they've benefited from their accidental friendship. Dench told *Arizona's Family*, "I've changed my view so much on the younger generation...I didn't change their life; they changed mine."

Do not neglect to show hospitality to strangers, for by doing that some have entertained angels. (Hebrews 13:2)

Teach us, Jesus, the value of gratitude and friendship.

Reasons for Gratitude

As Thanksgiving Day approached, Father Peter John Cameron, O.P., found himself reflecting on reasons for gratitude. Writing at *Aleteia,* he explained that the air we breathe, the food we eat, and the water we drink are all provided by God, so it is natural to express our thanks to Him.

We also give thanks to "create communion" with other people, Father Peter said: "The thanks we give acknowledge how much we rely on others for our well-being. The more thankful we are, the more we belong to each other."

The words of St. Bernard also offer insight: "Happy the person who gives thanks from the bottom of their heart, even for the least blessings, regarding everything they receive as a purely gratuitous gift."

And the late theologian and minister Dietrich Bonhoeffer, who was murdered by the Nazis, offered this piece of wisdom on finding meaning in our lives: "In ordinary life, we hardly realize that we receive a great deal more than we give, and that it is only with gratitude that life becomes rich."

Thanks be to God for His indescribable gift! (2 Corinthians 9:15)

Teach me to be appreciative of the gift of life, Creator.

The Root of Gratitude

"To be happy is to be grateful." So writes the Editorial Board of *Our Sunday Visitor* in a Thanksgiving reflection. And surely, as we take stock of the blessings in our lives, we know that statement is true. When we appreciate what each day brings—and what we already have—we find ourselves happier.

Our perspective on thankfulness, however, can always be broadened. As *OSV* further observes, "In the hustle and bustle of life, it's easy to overlook the many small miracles and blessings surrounding us. We should strive to continually offer thanks, not only when the sun shines but even—especially—when the storms gather, for it is in those moments that gratitude truly becomes an act of faith. Gratitude is the pathway to a life lived in awareness of God's boundless love and grace, where each day is an opportunity to say, 'Thank You, Lord, for the gift of life and for the privilege of sharing it with those we hold dear.'"

If you know anyone who is enduring loneliness or hardship this holiday season, consider being a blessing to them and giving them a reason to be grateful themselves.

Give thanks in all circumstances.
(1 Thessalonians 5:18)

Help me see my life through the eyes of gratitude, Savior.

Advent of Kindness

In addition to buying Advent calendars that include little pieces of chocolate behind each window, some people are using "Advent of Kindness" calendars, which offer suggestions for each day of December. Here are a few ideas:

■ While waiting on line in a store, allow someone to go in front of you.

■ Get in touch with an old friend or relative whom you've lost contact with. If you had a disagreement with that person, try your best to make peace.

■ Write a thank you note to someone. Express gratitude to anyone who helps you in the course of your day.

■ Bake Christmas cookies for a neighbor or offer to help put up a few decorations if they're unable to do so themselves.

■ Give a meal to someone who is hungry. Donate some clothes that you no longer wear—and that are in good condition—to a local organization that helps the less fortunate.

■ Pray—and work—to be more like Jesus, serving others with love.

Do not neglect to do good and to share what you have, for such sacrifices are pleasing to God. (Hebrews 13:16)

Teach me to be a role model of kindness, Savior.

Welcome Christ in Prayer and Song

Though it's been nearly 20 years since she was a freshman at New York's Fordham University, Jen Sawyer always attends the school's annual Festival of Lessons and Carols, held at St. Paul the Apostle Church on the first Saturday of December. This tradition remains a highlight of her Advent.

Writing at *Jesuits.org*, Sawyer describes a scene in which a female soloist, holding a single candle in the darkened church, begins singing, "Once in royal David's city/Stood a lowly cattle shed,/Where a mother laid her baby/In a manger for His bed:/Mary was that mother mild,/Jesus Christ her little child."

The rest of the choir then joins in, "as the flame from the single candle is passed from choir member to choir member until the once-dark church is fully illuminated by candlelight."

This experience has resonated with Sawyer since the first time she attended the festival. She wrote, "I listened attentively to the scriptural lessons and reflections, sang my heart out with my friends, and realized I was part of a community coming together in prayer and song to welcome Christ into our hearts."

They kindled a fire and welcomed all of us around it. (Acts 28:2)

Fill my Advent with prayer, song, and community, Jesus.

The Peace Light

Every Advent, a special package arrives at Kennedy Airport in New York: the Peace Light. As reported by *The Tablet's* Alicia Venter, the Peace Light is "a continuous flame originating in the Church of the Nativity in Bethlehem, where for more than 1,000 years oil lamps have continuously burned."

Brought from Vienna, Austria, by a group called the Messengers of Peace, a small ceremony, sponsored by the Boy Scouts of America, was held at the airport's Our Lady of the Skies Chapel in 2023.

"A gathering of faithful," Venter explained, "surrounded the flame and prayed for peace across the world—particularly in the war-torn Holy Land—before lighting their own lanterns with fire from the Peace Light flame, which is symbolic of universal peace, harmony and unity."

The irony of the Peace Light coming from the war-ravaged Middle East was not lost on attendees. Still, volunteers planned to drive the flame to different places across North America to spread the message of the Prince of Peace.

Give light to those who sit in darkness...guide our feet into the way of peace. (Luke 1:79)

Help us to choose peace over hatred and strife, Father.

A Pilgrimage of Light, Part 1

Back when Sister Ave Clark worked as a special education teacher, her students made her an Advent wreath. Only it wasn't perfectly round like the store-bought ones. Instead, it was noticeably crooked. Sister Ave still has that wreath and uses it as a decoration every year. Why? Because, as one student told her, "It's not perfect, but it sure was made with love."

In her book *Advent ~ Christmas: A Pilgrimage of Light,* Sister Ave looks at ways that each of us, imperfect as we are, can help the light of love be born again in our hearts during the four weeks of Advent, just as God's love entered the world in the person of His Son on Christmas day.

During a *Christopher Closeup* interview, Sister Ave noted that the candles on our Advent wreaths are there to make us reflect on hope, peace, joy, love, and, ultimately, Jesus: "Make time each day to take that pause and to feel the light within so that we [can] carry it better into a world that's shaking a lot with wars, violence, and discord."

Your word is a lamp to my feet and a light to my path. (Psalm 119:105)

Though I may not be perfect, remind me that I was created out of love, Father.

A Pilgrimage of Light, Part 2

Even though December can seem focused on the "go, go, go" of shopping and parties, Sister Ave Clark sees opportunities for stillness everywhere. While discussing her book *Advent~Christmas: A Pilgrimage of Light,* she said, "You can be still at a red light in the car…Just say, 'Lord, thank You for this moment.' Stillness can happen in a market when you're waiting on line.

"Stillness can happen at home, maybe when you carve out 10 to 15 minutes. But stillness isn't just sitting in a chair. It can be taking a walk, looking out your window. It could also be listening to somebody else on the phone telling you some good news—or some news they're asking for prayer [for]. I've discovered that stillness comes in a variety of ways."

Connection is vital, too. While Sister Ave was mailing her books at the post office, a stranger asked her what the book was about. Since she had an extra copy, she gave it to him as a gift. The man thanked her and promised to use it, even though he wasn't Catholic. Sister Ave relishes those moments when God shows up in unexpected people and circumstances.

Be still before the Lord, and wait patiently for Him. (Psalm 37:7)

Help me find stillness in my day, Father.

A Pilgrimage of Light, Part 3

Sister Ave Clark admits that seeing God in times of darkness takes effort. That was the case when her car was hit by a runaway train 20 years ago, and she had to endure a year of intense recovery and rehabilitation. She reflected, "Do I wish it didn't happen? Yes. But it brought different lights into my life, of understanding pain and having to adapt your life in a different way that you never thought you would."

"I said, 'I wonder what God wants me to learn along this way?' I can remember my first Christmas after that accident, not being able to go to shops or anything. I said, 'You know what? A phone call to somebody means a lot. A little note means a lot. Maybe the best gift we could give each other is that light of caring, the kind word, the extra listening, the forgiving, too.'"

"Advent can be a joyous, peaceful, loving, and hopeful time, and each one of us can make a difference in the world...[by] a kind word, a listening heart...But probably the most powerful is to pray, to give a prayer away to somebody...We have so much to give away and be thankful for."

Be kind to one another, tenderhearted, forgiving...as God in Christ has forgiven you. (Ephesians 4:32)

What non-material gifts can I share this Christmas, Jesus?

A Pilgrimage of Light, Part 4

Sister Ave Clark has a special place in her heart for those who are infirm or homebound, especially her fellow Dominican Sisters. Several of them are now in their 90s and 100s, living in Amityville, New York. "They used to be principals, nurses, college teachers, religious ed," she explained on *Christopher Closeup*. "Now, they're sitting in their rooms."

After receiving Sister Ave's book *Advent~Christmas: A Pilgrimage of Light,* the Sisters were taken by a quote on the back cover: "How will you be a Christ-bearer of the holy lights of Advent~Christmas time?"

They decided they would read the book as a group, reflect on its questions and insights, and share the answers in prayer. In other words, even though the Sisters can't be physically active anymore, they remain spiritually active.

Sister Ave observed, "Christ took on humanity, so that we would know God's love. So, we have to take on each other's humanity, the glory of it, and sometimes the weakness and frailty of it, not push it aside...God holds up each person's humanity, and that's the wonderful gift of the baby in the manger."

Do not ignore the discourse of the aged. (Sirach 8:9)

Lord, help me show Your love to my elders.

A Pilgrimage of Light, Part 5

As she makes her way through the Advent season, Sister Ave Clark looks to Mary, the mother of Jesus, as her guiding light. She noted, "Mary said yes, not knowing fully where these lights were going to take her...But she said yes, and it's the yes of trusting. I think that's what's needed in our world...Mary gave her son to everybody. Sometimes that's what we have to do with our love: to not hold it back, not just give it when it's comfortable or we're being applauded. Give it unconditionally."

That kind of love was witnessed by Sister Ave's brother, Dr. Paul Clark, many years ago when he served in Vietnam during the war. A nun named Sister San Quentin (yes, that was her name) lovingly took care of lepers and demonstrated to him "how those suffering people were fellow human beings." Dr. Clark said he "never forgot her brightness in the midst of war."

In addition, one night Dr. Clark looked up at the night sky and saw the stars shining brightly. That moment reminded him that "the light will never leave us. It can feel hidden at times, but light never leaves us."

Jesus said, "The light is with you...believe in the light." (John 12:35-36)

Help me to find the light when it is hidden, Jesus.

A Pilgrimage of Light, Part 6

One of the lights in Sister Ave Clark's life is James Palmaro, a poet who is blind. For Sister Ave's book, *Advent~Christmas: A Pilgrimage of Light,* James contributed the poem "The Advent Wreath." It beautifully captures the spirit of the season:

"The leaves are all gone,
the trees are barren and bare,
The autumn winds are chilling,
yet anticipation's everywhere.

It is the Advent season,
The winter nights grow near,
We search for the warmth inside ourselves,
Wreaths are everywhere.

Cousins to our Christmas trees
that bring us joy and brilliance,
We place them in and on our homes,
And they remind us of resilience.

Circular in shape, symbols of connection
That despite the cold and dark of night
We'll find light and resurrection."

A shoot shall come out from the stump of Jesse, and a branch shall grow out of his roots. (Isaiah 11:1)

Jesus, lead me towards light and resurrection.

Youngster's Pearl Harbor Mission

When 11-year-old Harrison Johnson heard the story of Japan's December 7th, 1941 attack on Pearl Harbor, which drew the U.S. into World War II, he was intrigued. The North Carolinian read everything he could about the "date which will live in infamy," as President Franklin Roosevelt called it.

After visiting the Pearl Harbor National Memorial in Oahu, Harrison became concerned that his generation might forget the American heroes of that day, both victims and survivors. So, in collaboration with Pacific Historic Parks, which oversees the Memorial, he began the project Harrison's Heroes, to raise money to create and promote history projects about Pearl Harbor.

At first, Harrison raised money door to door and through local events. After a website for Harrison's Heroes went online, donations boomed. Within two years, $100,000 had been collected. Harrison has been applauded by many, but the youngster remains humble. He told *WRAL*, "The real heroes are the men and women who sacrificed their lives to protect our freedom."

Let no one despise your youth, but set the believers an example in speech and conduct. (1 Timothy 4:12)

Today, I pray for the heroes of Pearl Harbor, Father.

A Holy Disruption

During Advent, Christopher Award-winning author Amy Julia Becker (*A Good and Perfect Gift*) took to her social media accounts to explore two Biblical figures' very different responses to the news of Jesus's coming.

Becker wrote, "When Mary hears the message that she has been chosen by God to be the mother of Jesus, Luke tells us she was 'troubled.' When King Herod hears from the three magi that Jesus has been born, Matthew tells us he was 'troubled.' The news that Jesus is coming disrupts their lives.

"Herod responds with denial and violence. Mary responds with surrender and acceptance and receptivity. The news of God's love entering our world disrupts our expectations. It challenges us. It proclaims our belovedness apart from our achievements or worth. It exposes injustice.

"The news of God's love entering the world invites us to healing and freedom. It threatens us with radical acceptance and grace. God's love is a holy disruption that might trouble us deeply. How will we respond?"

Here am I, the servant of the Lord; let it be with me according to Your word. (Luke 1:38)

Jesus, may I strive to surrender my heart and will to You.

The Silent Saint

During Advent, author Joy Clarkson reflected on the life of St. Joseph for *Christianity Today,* pointing out that he is "known as the silent saint...[because] he does not say a single word in any of the Gospels." Despite this, Clarkson notes that Joseph is "a man of decisive action emerging from a rich inner life."

For instance, when he learns of Mary's pregnancy—and suspects infidelity—Joseph does not subject her to public embarrassment or worse. Instead, he devises "a merciful and wise plan" to divorce her quietly. When an angel comes to him in a dream, telling him not to leave Mary because her baby was conceived of the Holy Spirit, Joseph obeys the angel.

Clarkson observes, "[Joseph] let people think that he, a thoughtful and self-controlled man, had gotten her pregnant...He took Mary's shame onto himself, perhaps foreshadowing what Jesus would do for all humankind. And all this he did without saying a word. Ours is a world drowning in words. In Joseph, the silent saint, I see a different way of being—a way of silence and action, where sometimes the most important words are the ones we don't speak."

The prudent are restrained in speech. (Proverbs 10:19)

God, in the silence of prayer, may we listen for Your call.

Kindness Eases Blue Christmas

After legendary singer Tony Bennett passed away in 2023, stories of his numerous successes filled the news. But, as with any life, there were also times of struggle. Christmas Eve, 1965, was one of those times.

As recounted by author Robert Sullivan in his book *Tony Bennett in the Studio,* the crooner was alone and depressed in New York City's Gotham Hotel that night. His marriage was headed towards divorce, and his two sons were spending the holiday with his wife. Professionally, the advent of rock music threatened Bennett's career performing American standards.

Meanwhile, a few blocks away, Bennett's old friend, bandleader Duke Ellington, was conducting a concert of sacred music. Ellington had invited Bennett to attend, but the singer was drowning so deeply in the blues, he didn't have the energy to go.

Later that evening, Bennett heard sounds outside his hotel room. When he opened the door, there stood the choir from Ellington's Sacred Concert, performing a private Christmas serenade to lift his spirits. Bennett relished that gesture of kindness for the rest of his life.

Show kindness...to one another. (Zechariah 7:9)

Help me make someone's blue Christmas brighter, Savior.

Operation Holiday Cheer

In 2004, a woman went to Dees' Nursery in Oceanside, New York, and asked if she could buy a fresh Christmas tree to ship to her son, who was serving in the U.S. military in Iraq. The nursery's owner, Tom Di Dominica Sr., was happy to give her the tree for free, but was unsure how to ship it overseas.

Di Dominica reached out for guidance to local businessman Jim Adelis, whose son was also stationed in Iraq. He, in turn, got in touch with the shipping company DHL Express, and their plan came to fruition. But they didn't just send one tree. They collected more than 100 trees, plus lights, menorahs, and holiday cards. The effort, dubbed Operation Holiday Cheer, has been going strong every year since then.

In December 2023, a caravan of volunteers traveled from Dees' Nursery to Kennedy Airport to deliver its donations. Jospeh Dee told *CBS News'* Jennifer McLogan that this effort brings soldiers stationed in the desert a beautiful touch—and aroma—of home. Volunteer Lucy Adelis added, "That's the least that we can do, besides praying for them to come home."

The fruit of the righteous is a tree of life. (Proverbs 11:30)

May those in the military feel Your love, Father.

A Sweet Memory of Christmas

"Shall we bake cookies today?" Every December, Jeffra A. Nicholson's grandmother greeted her with those words whenever she would come over to bake Christmas cookies as a child. Writing at *Guideposts.org,* Nicholson recalled they would laugh and tell stories while decorating their delicious snickerdoodles.

By the time Nicholson was a college senior, her grandmother lived in a nursing home because her body and mind were failing. While visiting her one December, Nicholson "prayed that God might awaken her spirit, just briefly, so I could see some spark of recognition in her eyes."

At first, Nicholson's attempts to trigger a memory in her grandmother failed. Then, they went for a walk in the sun. Nicholson was shocked when her grandmother suddenly asked, "How's school?" Nicholson happily responded with plenty of details, then noticed a look of determination on her grandmother's face, followed by the words, "Shall we bake cookies today?" With joy, Nicholson answered, "Absolutely!"

Nicholson still treasures this final, poignant memory with her grandmother.

The memory of me is sweeter than honey. (Sirach 24:20)

May all families create happy Christmas memories, Savior.

A Christmas Prayer for the Lonely

At *Guideposts.org*, Bob Hostetler shared a heartfelt Christmas prayer for the lonely and forgotten. Here is an excerpt:

"Lord God, in this special season, I come to You on behalf of those whose holidays are mournful reminders of loss or lack in their lives. I pray for those who, perhaps like Mary and Joseph upon their arrival in Bethlehem, feel forgotten or excluded over the holidays."

"I pray for those who, perhaps like the shepherds, are required to work while others sleep or celebrate. I pray for those who, perhaps like Simeon and Anna, have outlived many friends and loved ones…"

"I pray also for prisoners, patients…along with those who are stranded or sidelined during this blessed season."

"I cry out to You who 'is close to the brokenhearted' (Psalm 34:18 NIV). I ask You to be close to and shower Your favor on all of the above, in the name of Jesus, Your beloved and only-begotten Son, Amen."

Turn to me and be gracious to me, for I am lonely and afflicted. (Psalm 25:16)

Holy Spirit, help lonely people find companionship during this holy season and beyond.

Beauty in a Broken Manger

The Baby Jesus was missing, and the quest to find Him was on! This was the scene in Christine Lenahan's home as she and her family began to decorate for Christmas and were ready to set up the Nativity scene.

At first glance, their creche looked old and replaceable. After all, the small figures had taken a beating over many years. A donkey's leg was held on by Scotch tape, Lenahan wrote in *America*, and one of the wise men had lost his myrrh. Still, Lenahan saw a deeper meaning there.

She reflected, "This Nativity scene offers something a new one cannot. It has been uniquely touched by a family of fallible humans, and in its very brokenness is a reminder that Christ entered into our littleness. God came to be with us once, and God is still with us. Most of all, we believe that even in our brokenness, God will come among us again."

Thankfully, the baby Jesus was soon found in a corner of the living room. Lenahan concluded, "Our Nativity scene, in all its shining imperfections, is complete once more."

Remember, I am with you always, to the end of the age. (Matthew 28:20)

Help me to find You in this world of imperfections, Jesus.

Christmas Lights Unite Neighbors

In an essay for *Loyola Press*, Christopher de Vinck recalled his former colleague, Ralph, having a warm and welcoming personality—and always being full of the Christmas spirit. One year, having just moved into a new home with his wife, Ralph decorated the entire outside of his house with Christmas lights.

As Ralph admired his work, one of his neighbors came out and congratulated him on doing a wonderful job. Soon after, several more neighbors joined in and welcomed Ralph to the community. Ralph then asked when they would put their lights up. The neighbors chuckled, responding, "Ralph, we're all Jewish on this street...You are the first one ever on our street with Christmas lights, and we love it."

One of the neighbors invited Ralph and his wife to his home for the lighting of the menorah during Hanukkah, and Ralph happily accepted. Ralph told de Vinck, "When I went back into the house, I told my wife about how welcome they made me feel and how much our Christmas lights pleased them and how they all have menorahs. She said right away, 'Christmas lights, the menorah... Same light, Ralph.'"

In Your light we see light. (Psalm 36:9)

May Your love and light draw us closer to each other, God.

Expect to Meet the King of Angels

On the Daughters of St. Paul YouTube page, Sister Mary Martha offered words of wisdom about preparing our minds and hearts for the coming of Jesus.

She said, "Our lives are God's Bethlehem, the place where He dwells among us. God sanctified time and humanity when He entered our history and claimed it as His own in Jesus Christ. Thanks to this gift, we can encounter God at every moment and in every person. But if we are not looking for Him, we will most likely miss Him."

"The same Child born for us at Bethlehem comes to us at every Mass. We receive Him into the stable of our hearts at every Eucharist. Thus, even in the midst of Advent, Christmas joy is never far away. What would our lives look like if we approached every moment, every person, and above all every Eucharist expecting to meet the King of angels?"

My God in His steadfast love will meet me. (Psalm 59:10)

I don't want to miss seeing You, Jesus. Open my eyes and my heart to Your presence in every person and moment.

Christmas Gifts of Hope, Part 1

Charlotte Maya wasn't feeling the Christmas spirit. Earlier that year, her husband, Sam, had committed suicide, leaving her a widow with two young boys.

One evening, the doorbell rang in their Los Angeles home. Maya's six-year-old son answered the door, but all he found was a package containing a kit to make a gingerbread house. The gift tag read, "On the first day of Christmas…"

The family relished the mystery and joy this unusual experience brought them, but they didn't expect their doorbell to ring again the next night. This time, wrote Maya in *The New York Times*, a package with two snowman mugs and hot cocoa mix awaited them. The note read, "On the second day of Christmas…"

Now, the kids were getting excited and hoped to identify their benefactor when he or she came back. The person avoided detection, though, always showing up when nobody was around. Maya reflected, "In those dark days of intense grief, somebody was shining a light our way with a simple but powerful message: 'You are seen. You are loved.'" More tomorrow…

Every perfect gift is from above. (James 1:17)

Help me ease someone's grief, Prince of Peace.

Christmas Gifts of Hope, Part 2

Gifts kept showing up on Charlotte Maya's porch, much to the delight of her two young sons. The presents were always simple, she noted in *The New York Times*: "Six apples, seven clementines." She no longer wanted to know who was delivering the gifts, however, noting, "I made it my mission to protect their generous, sacred act."

Maya felt that the true gift brought by their benefactor in the aftermath of her husband's suicide was akin to the gift of Jesus's birth. She observed, "It was such a strange feeling to be wrenched so hard by grief and darkness on the one hand—and drawn so firmly to hope and light on the other."

On Christmas Eve, the family returned home to find 12 gifts on their porch. Four for each boy, and four for Maya. The note simply said, "Merry Christmas!" Maya concluded, "Fifteen years later, I still don't know who gave us those 12 days of hope...The not-knowing quickly became my favorite part. That mysterious light pushing its way into our ineffable darkness. Not a miracle. Not magic. Just generous, selfless, human love."

Serve one another with whatever gift each of you has received. (1 Peter 4:10)

Help me to practice generous, selfless love, Lord.

A Soldier's Musical Promise

It was Christmas Eve, and Frank Farmer found himself feeling lost and dejected. He had been a soldier in World War II and was now in a Denver, Colorado military hospital where doctors and nurses tended to his injuries—at least the physical ones. The emotional and spiritual wounds the war had inflicted on him would be harder to heal.

Suddenly, Frank heard carolers in the hallway singing the beautiful Christmas songs he remembered from his childhood. The melodies and lyrics served as a balm for his soul.

On her Instagram page, Christopher Award-winning writer/producer Martha Williamson (*Touched by an Angel; Signed, Sealed, Delivered*) shared Frank's story. She wrote, "That night, Frank promised God that if he ever got out of that hospital, he would start his own little choir of carolers and return to others the blessing of hope that he was given that Christmas."

That was the beginning of the Frank Farmer Octet, which spent the next 40 years caroling at Denver's hospitals every Christmas Eve. And for 30 of those years, Martha's father directed that choir. What a fitting hymn of praise!

Sing praises to the Lord. (Psalm 30:4)

Help me share the blessing of hope, Holy Spirit.

The Joy of the Giver

From the time she was a child, Molly Cahill looked forward to a unique tradition: every Sunday during Advent, her mother would give her and her sister a gift at dinnertime as they lit a candle on the wreath and read a prayer. The gifts were small, but always geared toward each girl's likes and personality.

Molly's mom has continued this tradition, even though her daughters have reached adulthood, and Molly works in New York City at America Media. She sends the gifts through the mail, and they connect as a family over Facetime each Sunday for the wreath-lighting, prayer, and gift-opening.

In 2022, Molly made it home for the fourth Sunday of Advent. She noticed the joy in her mother's eyes as she watched her daughters open their gifts. Molly observed, "For a couple of decades, I've felt the joy of being the recipient of this tradition. Looking at my mother's face, I sense the joy of the giver. The Christmas miracle came to us in the form of a person. Maybe the graces of this Advent season are little reflections of that miracle, given to us by people, too."

God loves a cheerful giver. (2 Corinthians 9:7)

Jesus, may people sense Your love through the gifts I give this Advent and Christmas season.

A Life-Saving Christmas Kindness, Part 1

The blizzard that hit Buffalo, New York, on Dec. 24, 2022, was the worst in half a century. That's why Sha'Kyra Aughtry was shocked when she heard someone crying outside her home.

As recounted in the *Washington Post,* Sha'Kyra and her boyfriend went outside and discovered a 64-year-old mentally disabled man named Joey White trapped in a snowbank. He had left his group home to go to work, even though he had been told not to. Sha'Kyra and her boyfriend carried Joey inside, deduced he had severe frostbite, and did their best to warm him up.

Joey remembered his sister Yvonne's phone number, so Sha'Kyra called to apprise her of the situation. Yvonne couldn't get out of her house, so she stayed in touch with Sha'Kyra by phone. It was soon evident, however, that Joey needed more help than home care could provide.

Sha'Kyra and Yvonne called 911 close to 100 times, but ambulances were having trouble getting around. All seemed hopeless until Sha'Kyra issued a cry for help and the best of humanity was revealed. More tomorrow...

In the shadow of Your wings I will take refuge, until the destroying storms pass by. (Psalm 57:1)

Allow me to be someone's shelter in the storm, Savior.

A Life-Saving Christmas Kindness, Part 2

Though mother of three Sha'Kyra Aughtry had gotten 64-year-old mentally disabled man Joey White out of the snow, his severe frostbite needed medical attention. With ambulances unable to get through the streets of Buffalo, both Sha'Kyra and Joey's sister, Yvonne, issued pleas for assistance on Facebook.

"Within half an hour," reported the *Washington Post,* "neighbors offered to help. Several showed up to plow around Aughtry's home. They wrapped Joey in a warm blanket and carefully transported him to the Erie County Medical Center. Aughtry accompanied him for the ride."

Though Joey needed to have all his fingers amputated, his life was saved. His boss, Ray Barker, who had told Joey not to come to work, said of Sha'Kyra, "This kind woman came out and heard a human being deep in distress and did something about it...She saved his life."

Yvonne added, "This stranger opened up her heart and opened up her home...This was such a Christmas miracle."

When they call to Me, I will answer them...I will rescue them and honor them. (Psalm 91:15)

Creator, instill us with the compassion to help human beings in distress.

The Star of Bethlehem Shines

In 1982, shortly before her death, Princess Grace of Monaco (aka actress Grace Kelly) filmed a clip for the Family Theater Productions Christmas special, *The Nativity*. She offered a reflection on the light of Christ. Here is an excerpt:

"Christian tradition tells us that Christ was born during the night. Usually, nighttime is associated with the dark side of life in which the familiar shape of our world dissolves, and we quickly lose some of our confidence. Indeed, we can sometimes lose our way. Isn't this a rather strange time for such a joyous event as the birth of the Savior? Not at all.

"Happily, God seems to come to us at an hour when He is most needed. The darkness of night is not only a realm of helplessness and fear. It can be a time of hope and healing...the time for the coming of truth and the incarnate love of God.

"The Star of Bethlehem might well have passed unnoticed in the blaze of noon. But set against the velvet of the midnight sky, the whole world knew its brilliance. A bright light that still shines through the dark, a light that darkness has not, and cannot, ever overpower."

**I have come as light into the world.
(John 12:46)**

Jesus, lighten the dark paths that lay before me.

The Wonder of Christ's Birth

In her book, *Have a Beautiful Terrible Day,* Christopher Award-winning author Kate Bowler shared a Christmas prayer. Here is an excerpt:

"You are here. What a wonder.

Robed in the everyday majesty of a newborn,
so beautiful, so soft, so new...

God become human...

All wisdom and power poured into a smallness
that knows hunger and gravity

and unseeing urgency for your mother's skin.

And Mary, so newly parted from you,

turns her thoughts to the impossible angelic
visitation that promised you'd come...

Blessed are we when our hearts warm with her.

You're here. And we are too,
newly come to worship

with kings and shepherds and
barn animals and angels

as you light up the world on this holiest,
loveliest night."

To you is born this day in the city of David a Savior, who is the Messiah. (Luke 2:11)

Prince of Peace, may Your light guide me always.

The Joys of Christmas

People often complain that secular Christmas celebrations leave out the religious aspects of the holiday. But Tom Hoopes prefers to look at what society gets right.

Writing at *Aleteia,* he says, "Our delight in receiving gifts is a beautiful proxy for our delight in receiving God." Though Hoopes decries consumerism, he relates getting gifts to receiving God's freely given love. And the fact that gift giving happens at Christmastime associates it with Jesus automatically.

In addition, says Hoopes, "Our delight in giving teaches us our true human vocation." Christmas, in other words, promotes selflessness and putting others ahead of ourselves. "This transforms people's purposes in exactly the way Jesus intended: Like His, our vocation is to give to all and not to count the cost."

Christmas also brings families together, reminding us that Jesus entered our world as part of a family. And finally, even in our secular world, Nativity scenes can be spotted all over. "[Jesus's] presence in a manger…shows that He is open to all of us, if we are willing to seek Him out."

Be rich in good works, generous, and ready to share. (1 Timothy 6:18)

May all the world see Your loving, giving nature, Jesus.

A Christmassy New Year's Resolution

Greg Erlandson's Christmas wish is that people actually celebrate Christmas for the full 12 days! He even thinks this would make a great New Year's resolution.

Writing at *OSV News,* Erlandson notes that Christians used to fast during Advent, so they made up for it by feasting for the full season of celebration which, in some cases, lasted until the Feast of Candlemas on February 2nd. But Erlandson would be happy convincing more people to keep the spirit of Christmas alive at least until the Feast of the Epiphany on January 6th.

Indulge in some favorite foods, and keep up your ornaments. Take extra time for prayer, and reflect on what you have to be grateful for in life. Reach out to an old friend or neighbor. Spread joy at work, and "say thanks to those who waited on you, rang up your groceries, and wrapped your presents during the Advent frenzy."

"If we have one New Year's Resolution to make this year," Erlandson concluded, "let's commit ourselves to celebrating what Christmas really means for just a bit longer."

Again, I will say, Rejoice. (Philippians 4:4)

Abba, may we keep the spirit of goodwill flowing throughout the Christmas season and beyond.

A New Year's Eve Miracle

Two years ago, on New Year's Eve morning, 17-year-old Griffin Evans was fast asleep when his dog, Macho, started barking and nipping at him, awakening the teenager and alerting him to the fire blazing around them.

Griffin's mother, Nicole, was out of town that day, but she received a Facetime call from her son and dog, once they were safely outside, letting her know what was happening. According to *WFLA News,* the house they had lived in for nearly two decades, was a "total loss." But Nicole maintained that thanks to Macho, they were able to save what was most important and "not replaceable"—her son and their heroic canine companion.

With a little help from their friends in Safety Harbor, Florida, the Evanses soon had the means to start over. According to *WTSP.com,* in just two days, "the community raised over $5,000" for them, not including "gift cards, food and house supplies."

"I'm overwhelmed," Nicole concluded, "Thank you...They're...just boats floating on an ocean of gratitude I'll never be able to express."

Give thanks in all circumstances.
(1 Thessalonians 5:18)

Savior, we thank You for the gift of good neighbors.

A Legacy of Remembrances

Father Michael J. Noonan was serving his second term as superior of the Priests of the Sacred Heart when he died suddenly one day. But his community continued to remember him decades later because he had a way with words.

The things he said and wrote are now known as "Noonanisms." Here are a few:

- "Hope is not a fire extinguisher to be used in case of discouragement. It's a muscle that must be flexed regularly, so that it can operate in times of aridity, like it was designed to."

- "The difference between the saint and the sinner is not that the saint never falls; it's that the saint never stops getting up. The only mistake one can make in the spiritual life is to quit trying."

- "All of God's demands upon me are the demands of one who loves me infinitely."

If you have gained wisdom in life and want to share it with future generations, set your thoughts down on paper or make a recording of them. People may turn to them time and again for support and inspiration.

The memory of the righteous is a blessing. (Proverbs 10:7)

Show me how to inspire others, God.

Breaking the Complaining Habit

Complaining is a natural part of life because we all get frustrated at times. When complaining becomes a habit, however, that is a problem. It is not healthy for you—or the people around you—to be in a negative mindset all the time. Writing at *Aleteia,* Krispin Mayfield offers suggestions on breaking the complaining habit:

- **Set boundaries.** If you are burdened by other people's demands on you, learn to say "no" sometimes. And if someone's behavior is constantly aggravating you, discuss it with them personally instead of complaining behind their backs.

- **Give yourself credit for completing a hard task.** This allows you to "replace feelings of frustration with pride and satisfaction."

- **Ask for help.** Instead of complaining about being overburdened, request support from those around you.

- **Connect in new ways.** Complaining can seem like a good way to connect with others. Instead, share the positive parts of your life, and build bonds based on those.

> **Do not grumble against one another, so that you may not be judged. (James 5:9)**

Help me to cultivate a more positive mindset, Jesus.

The Best Advice

Towards the end of 2023, *The New York Times'* Melissa Kirsch asked readers to send in the best advice they had received during the past year. Here are a few of the answers she received:

- "Keep a running list of the nicest things anyone has ever said to or about you. It's a lifesaver on days when the world is getting the best of you."

- "Life is too short not to tell the people you love that you love them."

- "Instead of calling someone out, call them in: Invite them into a judgment-free conversation with the intention of promoting understanding."

- "Every time you receive a box containing something you bought online, fill it with items to donate."

- "Before doing something, ask yourself, 'Is this something that someone who loves themselves would do?'"

**Listen to advice and accept instruction, that you may gain wisdom for the future.
(Proverbs 19:20)**

Open my mind and heart to wiser ways of living, Paraclete.

The Gift of a New Year

Theologian Henri Nouwen once shared these words on the best way to approach a new year: "We must learn to live each day, each hour, yes, each minute as a new beginning, as a unique opportunity to make everything new...Imagine that we could walk through the new year always listening to the voice saying to us: 'I have a gift for you and can't wait for you to see it!'"

"The problem is that...there are many cunning foxes jumping on our shoulders and whispering in our ears the great lie: 'There is nothing new under the sun.'...When we listen to these foxes, they eventually prove themselves right: our new year, our new day, our new hour become flat, boring, dull, and without anything new."

"We must open our minds and our hearts to the voice that resounds through the valleys and hills of our life saying: 'Let Me show you where I live among My people. My name is 'God-with-you.' I will wipe all the tears from your eyes; there will be no more death, and no more mourning or sadness. The world of the past has gone' (Revelation 21:2–5)."

**See, I am making all things new.
(Revelation 21:5)**

Jesus, guide my steps through the new year, and lead me towards a renewed sense of hope and joy.

Also Available

We hope that you have enjoyed *Three Minutes a Day, Volume 59*. These other Christopher offerings may interest you:

- **News Notes** are published 10 times a year on a variety of topics of current interest. Single copies are free; quantity orders available.

- **Appointment Calendars** are suitable for wall or desk and provide an inspirational message for each day of the year.

- **Annual Poster Contest for High School Students** and **Video Contest for College Students**

- **Syndicated "Light One Candle" newspaper columns**

- **Website—www.christophers.org—**has *Christopher Closeup* radio programs; links to our blog and social media pages; a monthly *What's New* update; and much more.

For more information about The Christophers or to receive News Notes, please contact us:

> The Christophers
> 264 West 40th Street, Suite 603
> New York, NY 10018
>
> Phone: 212-759-4050, ext. 241
> E-mail: mail@christophers.org
> Website: www.christophers.org

The Christophers is a non-profit media organization founded in 1945 by Father James Keller, M.M. We share the message of personal responsibility and service to God and humanity with people of all faiths and no particular faith. Gifts are welcome and tax-deductible. Our legal title for wills is The Christophers, Inc.